AT HOME WITH
MICROSOFT® WORKS

AT HOME WITH MICROSOFT® WORKS

by Doug Lowe

IDG BOOKS WORLDWIDE, INC.
AN INTERNATIONAL DATA GROUP COMPANY

Foster City, CA ■ Chicago, IL ■ Indianapolis, IN ■ Southlake, TX

At Home with Microsoft® Works

Published by

IDG Books Worldwide, Inc.

An International Data Group Company

919 E. Hillsdale Blvd., Suite 400

Foster City, CA 94404

Library of Congress Catalog Card No.: 96-79054

ISBN: 0-7645-3026-7

Printed in the United States of America

10 9 8 7 6 5 4 3 2 1

1DD/RS/RS/ZW/FC

Distributed in the United States by IDG Books Worldwide, Inc.

Distributed in Canada by Macmillan of Canada, a Division of Canada Publishing Corporation; by Computer and Technical Books in Miami, Florida, for South America and the Caribbean; by Longman Singapore in Singapore, Malaysia, Thailand, and Korea; by Toppan Co. Ltd. in Japan; by Asia Computerworld in Hong Kong; by Woodslane Pty. Ltd. in Australia and New Zealand; and by Transworld Publishers Ltd. in the U.K. and Europe.

For general information on IDG Books Worldwide's booksin the U.S., please call our Customer Service department at 800-762-2974. For reseller information, including discounts and premium sales, please call our Reseller Customer Service department at 800-434-3422.

For information on where to purchase IDG Books Worldwide's books outside the U.S., contact IDG Books Worldwide at 415-655-3021 or fax 415-655-3295.

For information on translations, contact Marc Jeffrey Mikulich, Director, Foreign and Subsidiary Rights, at IDG Books Worldwide, 415-655-3018 or fax 415-655-3295.

For sales inquiries and special prices for bulk quantities, write to the address above or call IDG Books Worldwide at 415-655-3200.

For information on using IDG Books Worldwide's books in the classroom, or ordering examination copies, contact the Education Office at 800-434-2086, or fax 508-750-4470.

For authorization to photocopy items for corporate, personal, or educational use, please contact Copyright Clearance Center, 222 Rosewood Drive, Danvers, MA 01923, or fax 508-750-4470.

is a trademark under exclusive license to IDG Books Worldwide, Inc., from International Data Group, Inc.

ABOUT IDG BOOKS WORLDWIDE

Welcome to the world of IDG Books Worldwide.

IDG Books Worldwide, Inc., is a subsidiary of International Data Group, the world's largest publisher of computer-related information and the leading global provider of information services on information technology. IDG was founded more than 25 years ago and now employs more than 8,500 people worldwide. IDG publishes more than 275 computer publications in over 75 countries (see listing below). More than 60 million people read one or more IDG publications each month.

Launched in 1990, IDG Books Worldwide is today the #1 publisher of best-selling computer books in the United States. We are proud to have received eight awards from the Computer Press Association in recognition of editorial excellence and three from *Computer Currents'* First Annual Readers' Choice Awards. Our best-selling ...*For Dummies*® series has more than 30 million copies in print with translations in 30 languages. IDG Books Worldwide, through a joint venture with IDG's Hi-Tech Beijing, became the first U.S. publisher to publish a computer book in the People's Republic of China. In record time, IDG Books Worldwide has become the first choice for millions of readers around the world who want to learn how to better manage their businesses.

Our mission is simple: Every one of our books is designed to bring extra value and skill-building instructions to the reader. Our books are written by experts who understand and care about our readers. The knowledge base of our editorial staff comes from years of experience in publishing, education, and journalism — experience we use to produce books for the '90s. In short, we care about books, so we attract the best people. We devote special attention to details such as audience, interior design, use of icons, and illustrations. And because we use an efficient process of authoring, editing, and desktop publishing our books electronically, we can spend more time ensuring superior content and spend less time on the technicalities of making books.

You can count on our commitment to deliver high-quality books at competitive prices on topics you want to read about. At IDG Books Worldwide, we continue in the IDG tradition of delivering quality for more than 25 years. You'll find no better book on a subject than one from IDG Books Worldwide.

John J. Kilcullen

John Kilcullen
President and CEO
IDG Books Worldwide, Inc.

**Eighth Annual
Computer Press
Awards ≥1992**

**Ninth Annual
Computer Press
Awards ≥1993**

**Tenth Annual
Computer Press
Awards ≥1994**

**Eleventh Annual
Computer Press
Awards ≥1995**

IDG Books Worldwide, Inc., is a subsidiary of International Data Group, the world's largest publisher of computer-related information and the leading global provider of information services on information technology. International Data Group publishes over 275 computer publications in over 75 countries. Sixty million people read one or more International Data Group publications each month. International Data Group's publications include: **ARGENTINA:** Buyer's Guide, Computerworld Argentina, PC World Argentina; **AUSTRALIA:** Australian Macworld, Australian PC World, Australian Reseller News, Computerworld, IT Casebook, Network World, Publish, Webmaster; **AUSTRIA:** Computerwelt Osterreich, Networks Austria, PC Tip Austria; **BANGLADESH:** PC World Bangladesh; **BELARUS:** PC World Belarus; **BELGIUM:** Data News; **BRAZIL:** Annuário de Informática, Computerworld, Connections, Macworld, PC Player, PC World, Publish, Reseller News, Supergamepower; **BULGARIA:** Computerworld Bulgaria, Network World Bulgaria, PC & MacWorld Bulgaria; **CANADA:** CIO Canada, Client/Server World, ComputerWorld Canada, InfoWorld Canada, NetworkWorld Canada, WebWorld; **CHILE:** Computerworld Chile, PC World Chile; **COLOMBIA:** Computerworld Colombia, PC World Colombia; **COSTA RICA:** PC World Centro America; **THE CZECH AND SLOVAK REPUBLICS:** Computerworld Czechoslovakia, Macworld Czech Republic, PC World Czechoslovakia; **DENMARK:** Communications World Danmark, Computerworld Danmark, Macworld Danmark, PC World Danmark, Techworld Denmark; **DOMINICAN REPUBLIC:** PC World Republica Dominicana; **ECUADOR:** PC World Ecuador; **EGYPT:** Computerworld Middle East, PC World Middle East; **EL SALVADOR:** PC World Centro America; **FINLAND:** MikroPC, Tietoverkko, Tietoviikko; **FRANCE:** Distributique, Hebdo, Info PC, Le Monde Informatique, Macworld, Reseaux & Telecoms, WebMaster France; **GERMANY:** Computer Partner, Computerwoche, Computerwoche Extra, Computerwoche FOCUS, Global Online, Macwelt, PC Welt; **GREECE:** Amiga Computing, GamePro Greece, Multimedia World; **GUATEMALA:** PC World Centro America; **HONDURAS:** PC World Centro America; **HONG KONG:** Computerworld Hong Kong, PC World Hong Kong, Publish in Asia; **HUNGARY:** ABCD CD-ROM, Computerworld Szamitastechnika, Internetto online Magazine, PC World Hungary, PC-X Magazin Hungary; **ICELAND:** Tolvuheimur PC World Island; **INDIA:** Information Communications World, Information Systems Computerworld, PC World India, Publish in Asia; **INDONESIA:** InfoKomputer PC World, Komputek Computerworld, Publish in Asia; **IRELAND:** ComputerScope, PC Live!; **ISRAEL:** Macworld Israel, People & Computers/Computerworld; **ITALY:** Computerworld Italia, Macworld Italia, Networking Italia, PC World Italia; **JAPAN:** DTP World, Macworld Japan, Nikkei Personal Computing, OS/2 World Japan, SunWorld Japan, Windows NT World, Windows World Japan; **KENYA:** PC World East African; **KOREA:** Hi-Tech Information, Macworld Korea, PC World Korea; **MACEDONIA:** PC World Macedonia; **MALAYSIA:** Computerworld Malaysia, PC World Malaysia, Publish in Asia; **MALTA:** PC World Malta; **MEXICO:** Computerworld Mexico, PC World Mexico; **MYANMAR:** PC World Myanmar; **NETHERLANDS:** Computer! Totaal, LAN Internetworking Magazine, LAN World Buyers Guide, Macworld Netherlands, Net, WebWereld; **NEW ZEALAND:** Absolute Beginners Guide and Plain & Simple Series, Computer Buyer, Computer Industry Directory, Computerworld New Zealand, MTB, Network World, PC World New Zealand; **NICARAGUA:** PC World Centro America; **NORWAY:** Computerworld Norge, CW Rapport, Datamagasinet, Financial Rapport, Kursguide Norge, Macworld Norge, Multimediaworld Norge, PC World Ekspress Norge, PC World Nettverk, PC World Norge, PC World ProduktGuide Norge; **PAKISTAN:** Computerworld Pakistan; **PANAMA:** PC World Panama; **PEOPLE'S REPUBLIC OF CHINA:** China Computer Users, China Computerworld, China InfoWorld, China Telecom World Weekly, Computer & Communication, Electronic Design China, Electronics Today, Electronics Weekly, Game Software, PC World China, Popular Computer Week, Software Weekly, Software World; **PERU:** Computerworld Peru, PC World Profesional Peru, PC World SoHo Peru; **PHILIPPINES:** Click!, Computerworld Philippines, PC World Philippines, Publish in Asia; **POLAND:** Computerworld Poland, Computerworld Special Report Poland, Cyber, Macworld Poland, Networld Poland, PC World Komputer; **PORTUGAL:** Cerebro/PC World, Computerworld/Correio Informático, Dealer World Portugal, Mac*In/PC*In Portugal, Multimedia World; **PUERTO RICO:** PC World Puerto Rico; **ROMANIA:** Computerworld Romania, PC World Romania, Telecom Romania; **RUSSIA:** Computerworld Russia, Mir PK, Publish, Seti; **SINGAPORE:** Computerworld Singapore, PC World Singapore, Publish in Asia; **SLOVENIA:** Monitor; **SOUTH AFRICA:** Computing SA, Network World SA, Software World SA; **SPAIN:** Communicaciones World, Computerworld España, Dealer World España, Macworld España, PC World España; **SRI LANKA:** Infolink PC World; **SWEDEN:** CAP&Design, Computer Sweden, Corporate Computing Sweden, Internetworld Sweden, it.branschen, Macworld Sweden, MaxiData Sweden, MikroDatorn, Nätverk & Kommunikation, PC World Sweden, PCaktiv, Windows World Sweden; **SWITZERLAND:** Computerworld Schweiz, Macworld Schweiz, PCtip; **TAIWAN:** Computerworld Taiwan, Macworld Taiwan, NEW ViSiON/Publish, PC World Taiwan, Windows World Taiwan; **THAILAND:** Publish in Asia, Thai Computerworld; **TURKEY:** Computerworld Turkiye, Macworld Turkiye, Network World Turkiye, PC World Turkiye; **UKRAINE:** Computerworld Kiev, Multimedia World Ukraine, PC World Ukraine; **UNITED KINGDOM:** Acorn User UK, Amiga Action UK, Amiga Computing UK, Apple Talk UK, Computing, Macworld, Parents and Computers UK, PC Advisor, PC Home, PSX Pro, The WEB; **UNITED STATES:** Cable in the Classroom, CIO Magazine, Computerworld, DOS World, Federal Computer Week, GamePro Magazine, InfoWorld, I-Way, Macworld, Network World, PC Games, PC World, Publish, Video Event, THE WEB Magazine, and WebMaster; online webzines: JavaWorld, NetscapeWorld, and SunWorld Online; **URUGUAY:** InfoWorld Uruguay; **VENEZUELA:** Computerworld Venezuela, PC World Venezuela; and **VIETNAM:** PC World Vietnam.   10/1/96

About the Author

Doug Lowe lives in sunny Fresno, California (where the motto is, "If you can't beat the heat, join it") with his wife Debbie, daughters Rebecca, Sarah, and Bethany, and a pair of female Golden Retrievers, Nutmeg and Ginger. He spends his days (and many of his nights too) toiling away at such books as *At Home with Microsoft Works* and expects that he will win a Pulitzer any day now.

In between writing computer books, Doug enjoys golfing and even got to play once in 1994. He helps coach various kids sports, but hates being called a "Soccer Mom."

Acknowledgments

Turn the page and you'll find a long list of dedicated and talented folks who helped out on this project. I'd like to thank them all, but most especially development editor Erik Dafforn, managing editor Andy Cummings, editor Judy Brunetti, and technical editor Beth Slick. Thanks everyone, and lets do it again real soon!

(The publisher would like to give special thanks to Patrick J. McGovern, who made this book possible.)

Credits

Senior Vice President & Group Publisher Brenda McLaughlin

Acquisitions Manager Gregory Croy

Marketing Manager Melisa M. Duffy

Managing Editor Andy Cummings

Editorial Assistant Timothy J. Borek

Production Director Andrew Walker

Project Coordinator Katy German

Supervisor of Page Layout Craig A. Harrison

Blueline Coordination Patricia R. Reynolds

Development Editor Erik Dafforn

Copy Edit Coordinator Barry Childs-Helton

Copy Editors Judy Brunetti

Technical Reviewer Beth Slick

Production Staff Ritchie Durdin, Jude Levinson, Dale Smith

Proofreader Kathy McGuinners

Indexer Ty Koontz

Cover Design Square Two

Contents at a Glance

Contents

INTRODUCTION

Greetings! Welcome to *At Home with Microsoft Works*, the only book written especially for folks who use Microsoft Works at home.

Works is the cool all-in-one program that comes preinstalled on just about every computer sold for home use. Works includes simple versions of the most commonly used computer programs: a word processor for creating letters, reports, and other documents; a spreadsheet for creating budgets and ledgers; a database for keeping track of information; and a communications program for connecting with other computers over the Internet.

There are plenty of other books about Works, and I'm sure many of them are excellent. But this is the only one that is specifically devoted to showing you how to do things you use Works for at home. With this book, you won't have to wade through chapter after chapter on boring subjects like Tabs and Spreadsheet Formulas and Database Filters. Instead, this book gets right to the point of why you bought that home computer anyway: to get stuff done at home.

You bought that computer because you figured it would help the kids with their schoolwork, would be great for printing party invitations, and would come in handy when you volunteered to put together the school directory or mail letters to everyone in the P.T.A.

That's what this book is all about. It's specifically designed to get you started — and finished — with the most common types of projects people like you and me use our home computers for.

About This Book

This book is unlike any other Works book you've seen. It isn't a 700-page tome about how to use every last feature of Works. Nor is it a tutorial that will teach you everything you need to know about Works in 137 simple lessons.

Rather, this is a project-oriented book. It contains complete instructions for how to create 31 projects that represent the kinds of things people actually do with their computers at home. For example:

- Printing up a calendar of who has to do household chores this week.
- Creating a class directory for your kids' school.
- Tracking batting statistics for your Little League team.

If these are the kinds of things you want to use your home computer for, you need look no farther than the pages of this humble book.

Foolish Assumptions

This book makes very few assumptions about who you are and how much you already know about computers. In fact, this book makes only two assumptions:

1. You have a computer at home which runs Windows 95.
2. That computer has Microsoft Works installed on it.

If you have a computer that runs Windows 95 at home, odds are you also have Microsoft Works. The overwhelming majority of home computers sold since the introduction of Microsoft Windows 95 — in fact, almost all of them — came with Microsoft Works all set up and ready to go.

Version Aversion

This book is designed to work with the Windows 95 version of Microsoft Works, which is formally known as Microsoft Works 4.0.

About a year after Windows 95 and Works 4.0 came out, Microsoft released a minor improvement to Works called Microsoft Works 4.01. The only difference of importance between Works 4.0 and Works 4.01 is that the newer version includes a few additional templates that aren't included with Works 4.0. This book will work fine with either version of Works.

How to Use This Book

The beauty of this book is that you don't have to read it through from start to finish. In fact, I'd start to wonder about you if you tried.

You should use this book like a cookbook. When you wake up the morning after volunteering to put together the class directory for your kids' school, pull out this book and look up the recipe for school directories. Follow the instructions carefully, be sure not to overcook it, and when you're done put the book away until you find yourself faced with another computer project.

For the most part, the projects are self-contained. In other words, you can go directly to a project and start following the instructions. However, there are a few basic Works skills you should try to pick up before launching into any of the projects. That's why this book starts with a *Crash Course* in Microsoft Works. This crash course consists of four chapters: a general introduction to Works, followed by a chapter on each of the three main programs contains in Works: the Word Processor, the Spreadsheet, and the Database.

What about Works' communication program? Frankly, the communication program is the weakest part of Works. In fact, although this communication program might have been useful three or four years ago, today it is virtually worthless. Especially since Windows 95 itself comes with much stronger communication programs. For that reason, this book virtually ignores the communication program that comes with Works.

How This Book is Organized

Inside this book are 18 chapters arranged into seven parts. Each chapter (except those in Part 1) is broken down into one or more Projects, which can be read independently of one another. The chapters and parts group related projects together, but you don't have to read the book in any particular order.

Here's the lowdown on what's in each of the seven parts.

Part I: A Crash Course in Microsoft Works

The four chapters in this part present a quick introduction to the basics of using Works. The first chapter covers Works features that apply to all of the Works tools, then the following three chapters delve more deeply into the Word Processor, Spreadsheet, and Database. If you're new to Works, you should read at least the first chapter before attempting any of the projects.

Part 2: Home Life with Works

The chapters in this part present nine projects that put Works to use around the house, from tracking a home inventory to creating a recipe book.

Part 3: Let's Get Personal

This part presents four projects that can help you organize your personal life, such as creating a To Do List or computerizing your address book.

Part 4: Fun Stuff

Works isn't all serious, and the six projects in this part prove it. You'll find projects for creating party invitations, creating your own crossword puzzles, and working with youth sports teams.

Part 5: You Volunteered for What?

If you're into volunteer work, the five projects in this part are for you. These projects show you how to keep membership roles, print a directory, and create a meeting agenda and minutes.

Part 6: Doing Homework with Works

The four projects in this part focus on using Works to do homework, including writing reports and book reports and studying math.

Part 7: The Home Office

The final part in this book is devoted to those of us who run businesses out of our homes and want to create a more professional appearance. The three projects in this part show you how to create professional looking letters, brochures, and resumes.

Look at All the Icons

As you work your way through the projects in this book, you'll come across several icons that appear in the margins to draw your attention to important information.

This icon points out a summary overview of a complicated procedure.

Several of the projects have additional suggestions marked by this icon. These suggestions involve a bit of extra work on your part, but can add professional polish to a project.

This icon points to where you can find additional information about a particular topic.

Pay attention; some interesting tidbit of information lurks nearby.

This icon points out a useful shortcut or a way of using a command that you may not have considered.

Danger! Danger! Stand back Will Robinson! This icon warns you about trouble lurking nearby.

Where to Go from Here

Yes, you can get there from here. With this book in hand, you're ready to put Works to use at home. Start by reading the Crash Course chapters in Part 1 to get your feet wet. Then, pick out a project and do it! And have fun.

PART I:

A CRASH COURSE IN MICROSOFT WORKS

CHAPTER ONE

WELCOME TO MICROSOFT WORKS FOR WINDOWS 95

In This Chapter

- Understanding Microsoft Works
- Starting Works and creating documents
- Saving and printing your work
- Getting help
- Exiting Works

This chapter is a gentle but quick introduction to Microsoft Works. Works is the all-in-one program that retailers include free with the majority of computers sold for home use. If you are already familiar with the basics of using Works (such as starting Works, creating new documents, and printing), skip this chapter or just skim over its contents. Don't be shy about referring to it at any time, however. The procedures covered in this chapter are referred to in most of the projects described in this book.

What Is Microsoft Works?

Microsoft Works is the Swiss Army Knife of software. It includes a variety of software tools all bundled into one convenient package. The cornerstones of Works are the following four software tools:

- **Word Processor:** Lets you create text-oriented documents such as letters, memos, reports, newsletters, brochures, flyers, and so on.
- **Spreadsheet:** Lets you create grids of numerically oriented information such as budgets and expense reports. In addition, Spreadsheet includes a built-in graphing tool that lets you create graphs and charts to add visual interest to otherwise boring numbers.
- **Database:** Lets you create files of records such as an address book, inventory file, or customer list.
- **Communications:** Lets you connect with various online services to send and receive files over telephone lines.

Of the four tools, the ones you'll use most are Word Processor, Spreadsheet, and Database. The Communications tool is an obsolete tool that doesn't get used much. As a result, you won't find much information on Microsoft's Communications tool within these pages. Instead, use the much more sophisticated communications tool found in Windows 95 called *Internet Explorer*, which is the subject of another book (*60 Minute Guide to Internet Explorer 3.0 or Internet Explorer 3.0 For Dummies* from IDG Books Worldwide would be a good place to start).

One of the nicest things about Works is that, as much as possible, all of the Works tools use similar commands to perform similar functions. Thus, once you learn how to open a file or print your document in the Word Processor, you already know how to do it in the Spreadsheet and the Database. There's no need to learn a different set of commands for each program.

Starting Works

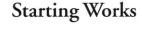

STARTING WORKS

- To start Microsoft Works, click the Start button. Then choose the <u>P</u>rograms⇨Microsoft Works 4.0⇨Microsoft Works 4.0 command.
- To start Works automatically whenever you start your computer, use the Start⇨ <u>S</u>ettings⇨<u>T</u>askbar command to add the Works program file (c:\Program Files\MSWorks\ MSWorks.exe) to the StartUp folder.

Here is the complete procedure for starting Microsoft Works:

1. Click the Start button to summon the Start menu.

You can usually find the Start button in the lower-left corner of your screen. If you can't find the Start button, point the mouse at the very bottom edge of the screen. If this does not summon the Start button, point the mouse at the left, top, and right edges of the screen. If all else fails, press Ctrl+Esc.

2. Click Programs to summon the Programs menu.

The Programs menu will also appear if you hover the mouse over the word Programs for a moment. The menu will appear sooner, though, if you click.

3. Click Microsoft Works 4.0 to summon the Works menu.

Again, you don't have to click, but the menu will appear sooner if you do.

4. Click Microsoft Works 4.0.

This time you do have to click.

If this is the first time you have ever used Works, you will see a dialog box inviting you to watch a brief program entitled *Introduction to Microsoft Works 4.0*. If you wish, you can view this introduction. It will take about 10 minutes and will give you a very general overview of the capabilities of each of the Works tools and let you know about some of Works' more interesting features. If you have the time, go ahead and view the introduction. It won't hurt.

When you have finished the introduction, Works displays its opening screen, called the *Works Task Launcher*. The Task Launcher is described in the section "Welcome to the Task Launcher" later in this chapter.

Other Ways to Start Works

One of the great things about Windows is that you can perform any given task in at least three ways. Works is no exception. The following sections describe a few alternate methods of starting Works.

Using My Computer

You can launch Works by double-clicking a Works document in My Computer. Start by double-clicking on the My Computer icon which resides on your desktop. This will display a view of the disk drives that are connected to your computer. Double-click the icon for your disk drive to display a list of the folders that are on the drive. You can continue double-clicking folder icons until you come to the folder that contains the Works document you want to access. Double-click the document's icon to start Works and open the document.

Using the Documents menu

The Start menu contains a Documents command, which keeps a list of the documents you have used most recently. You can quickly open any document you have worked on recently by clicking the Start button, then choosing the <u>D</u>ocuments command to reveal the menu of recently used documents. Double-click the document you want to open.

Creating a shortcut to Works

If you use Works a lot, you may want to create a shortcut to it. The shortcut is an icon which rests directly on your desktop. You can start Works by double-clicking this icon, so you don't have to fuss with the Start menu or My Computer. Shortcuts can be a real time saver.

Here are the steps for creating a shortcut to Works on your desktop:

1. Open a My Computer window and navigate your way to the c:\Program Files\MSWorks folder.

2. Use the right mouse button to drag the icon for the MSWorks.exe file out of the folder and onto the desktop.

3. When you release the button, a pop-up menu appears. Choose the Create Shortcut Here command to create a desktop shortcut.

Starting Works Automatically

If you use Works almost every time you use your computer, set up Windows 95 so that it automatically starts Works each time you turn on your computer. Just follow these steps:

1. Click the Start button and choose the <u>S</u>ettings⇨<u>T</u>askbar command.

2. Click the Start Menu Programs tab.

3. Click Add, and then click Browse.

4. Double-click the Works program file MSWorks.exe. You will find it in the c:\Program Files\MSWorks folder.

5. Click Next.

6. Double-click the StartUp folder. If you have many folders in your Start menu, you may have to scroll down the list a bit to find the StartUp folder.

7. Click Finish.

That's all! The next time you start your computer, Works will automatically start up.

If you get tired of Works starting up each time, you can remove it by choosing the Start⇨<u>S</u>ettings⇨<u>T</u>askbar command and clicking the Start Menu Programs tab, clicking <u>R</u>emove, locating the MSWorks.exe command, and clicking <u>R</u>emove.

Welcome to the Task Launcher

The control hub of Works is called the *Works Task Launcher*. It is shown in Figure 1-1.

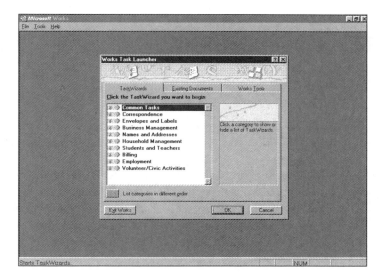

Figure 1-1
The Works Task Launcher.

The Works Task Launcher will be an almost constant companion throughout your Works journeys. As you can see, the Task Launcher (I usually call it that instead of the *Works* Task Launcher) consists of three tabbed sections. You can call up any of these tabbed sections by clicking on the tabs that appear across the top of the Task Launcher dialog box.

Each of the three tabbed sections of the Task Launcher provide a different means of entering the Works tools:

- **TaskWizards:** Lists the Works *TaskWizards*, which automatically create the common types of documents for you. The TaskWizards are described in the section "Creating a New Works Document."
- **Existing Documents:** Lists the documents you have been working with most recently. You can open one of these documents by double-clicking it. Or, you can click "Open a document not listed here" to open any other document located on your hard disk.
- **Works Tools:** Lets you directly access the Word Processor, Spreadsheet, Database, or Communication programs without creating a new document.

The Task Launcher automatically appears whenever you close all documents. If you ever find yourself starting at a blank Works screen, with no documents open and no Task Launcher in sight, you can recall the Task Launcher by choosing the File⇨New command.

Creating a New Works Document

■ To create a new document in Works, use one of the TaskWizards available from the Works Task Launcher dialog box.
■ To create a blank document, choose the Start from Scratch Wizard from the Works Task Launcher dialog box. You can also click the Tools tab and select the program you want to run.

When you start up Works, the Works Task Launcher is displayed. The Task Launcher is your portal to the many functions that are available from within Microsoft Works.

As you can see in Figure 1-1, the Task Launcher displays a list of TaskWizards that you can use to create a new Works document. TaskWizards simplify the process of creating certain types of documents by asking you a few questions about how you want the document to appear. Then Works automatically creates the document for you. You can then customize the document to suit your particular needs.

About the TaskWizards

The TaskWizards are organized into the following categories:

■ Common Tasks
■ Correspondence
■ Envelopes and Labels
■ Business Management
■ Names and Addresses
■ Household Management
■ Students and Teachers
■ Billing
■ Employment
■ Volunteer/Civic Activities

You can click any of these categories to reveal a list of the TaskWizards for that category. For example, Figure 1-2 shows the TaskWizards that are available under the Household Management category. Table 1-1 lists all TaskWizards that come with Microsoft Works and shows what category or categories each TaskWizard can be found under. (Some of the TaskWizards are listed under more than one category.)

The icon that appears next to each TaskWizard indicates which Works tool is used by the TaskWizard, as follows:

Word Processor
Spreadsheet
Database

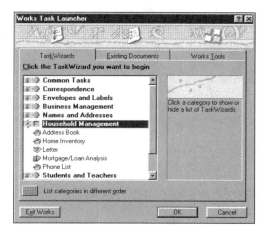

Figure 1-2
The Household
Management
TaskWizards.

TABLE 1-1: THE TASKWIZARDS THAT COME WITH MICROSOFT WORKS

TASKWIZARD	DESCRIPTION	CATEGORY
Accounts	Creates a database to keep track of your accounts receivable, accounts payable, or checking accounts.	Business Management
Address Book	Creates an address book to keep in touch with your business contacts, clients, family, friends, or employees.	Common Tasks
Bibliography	Creates a bibliography to list your reference sources in MLA, APA, or annotated bibliography styles.	Students and Teachers
Bids	Creates bid forms to estimate labor costs, material costs, and both labor and material costs for your customers.	Correspondence
Brochure	Creates a side-fold or three-panel brochure design for your business advertisements.	Correspondence
Business Inventory	Creates a database of the items and equipment you use, so you can calculate costs, current supplies, profits, or losses.	Business Management
Certificate	Creates one of three special certificates to acknowledge a special student, employee, or team member.	Correspondence
Customers or Clients	Creates an address book to keep track of key information about your customers or clients.	Names and Addresses

continued

Table 1-1: The TaskWizards That Come with Microsoft Works (*continued*)

TASKWIZARD	DESCRIPTION	CATEGORY
Employee Profile	Creates information sheets to store your employees' names, addresses, emergency contacts, employment history, and benefits.	Business Management
Employee Time Sheet	Calculates weekly, bi-weekly, and monthly time and wages for your hourly employees.	Business Management
Envelope	Prints an envelope for one or more people.	Envelopes and Labels
Fax Cover Sheet	Creates one of three designs to create an eye-catching cover sheet for your faxes.	Correspondence
Flyer	Create flyers to advertise special events at your business, school, organization, or household with a specially designed flyer.	Correspondence
Form Letter	Creates a form letter to send to the people in your address book.	Correspondence
Grade Book	Calculates student averages for a series of tests or assignments, and record the number of incomplete tests and assignments for each student.	Students and Teachers
Home Inventory	Stores important information about your possessions for insurance policies and household recordkeeping.	Household Management
Invoice	Creates sales or service invoice forms and has Works do the calculations, or print the forms for your customers.	Business Management
Labels	Creates a label for one or more people in your database.	Envelopes and Labels
Letter	Choose a letter from a list of prewritten letters that suites your needs, or create your own letter with suggestions from the TaskWizard.	Common Tasks
Letterhead	Creates professionally designed business or personal stationary for all your correspondence.	Common Tasks
Memo	Creates memos for your business, school, or club in three different designs.	Correspondence
Mortgage/ Loan Analysis	Calculates the cost of obtaining a fixed-rate mortgage or loan, the size of mortgage or loan you can qualify for, or the amount you can save by making extra payments.	Business Management
Newsletter	Creates a one-, two-, or three-column newsletter for your school, business, or organization in a few easy steps.	Common Tasks
Order Form	Creates order forms for your customers or to order goods from a store or supplier.	Business Management

TASKWIZARD	DESCRIPTION	CATEGORY
Phone List	Creates a phone directory of friends, family, contacts, associates, and emergency numbers, then organizes, sorts, and prints the information as needed.	Names and Addresses
Price List	Creates price lists for your customers' orders and to advertise your products and prices.	Business Management
Proposal Form	Creates a single- or multiple-page form to help you prepare a proposal.	Correspondence
Proposal Letter	Creates a proposal letter chosen from a list of prewritten proposals, cover letters, and follow-up letters, or write your own with help from professional guidelines.	Correspondence
Quotations	Creates forms to submit standard quotes, quotes with shipping procedures, or quotes with shipping procedures and discounts.	Correspondence
Resume (CV)	Creates a resume with a chronological, qualifications, or CV format, and the professionally designed layouts will assure an attractive appearance for your resume.	Common Tasks
Return Address Labels	Creates a return address label to use for your correspondence.	Envelopes and Labels
Sales Contacts	Creates an address book to keep track of key information about your sales contacts and to keep track of your follow-up requirements and dates.	Business Management
Schedule	Creates forms to schedule classrooms, write lesson plans, or plan work activities.	Students and Teachers
School Report/ Thesis	Creates a book report, essay, or term paper layout to help you get started on your school assignments.	Correspondence
Start from Scratch	Answer a few questions about the kind of document you want, and the TaskWizard will quickly set it up so you can start working right away.	Names and Addresses
Statements	Creates monthly statements or overdue notices for your customers, showing their purchases, payments, credits, and the current amount due.	Business Management
Student and membership Information	Creates an address book to keep record names, addresses, emergency numbers, and medical information for your students, club members, or teammates.	Names and Addresses
Suppliers and Vendors	Creates an address book to keep track of key information about your vendors and suppliers.	Business Management
Tests	Creates a preformatted layout to help you prepare a true/false, multiple-choice, or essay test.	Students and Teachers

Using the TaskWizards

Many of the projects in this book will use the TaskWizards. This section presents the basics of using TaskWizards; the details for using specific TaskWizards are found in the projects throughout this book.

To select a TaskWizard, click on one of the categories to display the TaskWizards for that category, then click the TaskWizard you want to select. If the TaskWizard isn't in the category you expanded, you can select another category to see its TaskWizards. And if you wish, you can click a category you've already expanded to hide that category's TaskWizards.

Notice that when you click a TaskWizard to select it, Works displays a brief explanation of what the TaskWizard does in the lower right corner of the Task Launcher dialog box. To run a TaskWizard, double-click it or select it and click the OK button.

When you run a TaskWizard, Works displays a dialog box asking if you really want to run the TaskWizard, as shown in Figure 1-3. To start the TaskWizard, click the button next to "Yes, run the TaskWizard." (If this dialog box annoys you, uncheck the Always display this message option.)

The TaskWizard you selected appears. Each TaskWizard has its own unique display. Figure 1-4 shows the Address Book TaskWizard, which is a typical TaskWizard that comes with Works.

All of the TaskWizards include an Instructions button. This button leads to a graphical explanation of how to use TaskWizards in general — it does not lead to detailed help for a particular TaskWizard.

Most of the TaskWizards begin with a display of several alternative formats for the document, spreadsheet, or database you are trying to create. Click the option for the style you want to use.

Many of the TaskWizards require more than one screen to gather the information they need to create your document. Click the Next button to move on to the next screen. You can also click the Back button to move back to the previous screen in case you want to change a previously selected option. When the TaskWizard has gathered all the information it needs, the Next button will be replaced by a Create It! button.

When you click the Create It! button, a special Check List screen appears. This screen summarizes the choices you made in the TaskWizard. From this screen, you can click the Create Document button to create the document based on your instructions. When you click the CreateIt! button, the TaskWizard will create the document for you. Then the TaskWizard will exit, leaving you in the Works tool used to create the document — the Word Processor, Spreadsheet, or Database, depending on which TaskWizard you chose. You can then customize the document for your needs.

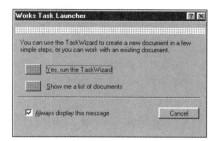

Figure 1-3
Works asks if you are
sure you know what
you're doing.

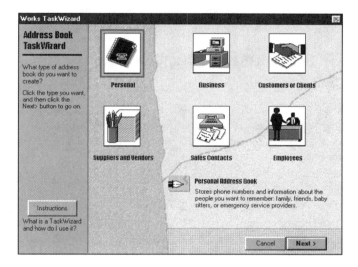

Figure 1-4
The Address Book
TaskWizard.

Creating a document from scratch

The TaskWizards are great for creating certain specific types of documents. But what if you need to create a type of document that isn't covered by any of the TaskWizards? That's when you need to start from scratch.

The Task Launcher gives you two ways to create a document from scratch. First, you can select the Start from Scratch TaskWizard, found under the Common Tasks category. The Start from Scratch Wizard lets you select whether you want to create a word processing, spreadsheet, or database file. It also lets you set up a basic format for the new file as described here:

- For a word processing document, you can choose one of four text styles (Prestige, Contemporary, Typewriter, or Whimsical), and you can add a border to the page. Each of these four styles is illustrated by a picture in the Wizard.
- For a spreadsheet, you can choose whether to include page headers and footers, select one of three text styles, and specify the page orientation (Landscape or Portrait). These options are illustrated by pictures in the Wizard.

■ For a database, you can choose the text style, and you can direct the Wizard to automatically add fields for names and addresses or generic fields named Field1, Field2, Field3, and so on. (If you're unsure about what a database field is, don't worry about it for now. Chapter 4 introduces this concept and other important database terms and shows you how to use the Database tool.)

The second way to create a document from scratch is to click the Works Tools tab in the Works Task Launcher and run the tool you want to use to create your new document (Word Processor, Spreadsheet, or Database). The tool you select will be started, and a new, empty document will be created.

Opening an Existing Document

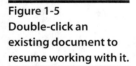

OPENING A FILE

1. To open a file you have recently used, click the <u>E</u>xisting Documents tab in the Works Task Launcher and double-click the file from the list of recently used files.
2. If the file you want doesn't appear in the list, click <u>O</u>pen a document not listed here and locate the file.

If you have previously created and saved a document, you can retrieve the document to work on it. The easiest way to open an existing document is from the Works Task Launcher. Just click the <u>E</u>xisting Documents tab and the dialog box shown in Figure 1-5 appears. (Of course, your filenames will be different, but you get the idea.)

As you can see, this dialog box lists files that you have recently used in Works. To open any of these files, click the file name and then click OK. Or just double-click the file.

Figure 1-5
Double-click an existing document to resume working with it.

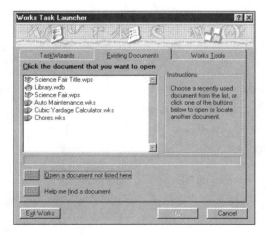

If the file you want to open doesn't appear in the list of recently used files, click Open a document not listed here. The browser dialog box shown in Figure 1-6 appears.

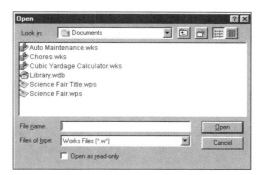

Figure 1-6
Opening a file that doesn't appear in the list of recently used files.

This dialog box lets you access any Works file that is on your hard disk. The Open dialog box displays one folder worth of files at a time. To change the folder that is displayed, use the Look in drop-down list which appears at the top of the dialog box. To move to the current folder's parent folder, click the Up One Level button.

Another way to open an existing document is to go directly to one of the Works tools via the Works Tools tab of the Task Launcher, then use the File⇨Open command. This will display an Open dialog box.

Also, Works adds the four files you have most recently worked with to the bottom of the File menu for each of the Works tools. Thus, when you are in the Word Processor, you can access the four word processing documents you have most recently used directly from the File menu. The same practice applies to the Spreadsheet and Database tools.

Saving a Document

■ Whenever you have made substantial changes to a document that you do not want to lose, choose the File⇨Save command to save the file. If this is the first time you have saved the file, a Save As dialog box will appear. Type a file name and click Save.
■ As an alternative to the File⇨Save command, you can use the keyboard shortcut Ctrl+S or click the Save toolbar button.
■ To save a document under a new name, choose the File⇨Save As command, type a new name for the file, and click OK.

FAST TRACK

SAVING A FILE

When you finish working with a word processing document, spreadsheet, or database file, you can just turn off your computer, right? Wrong! Big mistake!

Before you quit Works and turn off your computer, save your file to disk. Otherwise, you will lose your work. There are three ways to save the file you are working on, and all three work whether you are using the word processor, spreadsheet, or database. They are:

- Click the Save button on the toolbar.
- Choose the File⇨Save menu command.
- Press Ctrl+S.

The first time you save a new file, the dialog box shown in Figure 1-7 will appear. Type a name for your file in the Name field, and then click Save to save the file.

Don't work on a document for hours on end without saving it! In fact, you should get into the habit of saving your work every five minutes or so. Many of the projects in this book include several reminders to save your work at key points in the project, but you should probably save your work even more often than the projects recommend.

Figure 1-7
Specifying a name for a new file.

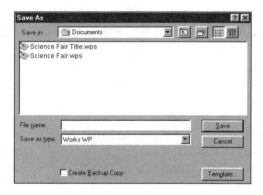

Printing a Document

FAST TRACK

PRINTING A DOCUMENT

1. Open the file you want to print (if it isn't already open).
2. Choose the File⇨Print command or press Ctrl+P.
3. Verify the setting in the Print dialog box.
4. Click OK.

Or, just click the Print button (it's that easy).

To print a document, first make sure your printer is plugged in, turned on, loaded with paper, and ready to print. Then open the document and summon the Print dialog box by choosing the File➪Print command or pressing Ctrl+P. The Print dialog box is illustrated in Figure 1-8.

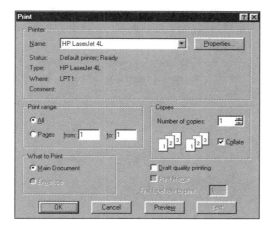

Figure 1-8
The Print dialog box.

Verify that the settings in the Print dialog box are correct. If you have more than one printer connected to your computer, or if you have access to a networked printer, make sure the Printer Name is correct. If you want to print just certain pages of the document, type the page numbers in the From and To fields. If you want to print more than one copy of the document, change the Number of Copies setting.

When the Print dialog box settings are to your liking, click OK to print the document. Or, if you decide you don't want to print the document, click Cancel. If you're not sure what the document will look like when printed, click the Preview button to see a preview of the printout.

The first time you print something in Works, a First Time Help dialog box will appear offering to take you on a tour of printing. If you're interested in such explanations, take the tour. It will last only a few minutes and will give you an overview of how printing works.

Closing a Document

There are three ways to close a file:

- Choose the File➪Close menu command
- Press Ctrl+W
- Click the Close button, which is the "X" button located at the top right corner of the document window.

FAST TRACK

CLOSING A DOCUMENT

To close a file, choose File⇨Close or use the keyboard shortcut Ctrl+W. If the file has changed since you last saved it, Works will ask if you want to save the file to disk before closing the file.

You can also close a file by clicking the close button at the top right corner of the document window. Note that if you have maximized the document window so that it fills the entire Works window, the document window's close button appears beneath the Works close button at the top right corner of the Works window.

You do not have to close the file before you exit the Works. If you exit Works while files are open, Works will automatically close all the files. Again, Works will ask if you want to save any files that have changed since you last saved them.

When you close all open documents, Works automatically summons the Task Launcher.

Getting Help

FAST TRACK

GETTING HELP

- **Choose Help⇨Index or press F1 to search for help by keywords.**
- **Choose Help⇨Contents to browse help by categories.**
- **Choose Help⇨Hide Help to hide the help information that appears at the right of the Works screen. Choose Help⇨Show Help to restore the help information.**

Although Works is not difficult to use, even some experts need help remembering how to use a seldom used feature or learning how to use a previously unused feature. Fortunately, Works has an excellent built-in help facility that displays help on the screen while you work.

Works provides several ways to summon help:

- Choose the Help⇨Contents command. This command summons a list of help categories which you can browse to find the help you're looking for.
- Choose the Help⇨Index command. This command displays an extensive list of help topics arranged in alphabetical order.

The Help⇨Contents and Help⇨Index commands actually summon the same Help Topics dialog box. This dialog box has two tabs: Contents and Index. Thus, if you choose Help⇨Contents, but then decide you want to look up a keyword, you can click the Index tab to display the index. And vice-versa.

- Press F1. This command also summons the help index.
- If a dialog box has a question mark button in its upper right corner, you can click the question mark, then click any control in the dialog box for an explanation of what the control does.
- If you missed the exciting Introduction to Works that was offered the very first time you started Works, you can summon it via the Help⇨Introduction to Works command.
- Use the Help⇨How to use help command to get an on-screen explanation of how to use help.

Figure 1-9 shows the Help Topics dialog box with the index tab shown. To search for help on a particular topic, type a word or phrase in the text box. Then, to display help information, click the help topic in which you are interested.

When working with the Contents tab of the Help Topics dialog box, help is categorized by topic. You can click on a topic, which is indicated by a folder icon, to reveal a list of help items for that topic. Some topics contain subtopics, so you may need to work your way down through several levels before you get to the help you want.

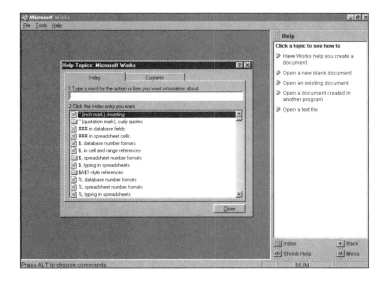

Figure 1-9
Help is at hand!

Notice in Figure 1-9 that the help information has taken over the right side of the Works screen. You can also select topics from this Help pane to find help with specific tasks. As you use Works, the topics presented in the Help pane change depending on what you are doing. For example, when you create a blank spreadsheet document, topics such as "Name and save your spreadsheet or chart" and "Type and correct entries" will appear.

You can shrink the Help pane to a thin vertical bar by clicking the Shrink Help button. Later, you can click this button again to expand the Help pane to its normal size. To hide the Help pane altogether, choose the Help⟳Hide Help command. To redisplay it, choose Help⟳Show Help.

You can also work your way back through previously displayed help topics by clicking the Back button, which appears at the bottom of the Help pane.

If you want to print a help topic, click the Print this topic button, which appears at the bottom of each Help topic.

Works comes with separate help file which contains Frequently Asked Questions — a list of the most commonly asked questions about Works, along with the answers. To access the Frequently Asked Questions, click the Windows 95 Start button, then choose Programs⟳Microsoft Works 4.0⟳Frequently Asked Questions.

Exiting Works

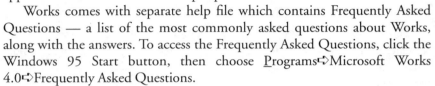

GETTING HELP

Use the File⟳Exit Works command, press Alt+F4, or click the close button at the upper-right corner of the Works toolbar.

If you've had about as much Works as you can take for one day, you can use one of the following techniques to exit Works:

- Choose the File⟳Exit Works command.
- Press Alt+F4.
- Click the close button, the "X" which appears in the upper-right corner of the Works window.
- From the Task Launcher, click the Exit Works button.

If you are working on an unsaved document when you give the command to exit the program, Works will ask if you want to save the document to disk before quitting. Say "Yes" to direct Works to save your file before exiting.

Note that the Task Launcher has an Exit Works button and a Cancel button. The Exit Works button actually quits Works, but the Cancel button merely dismisses the Task Launcher, leaving Works still active. You can summon the Task Launcher back by choosing the File⟳New command.

CHAPTER TWO

USING THE WORD PROCESSOR

In This Chapter

- Moving, copying, and selecting text
- Finding and replacing text
- Formatting text
- Using tabs, bulleted lists, and borders and shading
- Using easy formats
- Using Spell Check

The Word Processor is the Works tool most people use most often. It lets you create text-based documents of any type. With the Word Processor, you can create letters, reports, newsletters with columns, certificates, signs, brochures, flyers, proposals, and just about any other type of text document you can think of.

Although Microsoft Works Word Processor is not nearly as powerful as its older brother, Microsoft Word, it does offer a surprisingly powerful subset of that Word Processing giant's features. For example, Works has a simplified version of Word's powerful style sheets feature called *Easy Formats*, and a simplified version of Word's AutoText feature called *Easy Text*. Works can create multicolumn layouts, bulleted lists, tables, and it can even handle complicated mail merges.

Although Works Word Processor provides many valuable features, this chapter cannot cover all of them. Instead, this chapter focuses mostly on the Word Processor skills you need to create the projects described in the rest of this book.

The Word Processor Screen

When you first start the Word Processor, Works presents you with a blank document in a screen similar to the one shown in Figure 2-1. This screen has enough "doohickeys" and controls on it to make you long for your old Underwood typewriter. But don't be dismayed. Stare at this screen long enough and the various bits and pieces of it will slowly come into focus.

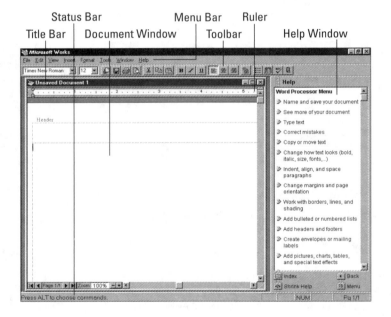

Figure 2-1
The Word Processor screen.

Several items on the Word Processor screen are worthy of comment:

■ At the top of the screen, just below the Microsoft Works title bar, is the *menu bar*. Within the menu bar lurk the mysterious secrets of the Word Processor. Learn the commands on these menus and you will have mastered the Word Processor.

■ Just below the menu bar is the *toolbar*. The toolbar is host to a series of buttons that make the most commonly used Word Processor features available with a single mouse click. If the toolbar doesn't appear, you can summon it by choosing the View➪Toolbar command.

To quickly figure out what a toolbar button does, hover the mouse pointer over the button. After a moment, the name of the button will appear in a small box just below the button. For a more complete description of the button's function, look down at the status bar.

■ In the middle left of the screen is the *document window*, which contains the document on which you are working. This is where you type the text for your document.

The document window shows the document in one of two views: Page Layout and Normal. Figure 2-1 shows the document in Page Layout view, which is my preferred mode of working because Page Layout view shows the exact appearance of various elements of the page, such as headers, footers, columns, and footnotes. If you prefer a simpler view, you can switch to Normal view by choosing the View↪Normal command. To switch back to Page Layout view, choose View↪Page Layout.

At the top of the document window is a *ruler* that you can use to gauge the position of text on the page. You can also use the ruler to set tab stops and control paragraph indentation. If the ruler doesn't appear, you can call it up by choosing the View↪Ruler command.

Notice also that Works provides several controls at the bottom of the document window. These controls allow you to move forward or backward through your document one page at a time. They also allow you to change the zoom factor. Increase the zoom factor and the document's text will appear larger in the document window. Decrease the zoom factor to decrease the size of the text so that more of the document can be seen at once.

If you have more than one document open at a time, each will be shown in its own document window. You can switch among the open document windows by choosing the document you want to view from the Window menu.

■ The right two-thirds of the middle portion of the screen contains the *Help window*, which displays a list of the most commonly used help topics for the Word Processor.

You can hide the Help window by clicking the Shrink Help button that appears at the bottom of the help window. The Help window will shrink down to a narrow bar at the right edge of the screen, just wide enough to retain the Shrink Help button. You can click the Shrink Help button again to restore the Help window to its normal size. You can also turn off the Help window by choosing the Help↪Hide Help command.

■ At the bottom of the screen is the *status bar*, which displays informative messages about what you are doing and what certain commands mean. These messages change frequently as you work.

Typing Text

The most basic task of a word processor is to allow you to type text. To enter text into your document, all you have to do is position the insertion point cursor where you want the text to appear and start typing.

Typing text in Works is much like using a typewriter, but there are several important dos and don'ts I want to point out:

- Do not press the Enter key at the end of each line of text. When you get to the end of a line, just keep typing. Works will automatically begin a new line for you and will break the line cleanly between words.
- Do press the Enter key at the end of a paragraph. To leave a blank line between paragraphs, press the Enter key twice.
- Do not use the space bar repeatedly to line up columns of text. Instead, use the Tab key.
- Do use the tab key to indent the first line of a paragraph.
- Do not use the backspace key to move the insertion point cursor back to retype text. The backspace key erases a character each time you press it. If you discover a mistake ten characters back and press the backspace key ten times to get to it, you'll have to retype all those characters you needlessly erased.
- Do use the backwards arrow key that is clustered with the other arrow keys to move backwards to correct text. This key moves the insertion point cursor back one character without deleting that character.

Moving and Selecting

The following sections describe some of the most basic procedures for working with Word Processor documents, such as moving the insertion point around the page and selecting text.

Moving around

Works provides you with many ways to move around within a document. For starters, you can click the mouse at any location on the screen where there is text to move the insertion point to that location. You can also use the scroll bar at the right of the document window to scroll forward or backward through the document. If the page is too wide to fit on the screen (this usually happens when the help window is displayed), you can also use the scroll bar at the bottom of the document window to scroll left and right.

You can also click the Shrink Help button to remove the Help window that takes up nearly a third of the screen. This will increase the width of the document window so that more of your document is visible at once.

To move from page to page, use the page control buttons that appears at the bottom left of the document window, as follows:

- ⏮ Moves to the first page of the document.
- ◀ Moves to the previous page.
- ▶ Moves to the next page.
- ⏭ Moves to the last page of the document.

If you're a keyboard aficionado, you can use the keyboard tricks in Table 2-1 to move around.

Table 2-1: Moving with the Keyboard

KEY OR KEY COMBINATION	WHAT IT DOES
Right Arrow	Moves right one character
Left Arrow	Moves left one character
Ctrl+right arrow	Moves right one word
Ctrl+left arrow	Moves left one word
Home	Moves to the beginning of the current line
End	Moves to the end of the current line
Up Arrow	Moves up one line
Down Arrow	Moves down one line
Page Up	Moves up one screen at a time
Page Down	Moves down one screen at a time
Ctrl+Page Up	Moves to the top of the screen
Ctrl+Page Down	Moves to the bottom of the screen
Ctrl+Home	Moves to the beginning of the document
Ctrl+End	Moves to the end of the document

Using the Go To command and bookmarks

To go directly to any page in your document, choose the Edit⮂Go To command or press its keyboard shortcut, Ctrl+G. This command summons the Go To dialog box, shown in Figure 2-2. Type the page number you want to go to, then click OK.

Figure 2-2
The Go To dialog box lets you jump to any page.

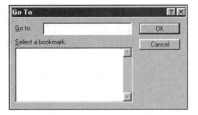

Another way to go to specific locations in a document is to create *book-marks* where you frequently need to go. A bookmark is simply a name of your own creation which you assign to a specific location in a document. To create a bookmark, move to the location that you want to bookmark and choose the Edit⇨Bookmark command. The Bookmark Name dialog box appears, as shown in Figure 2-3. Type the name you want to use for your bookmark, then click OK.

Figure 2-3
The Bookmark Name dialog box.

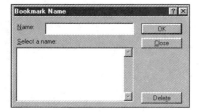

After you create a bookmark, you can go to the location marked by the bookmark at any time by choosing the Edit⇨Go To command (or pressing Ctrl+G) and double-clicking the bookmark name from the list of bookmarks that appears in the Go To dialog box.

If you decide you no longer need a bookmark, you can delete it by choosing the Edit⇨Bookmark command, selecting the bookmark you want to delete, and clicking the Delete button.

Tricks for selecting text

Many Word Processor functions (such as deleting and copying) require that you first select the text you want to change. For example, to delete text, you must first select the text you want to delete, then press the Delete key. To copy text, first select the text you want to copy, then choose the Edit⇨Copy command.

The easiest way to select text is to simply drag the mouse over the text you want to select. You can also select an entire word by double-clicking anywhere in the word you want to select.

To select text with the keyboard, move the insertion point to the beginning of the text you want to select. Then, to move the insertion point to the end of the text you want to select, hold down the shift key while you press any of the keyboard movement keys listed in Table 2-1.

To select an entire document, choose the Edit➪Select All command or press Ctrl+A.

If you select the wrong text, just click the mouse anywhere in the document to unselect the text. Then try again.

Moving and Copying Text

One of the basic joys of word processing is moving text around. As with any Windows word processor, Works provides several ways to do this. The following sections describe the most commonly used procedures.

If you make a mistake during any of these procedures, choose the Edit➪Undo command to immediately undo the damage. Then try again.

Dragging and dropping text

To move text from one point to another, use the drag-and-drop technique described in the following procedure:

1. Select the text you want to move.

2. Place the mouse pointer over the text you selected. When the word "drag" appears beneath the mouse pointer, click and hold the left mouse button.

3. Drag the text to its new location and release the mouse button.

To make a duplicate copy of selected text using the drag-and-drop method, hold down the Ctrl key while you drag the text.

If the mouse pointer never changes to the drag cursor, pop up the Tools➪Options command, click the General tab, and check the "Enable drag-and-drop editing" feature. Click OK, then try again.

Using the Cut, Copy, and Paste commands

Dragging and dropping is fine for moving or copying small bits of text a short distance, but serious moving and copying requires that you use the clipboard — a special "holding area" where Works temporarily stores text so it can be moved or copied from one location to another. Follow these steps:

1. Select the text you want to copy or move.

2. To copy text, choose the Edit➪Copy command, press Ctrl+C, or click the Copy button. Or, right-click the selected text and choose Copy from the shortcut menu that appears.

To move text, choose the Edit➪Cut command, press Ctrl+X, or click the Cut button. Or, right-click the selected text and choose Cut.

3. Move the insertion point to the location where you want the text copied or moved.

4. Choose the Edit⇨Paste command, press Ctrl+V, or click the Paste button. Or, right-click where you want the text pasted and choose the Paste command.

Here are a couple of pointers to keep in mind while pasting:

■ Once you copy or cut something to the clipboard, you can paste it more than once. For example, if you want to duplicate a line of text ten times, copy the text to the clipboard, then paste it nine times.

■ You can paste to a different document than you cut or copied from. After you have copied or cut, switch document windows or open another document, then paste.

■ Remember that copying or pasting permanently erases whatever was previously in the clipboard. So if you cut or copy something, be sure to paste it before you cut or copy something else.

Finding Text

You can use the Edit⇨Find command to find any occurrence of a particular word or phrase anywhere in a document. Just choose the Edit⇨Find command or press Ctrl+F to bring up the Find dialog box, shown in Figure 2-4. Type the text you want to look for, then click Find Next.

Figure 2-4
The Find dialog box.

When Works finds the text, it highlights the text on-screen. If this is the word you were looking for, click Cancel or press Escape to banish the Find dialog box. Note, however, that the Find dialog box remains on-screen so that you can click Find Next to find yet another occurrence of the text. If you start the search in the middle of a document, Works will ask if you want to continue the search from the beginning when the search reaches the end of the document.

The two buttons beneath the "Find what" text field let you search for tabs and paragraph marks. The two options at the bottom of the Find dialog box let you indicate whether you want to restrict the search to whole words, so Works won't find "love" within the word "glove," and whether capitalization matters, so that "Glove" is considered the same as "glove," "GLOVE," or even "gLoVe."

Replacing Text

You can use the Edit⇨Replace text to replace all occurrences of a particular word or phrase with some other text. For example, to replace all occurrences of "Rush Limbaugh" with "Ted Kennedy," use the Edit⇨Replace command. (Whether you would *want* to do so depends of course on your political persuasion.) When you choose the Edit⇨Replace command or use its keyboard shortcut Ctrl+H, the dialog box shown in Figure 2-5 appears. Here you can type in the old text you want to replace in the Find What box and the new text you want to replace the old text with in the Replace With box.

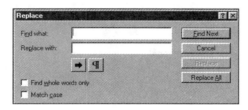

Figure 2-5
The Replace dialog box.

Click Find Next to find an occurrence of the old text, then click Replace if you want the text replaced. You can then click Find Next again to find the next occurrence of the text. Or, if you're in a daring mood, click Replace All to blindly replace all occurrences of the old text in your document, without confirming each one. (If you do this, then realize it was a mistake, choose the Edit⇨Undo command to undo the replace all.)

Here are some additional thoughts to ponder concerning the Replace command:

- Make sure you do not have any text selected before you invoke the Replace command. If you have text selected, the Replace operation will be limited to the selected text and won't be applied to the entire document.
- You can replace text with nothing. For example, if you want to remove all occurrences of the word "Democrat," type "Democrat" in the Find What field and leave the Replace With field empty. (Of course, just to give equal time, you could also eliminate all occurrences of the word "Republican" in the same manner. You would then have a truly nonpartisan document.)

Formatting Text

Works allows you to apply various formats to your text to change the text's appearance or give the text special emphasis. The following sections present the most common formatting procedures.

Setting the font and style

To set the font and style of text, use the following procedure:

1. Highlight the text to which you want to apply the formatting. (If you skip this step, formatting is applied to all new text you type until you repeat the procedure to deactivate the formatting.)

2. Choose the Format⇨Font command.

The Format Font and Style dialog box appears, as shown in Figure 2-6.

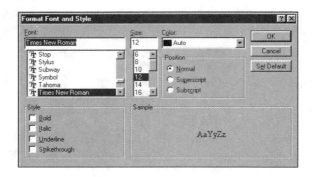

3. Use the controls on the Format Font and Style dialog box to set the font, size, color, position, and style for the font. Some sample text appears in the lower-right corner of the Format Font and Style dialog box so you can see the effect of the font and style settings on your text.

4. Click OK to apply the font and style settings.

For even faster formatting, use the following toolbar buttons or keyboard shortcuts instead of choosing the Format⇨Font command:

CONTROL	KEYBOARD SHORTCUT	FORMAT
Times New Roman		Font
12		Size
B	Ctrl+B	Bold
I	Ctrl+I	Italic
U	Ctrl+U	Underline

Setting indentation and alignment

To set indentation and alignment for a paragraph, use the following procedure:

1. Click anywhere in the paragraph you want to format.

Or, to change indentation and alignment settings for more than one paragraph, select the paragraphs you want the formatting to apply to.

2. Choose the Format⇨Paragraph command. The Format Paragraph dialog box appears, as shown in Figure 2-7.

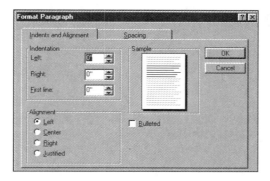

Figure 2-7
The Format Paragraph dialog box.

3. Use the controls on the Format Paragraph command to set the indentation and alignment. The Indents and Alignment tab allow you to set three types of indents: Left, Right, and First Line. You can also choose from four types of alignment: Left, Center, Right, and Justified. And you can add a bullet to the paragraph. (More on bullets later in this chapter, in the section "Bulleted Lists")

4. Click the Spacing tab to reveal the spacing controls. Figure 2-8 shows the spacing controls.

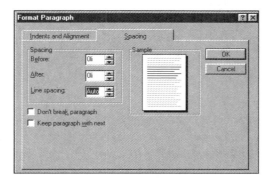

Figure 2-8
The spacing controls on the Format Paragraph dialog box.

5. Set the spacing options. You can increase or decrease the amount of spacing Before and After the paragraph and set the Line Spacing. You can also indicate that the paragraph should not be split over two pages, or that it should always appear on the same page as the next paragraph. (The latter option is useful for headings, as it prevents headings from being orphaned at the bottom of a page.)

6. Click OK to apply the formats. Another way to apply formats is to use the toolbar controls and keyboard shortcuts described in Table 2-2.

TABLE 2-2: BUTTONS AND KEYBOARD SHORTCUTS FOR FORMATTING

CONTROL	KEYBOARD SHORTCUT	FUNCTION
	Ctrl+L	Left aligns a paragraph
	Ctrl+E	Centers a paragraph
		Right aligns a paragraph
	Ctrl+J	Justifies a paragraph
	Ctrl+0 (zero)	Sets space before to 1 line
	Ctrl+1	Single-spaces a paragraph
	Ctrl+2	Double-spaces a paragraph
	Ctrl+5	Sets line spacing to 1.5
	Ctrl+Q	Removes all paragraph formatting

Using Tabs

Tabs allow you to line up columnar information in paragraphs. Whenever you press the Tab key in a paragraph, the text jumps ahead to the next tab stop. By default, tab stops occur every half inch. You can, however, add your own tab stop at any point you want by clicking on the ruler where you want the tab stop to be positioned. A little "L" character will appear on the ruler to mark the tab stop. Note that wherever you place a tab stop, all the default half-inch tab stops that came before the tab stop you created are ignored. In other words, if you create a tab stop at 1.5", the default .5" and 1.0" tab stops are no longer used.

To remove a tab stop, simply drag the tab stop off the ruler. Just position the mouse directly over the tab stop, click and hold the mouse button, drag the mouse straight down until it no longer points at the ruler, and release the button. The "L" character will vanish. Be careful to position the mouse exactly over the tab stop before you click; otherwise, you'll create a new tab stop instead of deleting one.

Each paragraph in your document can have different tab stops. So, changes you make to tab stops apply only to the paragraph or paragraphs that are selected when you make the change. If you want to change tab stops for several paragraphs, you must first highlight those paragraphs before you make the tab stop changes.

When you create a tab stop by clicking on the ruler, you create a left tab stop. In a left tab, text is left-aligned at the tab stop. Works also lets you create centered, right-aligned, and decimal tabs, in which numbers are centered over the decimal point. To create one of these more exotic tabs, double-click the ruler where you want the tab stop to be positioned. The Format Tabs dialog box appears, shown in Figure 2-9. Select the type of tab you want to create, then click OK.

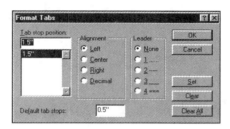

**Figure 2-9
The Format Tabs dialog box.**

The Format Tabs dialog box also lets you create leader tabs, which are tabs that have rows of dots, dashes, underlines, or double-underlines instead of spaces between tab stops. These tabs are perfect for tables of contents, indexes, menus, concert programs, and other similar documents.

Bulleted Lists

Bulleted lists are often used to draw attention to a series of related paragraphs. To create a bulleted list, follow these steps:

1. Select the paragraph or paragraphs to which you want to add bullets.
2. Click the Bullets button on the Formatting toolbar.

To add additional paragraphs to the bulleted list, position the cursor at the beginning or end of one of the bulleted paragraphs and press Enter. Because the bullet is part of the paragraph format, it carries over to the new paragraph.

To remove bullets, select the paragraphs from where you want to remove the bullets, then click the Bullets button again. (Note that when you highlight text, the bullet character itself will not be highlighted. That's because the bullet character is not a character you typed. Therefore, you can't select it. To remove the bullet, you must click the Bullets button.)

If you want to create a bulleted list as you go, start by formatting the first paragraph with a bullet; then the bullet format is propagated to subsequent paragraphs as you type them. After you finish, press Enter and then click the Bullets button again to deactivate bullets.

To change the bullet character, choose Format⇨Bullets to summon the Format Bullets dialog box, shown in Figure 2-10. Pick the bullet you want to use, then click OK.

Figure 2-10
The Format Bullets dialog box.

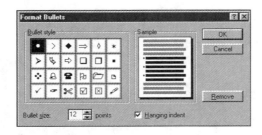

Borders and Shading

You can add a border all the way around a paragraph, or you can selectively add borders above, below, to the left, or to the right of a paragraph. To add a border around a text paragraph, follow these steps:

1. Place the insertion point anywhere in the paragraph to which you want to add a border. If you want to border several paragraphs, select them all.

2. Choose the Format⇨Borders and Shading command. The Borders and Shading dialog box appears with the Borders tab selected, as shown in Figure 2-11.

Figure 2-11
The Bullets and Shading dialog box.

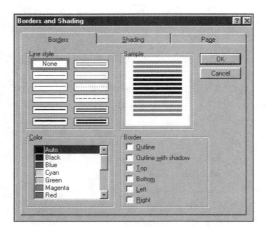

3. Select the Line style you want to use. A variety of line styles are available, including thin and thick solid lines, dashed lines, and doubled lines. To remove a border, choose None as the Line style.

4. Pick a color for the border. Unless you use a color printer, stick with black or a shade of gray.

5. Check the Border options you want to use. You can select Outline or Outline with Shadow to draw a box completely around the paragraph. Or, you can choose any combination of Top, Bottom, Left, or Right.

6. Click OK to apply the border. To apply shading, the paragraph or paragraphs you want to shade, choose the Format⇨Borders and Shading command, and click the Shading tab. The Shading options appears, as shown in Figure 2-12.

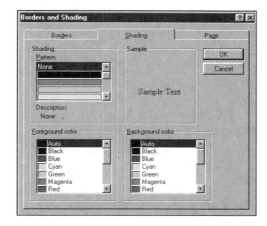

Figure 2-12
Shading a paragraph.

The Shading options may seem confusing at first. To shade a paragraph, you must choose three option settings: a pattern, a foreground color, and a background color. The default pattern is None. The first pattern in the list after None is a solid color, which uses only the foreground color you choose. The remaining patterns use a combination of foreground and background colors to create various types of shading. The best way to learn how these shading patterns work is to experiment with different combinations of patterns, foreground, and background colors. You should also experiment by printing out results of various shading patterns and colors, as printed output will vary a bit from how the shading and coloring appears on the screen.

You can also apply a border to an entire page by displaying the Borders and Shading dialog box and clicking the Page tab, shown in Figure 2-13. Here, you can select one of several line styles and colors for the border. You can also add a shadow, specify that the border should appear only on the first page of the document, and control the distance of the border from the edge of the page.

Figure 2-13
Applying a border to a
page.

Figure 2-13
Applying a border to a
page.

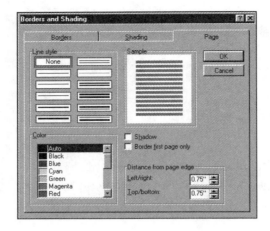

Using Easy Formats

Easy Formats let you apply a group of formatting options with a single
mouse click. An Easy Format is a collection of formatting options, such as
font, size, style (bold, italic, or underline), paragraph spacing and indentation, and even border and shading options. Works comes with a collection of
25 Easy Formats already defined for you. In addition, you can create your
own Easy Formats to supplement the 25 that come with Works.

Figure 2-14
The Easy Formats
dialog box.

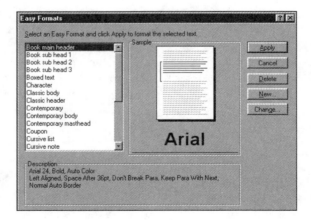

Applying an Easy Format

To apply an Easy Format, follow these steps:

1. Place the insertion point anywhere in the paragraph you want to format. You don't need to highlight the entire paragraph. But you can, if you wish, highlight more than one paragraph.

2. Choose the Format⇨Easy Formats command. The Easy Formats dialog box appears, as shown in Figure 2-14.

3. Select the Easy Format you want to use for the paragraph. When you select an Easy Format, a sample of how text will appear when the Easy Format is applied appears in the dialog box along with the name of the font that will be used. In addition, a description of the Easy Format's formatting options appears at the bottom.

4. Click Apply. The Easy Format will be applied to the text. The effect should be immediately apparent. If you applied the wrong Easy Format, don't panic. Just choose the Edit⇨Undo command to remove the Easy Format.

Another way to apply an Easy Format is to use the Easy Formats button in the toolbar. Select the paragraph or paragraphs you want to format, then click the Easy Formats button. A list of commonly used Easy Formats will appear. Click the one you want to use, or click More Easy Formats to summon the Easy Formats dialog box.

Creating a new Easy Format

To create an Easy Format of your own, follow these steps:

1. Format a paragraph the way you want the Easy Format to be formatted. Apply whatever font, size, style, line spacing, indentation, borders, and shading you want the Easy Format to reflect.

2. Choose the Format⇨Easy Formats command. The Easy Formats dialog box appears. (Refer to Figure 2-14.)

3. Click the New button. The New Easy Format dialog box appears, as shown in Figure 2-15.

4. Type a name for your Easy Format. Use a sensible name that will help you remember what the new Easy Format can be used for.

5. Click Done. The Easy Formats dialog box reappears. The name of the new Easy Format you just created also appears alphabetically.

6. Click Close to dismiss the Easy Formats dialog box. If you prefer, you can use the buttons on the New Easy Format dialog box to manually set each of the new Easy Format's formatting options.

Figure 2-15
The New Easy Format
dialog box.

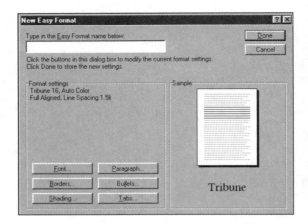

To remove an Easy Format, summon the Easy Formats dialog box, select the Easy Format you want to delete, and click the <u>D</u>elete button.

Spell Checking Your Document

If you count yourself among those who thought Dan Quayle was right when he stuck an "e" on the end of "Potato," you'll appreciate Works' spell checker feature. It compares every one of the words in your document against its built-in dictionary to see if you have misspelled any words. It even offers to correct your spelling mistakes for you.

To start the spell checker, first make sure no text is selected. Then choose the <u>T</u>ools➪<u>S</u>pelling command, press F7, or click the Spelling button. Whichever you choose, Works begins checking your spelling. If (or when) Works finds a misspelled word, it displays the Spelling dialog box as shown in Figure 2-16.

Figure 2-16
The Spelling
dialog box.

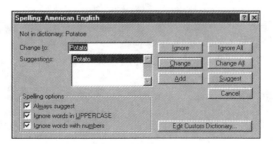

If the word really is misspelled, choose the correct spelling from the list of suggested spellings that appears in the dialog box and click the <u>C</u>hange button. If the correct spelling doesn't appear among the suggestions, type the correct spelling in the Change <u>T</u>o box and click the <u>C</u>hange button. If the word is correctly spelled as it is, click the Ignore button. Or, if you don't want the word to be flagged as a spelling error in the future, click the Add button to add the word to the Works spelling dictionary.

Works doesn't spell check the word you type as a replacement. So be careful! Also, note that ewe cannot count on the spell checker two correct words that are incorrectly used, such as sew called "homophone" errors, where words that sound alike are interchanged.

CHAPTER THREE

USING THE SPREADSHEET

In This Chapter

- Understanding spreadsheets
- Working with formulas
- Formatting cells
- Editing your spreadsheet
- Creating charts

The Spreadsheet is the mathematical brains of Works. It allows you to lay out a grid of rows and columns of numbers much like an old-fashioned ledger sheet. A spreadsheet lets you create formulas which cause calculations (such as totals and averages) to be automatically updated whenever you change any of the numbers in the spreadsheet. For example, in a budgeting spreadsheet, the total budget would automatically be recalculated whenever you change any of the individual budget lines. Or, in a baseball or softball team roster, each player's batting average would be automatically updated whenever you change the number of at-bats and the number of hits.

The ultimate spreadsheet program is Microsoft Excel. The Works Spreadsheet isn't nearly as powerful as Excel. If you are the manager of a billion-dollar mutual fund, or if you are plotting the orbital dynamics for the next Shuttle mission, you probably should use Excel instead. However, for simple spreadsheets such as budgets for home, small business, or volunteer organizations, the Works spreadsheet is ideal.

The Spreadsheet Screen

Figure 3-1 shows the screen that is initially displayed when you start up the Spreadsheet program with a blank spreadsheet. The resemblance to a ledger sheet should be immediately apparent.

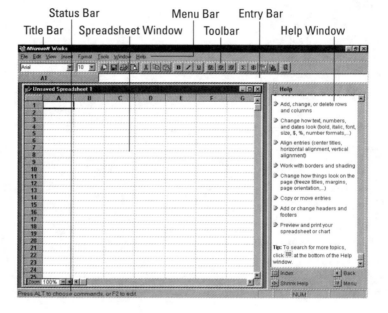

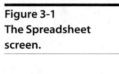

Figure 3-1
The Spreadsheet screen.

Here is a description of the major portions of the Spreadsheet screen:

■ The *title bar* is at the very top of the screen. It contains the title "Microsoft Works," plus the buttons which let you minimize the Works window, switch between a full-screen maximized window and a smaller window (which you can resize at will by dragging from the corner or edge), and close Works.

■ The *menu bar* is located beneath the title bar. The commands within the menu bar are the secret to getting work done with the Spreadsheet. Learn these commands and you will attain Spreadsheet mastery.

■ As usual, the *toolbar* is located just below the menu bar. This is where you will find buttons that provide shortcuts to the most commonly used Spreadsheet features. If the toolbar doesn't appear, you can call it up by choosing the <u>V</u>iew⇨<u>T</u>oolbar command.

If you're not sure what a particular button does, point at it for a moment with the mouse, without clicking the mouse button. After a second or two, the name of the button will appear next to the button, and a description of the button's function will appear in the status bar.

■ Beneath the toolbar is the *entry bar*, which provides a text box in which you can type data to be entered into a cell, or in which you can edit the contents of a cell.

■ The central portion of the screen is devoted to the *spreadsheet window*, wherein you will find the spreadsheet on which you are working. Across the top of the window are column headings in which each column is designated by a letter (A, B, C, and so on). Running down the left edge of the window are the row headers, designating the rows by numbers (1, 2, 3, and so on).

In a spreadsheet, a *cell* is the location at the intersection of a row and column in which you can type data. You can identify any cell in the spreadsheet by using a combination of its column letter and row number, such as A1, B5, and E19. In Figure 3-1, cell A1 is selected.

In Works, a spreadsheet can have as many as 230 columns and 16,384 rows. After the first 26 columns, double letters are used for the column names. Thus, after column Z comes columns AA, AB, AC, and so on up to AZ. Then comes columns BA, BB, BC and so on. The last column is column IV, which is appropriate because if you have to use a spreadsheet with that many columns, you probably will need an "IV." Stat.

■ To the right of the spreadsheet window is the familiar *Help window*, showing a list of common help topics for the Spreadsheet. As usual, you can hide the Help window by clicking the Shrink Help button, which allows more space for the spreadsheet window. The Shrink Help button will remain visible along the right edge of the screen; click it again to restore the Help window to its former glory.

■ At the bottom of the screen is the *status bar*, which displays information about what you're doing, or are about to do, and sometimes even advises you what you should do next.

Entering Data Into Spreadsheet Cells

To enter data into a spreadsheet cell, all you have to do is move the cell pointer to the cell you want to enter data into and start typing. The *cell pointer* is the large rectangle that indicates which cell is currently selected. You can move the cell pointer around the using the cursor control keys or by clicking the cell you want to move the pointer to. (For more information about moving the cell pointer around and selecting cells, see the section "Moving and Selecting" later in this chapter.)

Typing data into spreadsheet cells is a bit different than typing data onto a word processing page. Here are a few pointers to keep in mind:

- If you simply start typing text or a number, the data you type will be placed in the cell that is selected when you start typing. The characters you type will appear in the cell as you type them. The characters will also appear up in the entry bar (which is just beneath the toolbar).
- You can press the Enter key to end a cell entry. This places the data into the cell and leaves the cell selected.
- You can also use any of the arrow keys to end a cell entry. This not only places the data in the cell, but also moves the cell pointer one cell over in the direction indicated by the arrow you press. This can be handy, for example, when entering a series of values down a column of cells — just press the down-arrow key to end each entry, and the cell pointer will automatically move down to the next cell in the column.

To edit the contents of a cell, move the cell pointer to the cell you want to edit and press F2. This will activate a special cell-editing mode for the cell, in which the left and right arrow keys behave more like they do in a word processor: They move the insertion point one character to the left or right rather than move the cell pointer.

When editing a cell, you can use most of the normal Windows text-editing skills you already know. Use the delete and backspace keys to delete characters. To insert characters, use the arrow keys to move the insertion point to the location where you want to insert something and start typing.

When you are finished editing a cell's value, press the Enter key.

Most of the time, you will work directly in the cell when entering and editing cell contents. However, if the cell contains a lot of data (such as a long label or a complicated formula), you may want to work in the entry bar. To edit in the entry bar, select the cell you want to edit, then click the mouse in the entry bar's text box. Edit the cell contents however you wish, then press Enter.

The Tools⇨Options command allows you to change the way cells can be edited. Choose the Tools⇨Options command to summon the Options dialog box, then click the Data Entry tab to display the data entry options. This tab lists three cell data entry modes you can choose from:

- Edit in cells and in entry bar: This is the default data entry mode, and the most flexible. It allows you to edit cells both in the cell itself and in the entry bar at the same time. That's why when you type data into a cell, the data you type appears both in the cell and in the entry bar.
- Edit in entry bar, not in cells: This data entry mode forces you to work in the entry bar. Pressing F2 to edit a cell will take you directly to the entry bar.
- Edit in cells, not in entry bar: This data entry mode hides the entry bar so that you must edit cells directly in the cells.

Because the Edit in cells and in entry bar option provides the most flexible method of editing cells, I suggest you leave it set.

Moving and Selecting

Most of what you do in a spreadsheet requires you to move the cell pointer around to a particular cell, or to select a range of cells so that you can apply formatting or some other type of command. The following sections describe the procedures for moving around a spreadsheet and selecting ranges of cells.

Moving around

As I've already mentioned, the *cell pointer* refers to the heavy outline that marks the currently selected cell. When you click the mouse anywhere in the spreadsheet window, the cell pointer moves to the cell you clicked. You can also move the cell pointer with the keyboard by using the key combinations listed in Table 3-1.

TABLE 3-1: MOVING WITH THE KEYBOARD

KEY OR KEY COMBINATION	FUNCTION
Right Arrow	Moves right one column
Left Arrow	Moves left one column
Ctrl+right arrow	Moves to the right-most cell in a group of nonblank cells or to the last column (column IV) if the row is empty.
Ctrl+left arrow	Moves to the left-most cell in a group of nonblank cells or to the first column (column A) if the row is empty.
Home	Moves to the first cell in the current row (column A)
End	Moves to the rightmost column which contains data in the spreadsheet.
Up Arrow	Moves up one row
Down Arrow	Moves down one row
Page Up	Moves up one screen at a time
Page Down	Moves down one screen at a time
Ctrl+Home	Moves to the beginning of the spreadsheet (cell A1)
Ctrl+End	Moves to the end of the spreadsheet—that is, the right-most column which contains data in the last row which contains data.

Selecting ranges of cells

A *range* of cells is a rectangular block of cells that has been selected. A range can be described by designating the address of the cell in the top-left corner of the range, followed by a colon and the address of the cell in the bottom-right corner of the range. For example, the range of cells bounded by cell A1 and cell D4 is designated as A1:D4.

A range can consist of several cells in a single column or row, in which case either the row number or the column letter will be the same before and after the colon. For example, the range consisting of the cells in rows 5 through 20 of column D would be referred to as D5:D20. Likewise, a range marking columns B through E of row 7 would be B7:E7. You can select a range of cells in Works two ways: with the mouse or with the keyboard. To select a range with the mouse, simply drag the mouse over the range you want to select while you hold down the left mouse button. For example, to select the range B4:G19, point the mouse to cell B4, press and hold the left mouse button, and drag the mouse down to cell G19 and release the mouse button.

To select a range with the keyboard, first move the cell pointer to one of the corners of the range, then press and hold the Shift key and move the cell pointer to the opposite corner of the range. You can use any of the keyboard shortcuts listed in Table 3-1 when you select a range.

Labels, Values, Formulas, and Functions

A cell can contain two basic types of information: a label or a value. To properly use the Works spreadsheet, you must understand the difference between labels and values. You also need to understand how formulas and functions can be used in values to create spreadsheets that perform useful calculations.

Labels

A *label* is text that is not involved in any type of calculation. You use labels to provide titles, headings, and other similar information on a spreadsheet. In many spreadsheets, the first few rows of the spreadsheet are devoted to titles and headings. Often, the first row is a title for the entire spreadsheet, and the second or third row provides headings for each column in the spreadsheet. Similarly, the first column is often devoted to headings that apply to individual rows. For example, in a budget spreadsheet, the first column may contain a budget account description.

Whenever you type text into a cell, Works assumes you are entering a label. If you start typing a number, but then throw in some text, Works assumes that you are typing a label. For example, if you type **2001: A Space Odyssey**, Works will treat the text as a label even though it begins with a number.

If you want a simple number to be treated as a label, start your entry with a quotation mark. For example, suppose you are creating a spreadsheet about the glory years of disco, and you want to use 1975, 1976, and 1977 as column headings. If you simply type **1975** into a cell, Works will assume the cell contains a value. To tell Works to treat 1975 as a label, type "**1975** into the cell.

Values

A *value* is a numeric quantity that you can use in calculations. For example, 100, 49.5, -31833, 3.14159, and 0 are all examples of values.

Values can be simple numbers, but they can also be formulas such as 100*3.5, =B15*0.075, or =C3/(B2*B6/2)+200. Formulas are described in the next section.

Formulas

Formulas are like algebraic expressions and can include mathematical symbols such as +, -, * (for multiplication), / (for division), and ^ (for exponentiation — that is, raising a number to a power). Formulas can also include parentheses to change the order in which the math operations are carried out. Whenever you type a formula, you should always begin the formula with an equals sign so Works doesn't get confused and think you are trying to type a label instead. For example, to enter the formula 15+(2*9), type **=15+(2*9)**.

The real power of formulas is that they can include references to other cells in the spreadsheet. For example, you can add the values in cells D3 and D4 by using the formula =D3+D4. Or, you can multiply the value in cell B15 by 1.5 with the formula =B15*1.5. The advantage of this type of formula is that whenever you change the value of one of the cells mentioned in a formula, the formula is recalculated to give a new result.

Creating formulas that include cell references would be an awkward process if you had to type the cell references yourself. Fortunately, Works provides an easier method, which is best described with the following example. Suppose you want to create a formula in cell B9 that adds the values of cells B7 and B8. You could simply type **=B7+B8** into cell B9. An easier way, however, is to follow these steps:

1. Move the cell pointer to cell B9, where you want the sum to appear.

2. Type an = (equals) sign so Works will know you are about to enter a formula rather than a label.

3. Move the cell pointer to cell B7. The cell reference B7 is added to the formula in cell B9, and the formula now reads =B7.

4. Type a + (plus) sign. The formula now reads =B7+, =B7+, and the cell pointer is returned to cell B9.

5. Move the cell pointer to cell B8. The cell reference B8 is added to the formula in cell B9, and the formula now reads =B7+B8.=B7+B8.

6. Press Enter to complete the formula.

It's true that for this simple example, it would have been faster to just type **=B7+B8**. But trust me. For more complicated formulas, the technique just described is *much* easier than manually typing cell references into your formulas.

Functions

Functions let you perform calculations that are more complicated than simple addition, subtraction, multiplication, or division. Although Works offers many different functions from which to choose, the most popular functions are those that perform basic math operations on a range of cells rather than on a single cell. For example, suppose you want to add up the contents of cells B3 through B10. You could perform this addition with the following formula:

=B3+B4+B5+B6+B7+B8+B9+B10

An easier way, however, is to use the *SUM function*, which adds up all the cells in a given range. To use the SUM function, move the cell pointer to the cell where you want the sum to appear, then type the word **SUM** followed by the cell range in parentheses, as shown here:

=SUM(B3:B10)

Then press Enter.

Notice that the equals sign is typed *before* the SUM function. The placement of the equals sign tells Works that a formula (rather than a label) is being typed. Without the equals sign, Works would treat SUM(B3:B10) as a label.

Works provides dozens of different functions from which you can choose. The most popular functions are listed in Table 3-2. In this table, text which appears in italics refers to information which you must supply when you type the function. For example, in the ABS function, you must supply a *number* which Works uses to calculate the absolute value. You can either type a number directly into the formula, or use a cell reference, such as ABS(B3) to calculate the absolute value of the contents of cell B3.

When you type a function name in a formula, Works automatically displays a small help window, providing help information about the function you typed. This help window will remind you of the details for typing the function you are trying to use.

Also note that when you type a function, it doesn't matter whether you type the function name or cell references in upper-or lower-case letters. Thus, **SUM(B3:B19)** is the same as **sum(b3:b19)**.

TABLE 3-2: POPULAR SPREADSHEET FUNCTIONS

FUNCTION	WHAT IT DOES
ABS(*number*)	Returns the absolute value of *number*.
AVERAGE(*range*)	Calculates the average value of the cells in *range* by adding up the sum of the cells and then dividing the result by the number of cells in the range. Blank cells are not counted, but cells that contain the value zero are.
COUNT(*range*)	Returns the number of cells in *range*. Blank cells are not counted, but cells that contain the value zero are.
IF(*condition, true-value, false-value*)	Tests the condition spelled out in *condition*. If the condition is true, IF returns *true-value*. Otherwise, it returns *false-value*. For example, IF(B9>100,0.20,0) returns 0.20 if cell B9 is greater than 100; otherwise, it returns 0.
MAXIMUM(*range*)	Returns the largest value in *range*.
MEDIAN(*range*)	Returns the median value of the cells in *range*. When you sort the cells in order, the median value is the value in the cell that falls right in the middle of the sorted list. Half the cell values are larger than the median value, and the other half are smaller.
MINIMUM(*range*)	Returns the smallest value in *range*.
NOW()	Returns the current date and time. Nothing need be typed between the parentheses, but the parentheses are required nonetheless.
PMT(*principal, rate, term*)	Calculates payments for a loan. *Principal* is the amount of the loan. *Rate* is the interest rate per period. *Term* is the number of periods. For example, if the annual interest rate is 12 percent and you make payments monthly, the periodic interest rate is 1 percent. Likewise, if the loan is for three years and you make payments monthly, 36 periods exist.
PRODUCT(*range*)	Multiplies all the cells in the specified range.
ROUND (*number, digits*)	Rounds off the *number* to the specified number of *digits*. For example, ROUND(C1,2) rounds off the value in cell C1 to two decimal places.
SUM(*range*)	Adds the values of all cells in the specified range.
VLOOKUP (*value, range, col*)	Searches for the cell in *range* that contains *value*. VLOOKUP searches all the cells in the first column of the range specified for *range*. If it finds *value*, VLOOKUP returns the value of the corresponding cell in the *col* column of *range*. For example, to return the value in the corresponding cell in the second column of the range, specify 2 for *col*.

Formatting Cells

The Works spreadsheet lets you format individual cells in many ways. The following sections describe each of the cell-formatting options available in Works.

Number

You can format each cell with a number format, which determines how numeric values will be displayed. For example, you can display a number with or without dollar signs, commas, and decimal points. To apply a number format, select the cell or range you want to format, then choose the Format➪Number command. The Format Cell dialog box appears with the number formats visible, as shown in Figure 3-2.

Figure 3-2
Setting the number
format.

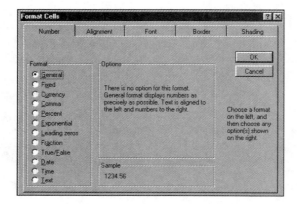

Table 3-3 lists the various number formats that are available from the Format Cell dialog box.

TABLE 3-3: NUMBER FORMATS

FORMAT	EXPLANATION	SAMPLE
General	The default format for numeric values. Decimals are displayed only if necessary, and commas are not used.	239.296
Fixed	Lets you set the number of decimal places to be displayed. Zeros are used if necessary. Commas are not used.	1000.00
Currency	Displays money amounts with a dollar sign and commas and lets you set the number of decimals to show.	$1,000.00
Comma	Uses commas where appropriate. You can set the number of decimal places to display.	1,200.00
Percent	Shows the number as a percentage, with a trailing percent sign.	56.5%
Exponential	Used by NASA to calculate Shuttle orbits.	1.655E+07
Leading Zeros	Lets you set how many digits are to be shown to the left of the decimal point. Leading zeros are used if necessary.	00034

FORMAT	EXPLANATION	SAMPLE
Fraction	Shows the value as a fraction. Great for fourth grade homework.	.2 1/2
True/False	Displays FALSE if the value is zero. Otherwise, displays TRUE.	TRUE
Date	Shows the value as a date. You can choose from several available date formats.	August 18, 1996
Time	Shows the value as a time by using a format you specify.	1:15 am
Text	Displays the Value as Text.	12345

Alignment

Cell alignment is set by the Format⇨Alignment command, which summons the alignment options shown in Figure 3-3. These options determine how information within a cell will be aligned. (Make sure you highlight the cells you want to apply the alignment options to before you call up the Format⇨Alignment command.)

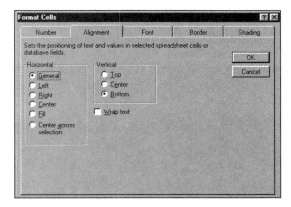

Figure 3-3
Cell alignment settings.

You can specify both a horizontal and a vertical alignment setting. For horizontal alignment, you have the following options:

■ **General:** This is the default alignment. Labels are left aligned and values are right aligned.

■ **Left:** The contents of the highlighted cell or cells are left aligned.

■ **Right:** The contents of the highlighted cell or cells are right aligned.

■ **Center:** The contents of the highlighted cell or cells are centered.

■ **Fill:** The Fill option causes the contents of the highlighted cell or cells to be repeated for the entire width of the cell. It is a good way to fill a cell with asterisks or some other symbol you want repeated.

■ **Center Across Selection:** This option causes the contents of a cell to be centered, but not just within the cell. Instead, the cell is centered over a range of columns. Use this option to create a heading that applies to several columns, or to center a spreadsheet title over the entire spreadsheet.

FAST TRACK

CENTERING A TITLE OVER SEVERAL CELLS

To create a title that is centered over several cells, follow these steps:

1. Type the title in the first cell of the range of cells over which you want the title to be centered. For example, to center a title over cells C3 through C7, first type the title in cell C3.
2. Select the cell in which you typed the title and any cells to the right over which you want the title to be centered. For example, select the range C3:C7.
3. Call up the Format⇨Alignment command and choose Center Across Selection.
4. Click OK.

Note that you can apply Left, Right, and Center alignment quickly by simply selecting the cells you want to align and clicking the appropriate toolbar button.

Font

The Format⇨Font and Style command lets you control the font settings using the dialog box controls shown in Figure 3-4. You can set the font name, font size, color, and style (Bold, Italic, Underline, or Strikethrough).

Figure 3-4
Font and style options.

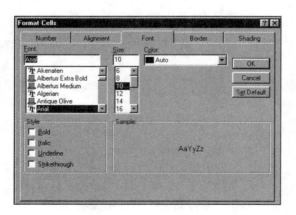

You can also use the following toolbar controls to set the font and size:

 Sets the font.

 Sets the size.

Border

Borders — lines which are drawn around a cell or range of cells — are one of the most useful formatting features in the Works spreadsheet. With the judicious use of borders, you can make even a complicated spreadsheet easy to read. Of course, you can also overdo the borders, making your spreadsheet look like something on which you'd want to play checkers. You can set borders by highlighting the cell or cells you want to apply borders to, then choosing the Format⇨Border command. This will summon the dialog box shown in Figure 3-5.

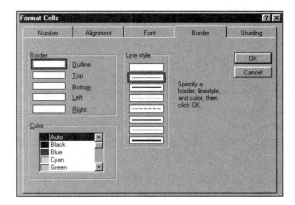

**Figure 3-5
Setting borders.**

To set a border, first click on the border you want to set: Outline, Top, Bottom, Left, or Right. (Outline borders apply to the outside edge of an entire range of cells.) Next, click the Line style and Color you want to use for the border. Note that you can set a different style and color for each border. For example, you could place a heavy line on the bottom, a thin line on the top, and no lines on the left or right. Or, you can place thin lines on the left and right and no lines on the top or bottom. Any combination you can devise will work, as long as the result looks good.

That's all there is to setting up borders. Although you may have to experiment getting the borders to look just the way you want them, don't hold yourself back. Be bold. If your borders end up looking terrible, you can always wipe them out by selecting a range that includes all the cells with borders and clearing all the border settings.

Shading

Shading is another way to make spreadsheets easier to read. It highlights key information, which draws attention to it. To apply shading, first select the cell or cells you want shaded. Then choose the Format⇨Shading command, which displays the dialog box shown in Figure 3-6.

Figure 3-6
A shady deal.

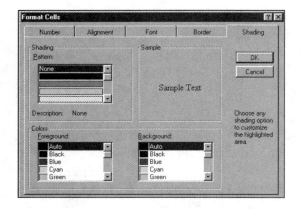

The Spreadsheet's shading options work just the same as the Word Processor's. You can choose from three shading options: a pattern, a foreground color, and a background color. Most of the patterns use both a foreground and a background color, so you can experiment with different combinations of pattern, foreground color, and background color to achieve different shading effects. The Sample area in the dialog box shows how each shading combination will appear. When you're done, click OK.

Using AutoFormat

Because formatting options — especially borders and shading — can be tricky to set up, the Works spreadsheet includes an AutoFormat feature which professionally applies designed formats to entire ranges of cells with just a few mouse clicks. The AutoFormat command sets up row and column headings, as well as optional total lines, and takes care of setting the borders and shading options properly.

To use AutoFormat, follow this procedure:

1. Create your spreadsheet as you normally would. The Format⇨Auto-Format command works best when the first row and the first column of the worksheet contain headings and the last row contains totals. The last column of the worksheet may also contain totals, but it doesn't have to. The AutoFormats work whether or not the last column contains totals.

2. Highlight the entire range of spreadsheet cells that contains the data you want formatted, as shown in Figure 3-7.

3. Choose the Format⇨AutoFormat command. The AutoFormat dialog box appears, as shown in Figure 3-8.

4. Select the format you want to use. A preview of each AutoFormat appears in the Sample portion of the AutoFormat dialog box.

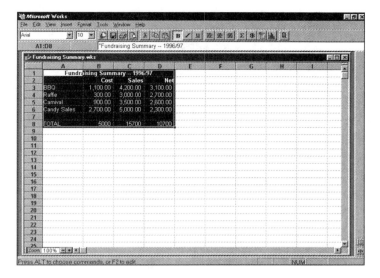

Figure 3-7
Highlighting a range
for the AutoFormat
command.

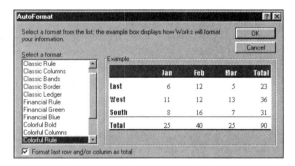

Figure 3-8
The AutoFormat
dialog box.

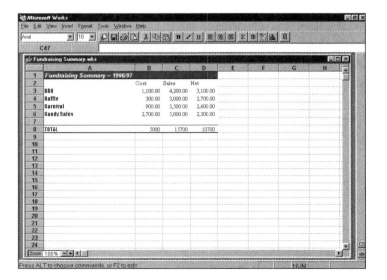

Figure 3-9
A spreadsheet that has
been improved with
the AutoFormat
command.

5. Click OK.

The AutoFormat is applied, as shown in Figure 3-9. If you don't like the formatting applied by the AutoFormat, you can always revert to the previous formatting by pressing Ctrl+Z or choosing the Edit⇨Undo command.

Inserting and Deleting Rows and Columns

No matter how thoroughly you think through your spreadsheet before you create it, you may still end up with too many or too few rows or columns. Fortunately, Works lets you easily add or remove columns and rows from your spreadsheet. The following paragraphs outline the procedures:

■ To insert a new row into a spreadsheet, select any cell in the row above which you want the new row to be inserted. Then choose the Insert ⇨Insert Row command.

■ To insert several rows, select a range of cells which spans the number of rows you want to insert. Then choose the Insert⇨Insert Row command. A corresponding number of rows will be inserted above the first row in your selection.

■ To insert a column, select any cell in the column that precedes the location where you want the new column inserted. Then choose the Insert ⇨Insert Column command.

■ To insert more than one column, select a range that includes the number of columns you want to insert and choose the Insert ⇨Insert Column command. A corresponding number of columns will be inserted to the left of the first column in your selection.

■ To delete a row or column, select any cell in the row or column you want to delete. Then choose the Insert⇨Delete Row or Insert⇨Delete Column command.

■ To delete the contents of a cell without actually removing the cell from the spreadsheet, select the cell and press the Delete key.

Changing the Column Width

Occasionally, you will find that a column is either too wide for the information it contains or, more likely, not wide enough. If a label is too long to fit in a column, Works simply spills the label into the adjacent column — provided the cell in that column is empty. If the cell is occupied, Works doesn't display the extraneous information. (The information isn't deleted from the cell; it just doesn't display because the cell isn't wide enough.)

Values aren't so lucky, however. Cutting off a value because it didn't fit could be dangerous. For example, there's a big difference between

1,022,587,212 and 1,022,587, even to Ross Perot. You wouldn't want Works to just cut off the last three digits because the column isn't wide enough to display them. So, instead of showing just part of the value, Works fills the overflowing cell with # symbols. In other words, if you see a cell that contains #######, it means the column isn't wide enough to display a value.

If you use the General number format, Works will use a peculiar scientific numbering notation for values that are too large. For example, 1,022,587,212 will appear as 1.023E+09. The # symbols appear if you designate a specific number format, such as Fixed, Currency, or Comma, and the number is too large to fit in the column.

Fortunately, changing the width of a column is easy. Just point the mouse between columns in the column heading area until the mouse pointer turns into a double arrow and the word "ADJUST" appears. Then click and drag the column to its new width. Or, you can simply double-click the header above a column. This procedure automatically resizes the column so it is just large enough to display the widest value in the column.

Another way to set the column width is to select a cell in the column, and then choose the Format⇨Column Width command. This procedure displays the dialog box shown in Figure 3-10. Here, you can type in an exact size for the column. Or, you can restore the column to the standard size (10) by clicking the Standard button, and you can set the width so it is large enough to display the widest cell in the column by clicking Best Fit.

Figure 3-10
The Column Width
dialog box.

Using the Fill Feature

The Fill feature makes it easy to create a series of cells, either in a single row or column, which has either the same value or values that change incrementally. For example, you can easily create a series containing the numbers **1** through 100. Start by typing the value **1** in the first cell of your series and **2** in the second cell. Then select both cells. Notice the small box at the lower-right corner of the selection box. When you position the mouse pointer directly over this box, the mouse pointer becomes a cross with the word *FILL* beneath it. When it does become a cross, click and drag the selection to include the rest of the cells you want filled with your series. When you release the mouse button, the cells will be filled in with your series.

Works uses a set of simple rules to determine how it should fill cells when you use the Fill feature. These rules are as follows:

- If only a single cell was selected when you started the fill, the contents of that cell is duplicated in the Fill selection.
- If two cells were selected and both contain values (as opposed to labels), Works determines the difference between the values of the two cells and uses that as the increment value for the rest of the series. For example, if the first two values are 1 and 2, the remaining cells will be filled with 3, 4, 5, and so on. But if the first two values are 5 and 10, the remaining cells will be filled with 15, 20, 25, and so on.
- If more than two cells were selected and those selected cells didn't all have the same increment, Works would simply duplicate the entire range of selected cells. For example, if you select cells with values 1, 4, and 9, Works would fill subsequent cells with 1, 4, and 9 in sequence.
- Fill works fine with dates. For example, type **January 1** and **February 1**, and then use Fill to create cells with March 1, April 1, May 1, and so on. Times work too.

Working with Charts

The Works Spreadsheet program includes a charting feature that can take boring numbers and convert them to exciting charts that even Ross Perot would be proud of. You can create pie charts, bar charts, area charts, line graphs, and even a funky graph called a *radar chart*.

Before you learn how to create a chart, you need to understand the concept of a *series*. A series is a set of numbers that is charted together. Many charts have just one series of numbers to be plotted. For example, if you want to chart your income for the past five years, you would have just one series, with five numbers representing income for five years. However, if you want to chart your income alongside your expenses for the past five years, you would have two series: one for income, the other for expenses. If you want to chart your income, expenses, and your savings, you would have three series.

All the chart types that Works can create, except pie charts, can handle more than one series. For a pie chart, you can only plot one series. That makes sense when you consider that the purpose of a pie chart is to show the relative proportions of several related numbers. For example, a pie chart could show how much of your income went to taxes, savings, and expenses, which would be a single series of numbers. However, you couldn't create a single pie chart that compared taxes, savings, and expenses for this year and last year; it would require two series and, therefore, would have to be plotted as two separate pie charts.

Creating a chart

The following procedure shows how to create a chart:

1. Create a spreadsheet that contains the numbers you want to chart.

For example, if you are creating a chart for a Science Fair experiment in which several brands of popcorn were popped on the stove and in a microwave oven to determine which method pops more corn, create a spreadsheet that lists the amount of popcorn popped for each brand in the microwave and on the stove, as shown in Figure 3-11. Note that you don't have to worry much about the appearance of this spreadsheet, unless you plan on printing the spreadsheet along with the chart.

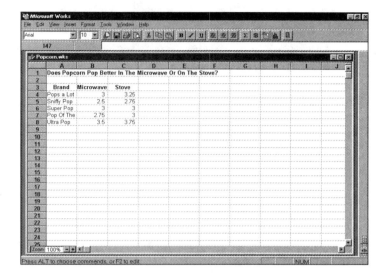

Figure 3-11
A spreadsheet ready to chart.

2. Select the portion of the spreadsheet that contains the data you want to chart.

For example, in Figure 3-11, select the range A3:C9. Include the column headings in the range; Works automatically treats the first row of the selection as a row of headings rather than data. (If your spreadsheet doesn't have headings, you can tell Works to treat the first row as a row of data rather than headings later.)

3. Click the New Chart button.

The New Chart dialog box appears, as shown in Figure 3-12. (If this is your first time creating a chart, a first-timer help dialog box will appear, offering to take you on a tour of charting. Click "To create a chart" to skip the tour.)

4. Select the type of chart you want to create.

The New Chart dialog box lists the basic chart types Works can create. Note that Works can also create several variations of each of these basic chart types. To use one of the variations, however, you must first create a chart by using one of the basic types. You can then change the chart type, as described later in the section, "Changing the chart type."

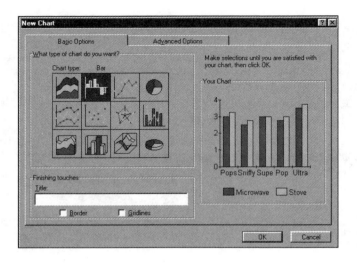

Notice that the preview area of the New Chart dialog box changes when you select the chart type. This preview shows how the data you selected will appear when charted.

5. If you want a title for your chart, type the title in the Title field.

The title appears in the preview area. However, because of a minor bug in Works, the title will not be shown in the correct size. As a result, longer titles will appear to be cut off in the preview. Don't worry about this. The entire title will be shown in the final chart.

6. Click the Border or Gridlines check boxes if you want a border or gridlines to be drawn on your chart.

Both are nice embellishments to add to your chart. You can always add or remove them later if you change your mind. (This options aren't available for pie charts.)

7. If the data does not appear to be charted correctly, click the Advanced tab and fiddle with the advanced chart options.

Figure 3-13 shows the Advanced chart options. These options let you change the orientation of your chart data and indicate whether the first row and column contain labels or data that should be charted. If the chart that appears in the preview area is not at all what you expected, changing these settings can often correct the problem.

8. Click OK to create the chart.

The chart appears in a new spreadsheet window, as shown in Figure 3-14.

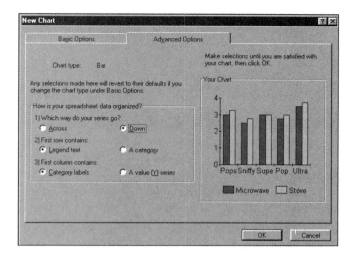

Figure 3-13
The Advanced chart options.

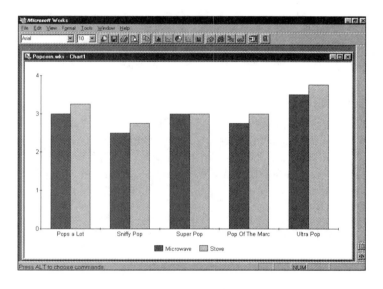

Figure 3-14
Voila! A new chart is born.

Help! Where did my chart go?

When you create a chart, the chart is saved along with the spreadsheet from which you created it. When you open a spreadsheet that contains a chart, however, the chart is not automatically opened. To open a chart that has been saved along with a spreadsheet, choose the View⇨Chart command. A View Chart dialog box appears that lists all the charts that have been saved with the current spreadsheet. Select the chart you want to open, and then click OK.

Changing the chart type

After you have created a chart, you can change the chart type by displaying the chart (use the View⇨Chart command as described in the previous section), then choosing the Format⇨Chart Type command. The Chart Type dialog box appears, as shown in Figure 3-15.

Figure 3-15
The Chart Type dialog box.

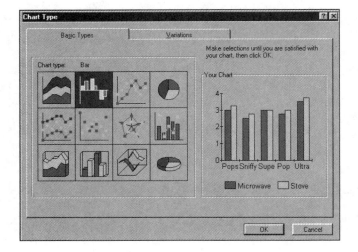

As you can see, the chart types listed in the Chart Type dialog box are the same as the types that were shown in the New Chart dialog box when you first created the chart. However, the Chart Type dialog box also has a Variations tab that shows you up to six variations for each chart type. For example, Figure 3-16 shows the variations that are available for the 3D Bar Chart type. Pick the variation you want, and then click OK to apply the new chart type.

Figure 3-16
The Variations tab provides many choices.

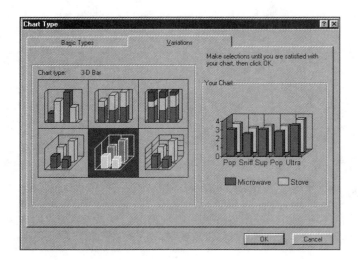

Other embellishments

The Edit and Format menu contains several other commands that you can use to add embellishments to a chart. These commands are described in the following list:

- **Edit⇨Titles:** Choose this command to add a chart title and subtitle, or to add titles for the horizontal and vertical axes of the chart.
- **Edit⇨Legend/Series Labels:** Use this command to add a legend that explains what the different colors used for each chart series represents, or to remove the legend if you later change your mind. (This option isn't available for pie charts.)
- **Format⇨Font and Style:** This command changes the font used to display the legends and labels.
- **Format⇨Shading and Color:** Use this command to change the color used to plot each data series.
- **Format⇨Horizontal (X) Axis:** This command lets you change various and sundry options for the horizontal axis.
- **Format⇨Vertical (Y) Axis:** Choose this command to change the options for the vertical axis.

Besides the commands just listed, you can also change many chart options by right-clicking an object on the chart. A pop-up menu of commands appears. Apply these commands to the object you clicked. For example, if you want to change the font or size of the chart title, right-click the chart title and choose the Font and Style command.

CHAPTER FOUR

USING THE DATABASE

In This Chapter

- Understanding databases
- Creating a database
- Entering data into a database
- Sorting and filtering records
- Creating reports
- Designing good-looking forms

The Works Database is the computer equivalent of the shoe box in which you store your important tax records such as receipts, canceled checks, and so forth. The main difference between the Works Database program and a shoebox is that Works keeps your records in order, lets you print reports that list and summarize your data in almost any form imaginable, and doesn't crumple up your papers.

The ultimate database program is Microsoft Access. If you're designing a database system for the IRS, Publisher's Clearinghouse, or Chase Manhattan Bank, you should probably consider using Microsoft Access instead of Works. But if you're setting up a database for your local Girl Scouts troup, a youth soccer league, or for your household inventory, the Works database is more than adequate.

What Is a Database?

A *database* is a collection of information. Here are some examples of databases from everyday life:

- Your personal address book
- The shoe box that contains your tax records for the year
- Your baseball card collection
- All those parking tickets conveniently stuffed into your car's glove compartment
- The phone book
- The pile of score cards that has been accumulating in the bottom of your golf bag for 15 years
- Your Rolodex file and Day Planner

You can think of each of these databases as a collection of records. A *record* consists of all the useful information you can gather about a particular thing. In your address book, each record represents a person that you know. For your tax records database, each receipt in the shoe box is a record. Each baseball card in your card collection is a record, as is each parking ticket stuffed into the glove box.

Each little snippet of information that makes up a record is called a *field*. The information put into each field is called the *value* of the field. Using the address book as an example once again, each person's record — that is, each entry in the address book — consists of several fields: name, street address, city, state, ZIP code, and phone number. It may also include other information, such as the person's birthday, whether you received a Christmas card from that person last year, and how much money that person owes you.

A Works database is much like these noncomputerized databases. Like your address book or shoe box full of tax records, a Works database is a collection of records, and each record is a collection of fields. The biggest difference is that when you use Works, your database is recorded on the computer's hard disk rather than on paper. When you use the hard disk, you give Works several distinct advantages over address books and shoe boxes. For example, searching a Works database for a particular receipt is much easier than riffling through an overstuffed shoe box.

Works automatically keeps records organized, enables you to conduct a search for particular records that is based on any field in the record, and then lets you print out the results in a report format of your choosing. For example, if you kept your address book as a Works database, you could quickly print a list of all your friends who live in Iowa and owe you more than $10. Try that trick with your noncomputerized address book.

Creating a New Database

Creating a new database in Works is easy. One method is to use the Start from Scratch TaskWizard as described in Chapter 1, which will create a database that has either a set of name and address fields or a set of generic fields with names such as Field1, Field2, and so on. Then you can modify this database by adding new fields or removing or changing the fields created by the TaskWizard.

Or, you can *really* start from scratch, as described in the following procedure:

1. To start the Database, choose Database from the Works Tools tab of the Task Launcher dialog box.

The Database comes to life, displaying the Create Database dialog box, as shown in Figure 4-1. (If this is the first time you've created a database, you'll see a special first-timer's help screen. Click on "Create a database" to get caught up.)

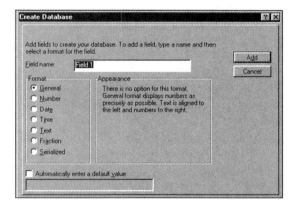

Figure 4-1
The Create Database dialog box.

2. Type a name for the first database field in the Field Name text box.

Choose a name that describes the intended contents of the field, such as Last Name, Address, or Phone Number.

3. Select the data format for the field.

Selecting the data format tells Works what kind of information you'll be storing in the field. Works lets you choose from several different types of data formats, as summarized in Table 4-1.

TABLE 4-1: FIELD FORMATS

FORMAT	EXPLANATION
General	The default format for database fields. Numbers are displayed using a generic number format, and text values are displayed as text.
Number	Lets you choose one of several number formats. Numbers can be formatted with or without commas, decimal positions, dollar signs, and exponents. You can also choose a True/False format in which zero represents False and any non-zero value represents True.
Date	The field will be used to store a date. There are several date formats to choose from.
Time	The field will be used to store a time. There are several time formats to choose from.
Text	Displays the value as text.
Fraction	The value of the field should be displayed as a fraction. Great for fourth grade homework.
Serialized	One of the most useful database field types, Serial fields are automatically assigned the next available number value for each new record inserted into the database.

4. If the field format you choose shows additional options in the Appearance portion of the Create Database dialog box, choose the option you want to use for the field.

All the field formats, except General and Text, have additional formatting options. Pick the one you want to use. (You can always change the field format later if you make a mistake.)

Unlike more sophisticated database programs such as Microsoft Access, Works does not place much emphasis on database field formats. In fact, the database field format is nothing more than a display of formats; you can enter any type of data into any database field, no matter how the field is formatted. Works lets you enter text into a Number field, and you can enter numbers into text fields.

5. Click Add to add the field to the database.

The field is added to the database, and the Create Database dialog box remains on the screen so you can create additional fields.

6. Repeat Steps 2 through 5 for each additional field you want to add to your database.

You can add as many fields as you want.

7. When you finish adding fields, click the Done button.

The Done button doesn't appear in Figure 4-1 because that figure shows how the Create Database dialog box appears *before* you add any fields to the database. When you add a field, the Cancel button changes to the Done button.

When you click the Done button, the Create Database dialog box disappears and the database is displayed, ready for you to enter data as described in the section, "Entering and Editing Data" later in this chapter.

8. Choose the File⇨Save command to save the database.

Type a meaningful name for your database, and then click Save.

Several of the examples that appear in the rest of this chapter work with a simple Batting Stats database, which is used to track batting averages for a baseball or softball team. If you'd like to follow along with these examples in Works, follow the procedure described in the preceding section ("Creating a New Database") to create a database with the following fields:

FIELD NAME	DATA FORMAT
Last Name	Text
First Name	Text
At Bats	Number, 0 decimal places
Hits	Number, 0 decimal places

Understanding Database Views

Figure 4-2 shows how a database appears after you have created it but before you've entered any data into it. This figure shows the database in a format that resembles a spreadsheet. Each row represents a single database record, and the database fields are represented as columns. This database view is called *list view*. It enables you to easily scan the contents of your entire database. You can also modify the design of your database from list view by adding new fields, deleting fields, or changing the name or format of fields.

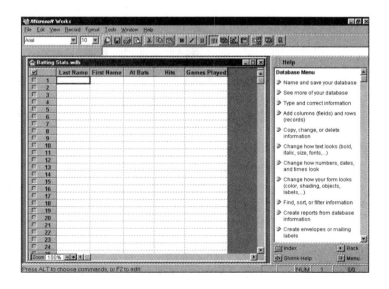

Figure 4-2
A database shown in list view.

The trouble with list view is that for all but the simplest databases, you won't be able to see the entire contents of an individual record without scrolling. For example, even a simple database with fields for Last Name, First Name, Address, City, State, Zip Code, and Phone Number is too wide to be displayed on the screen at one time. Form view shows just one record at a time, with each field on a separate line. Even though you can only see one record at a time in form view, you can usually see the entire contents of that record without scrolling horizontally. (Some databases have so many fields that you have to scroll horizontally to see the entire record even in form view.) Figure 4-3 shows a database in form view.

Figure 4-3
A database shown in form view.

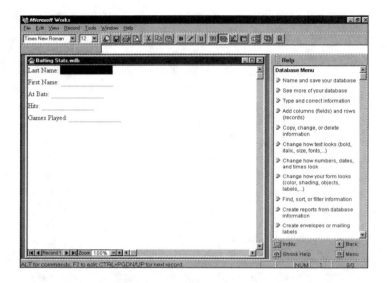

When you create a database, Works constructs a primitive form for you. This default form is unattractive, but it is functional. If appearances are important, you can modify the form design by rearranging fields, adding text and graphical elements, setting background colors changing fonts, and so on. All of this is explained later in this chapter, in the section titled, "Designing a Form."

To switch between list view and form view, use the following procedures:

 ■ To switch to form view, choose the View⇨Form command. Or press F9 or click the Form View toolbar button.

 ■ To switch to list view, choose the View⇨List command. Or press Shift+F9 or click the List View toolbar button.

Entering and Editing Data

After you create the database, you must enter data into it — quite a tedious chore, to say the least. In most cases, it's easiest to do your data entry in form view. To enter data into form view, type the contents of each field and use the

Tab key to move from field to field. When you finish the last field for a record, press the Tab key again. This procedure moves you to the first field of a new, blank record.

You can keep track of what record you are working on by watching the record indicator at the bottom of the form. The record indicator not only tells you which record is displayed on the form, but also provides controls that let you move to the next record, the previous record, the first record, or the last record.

Table 4-2 lists the keyboard shortcuts you can use to navigate through a database in form view.

Table 4-2: Navigation Keys for Form View

KEY	WHAT IT DOES
Tab	Moves to the next field. If you are already at the last field for a record, the Tab key moves to the first field of the next record.
Shift+Tab	Moves back one field.
Ctrl+PageDown	Displays the next record.
Ctrl+PageUp	Displays the previous record.
Ctrl+Home	Displays the first record in the database.
Ctrl+End	Displays the last record in the database. (Note that the last record is always a blank record, so that you can easily add new records to the end of the database.)

You can also move directly to a field by clicking the field with the mouse, and you can move forward or backwards through the database by clicking the left or right arrows that appear next to the record number at the bottom left of the form window.

To change the contents of an existing record, simply move to the record you want to change by using the keyboard shortcuts listed in Table 4-2. Then use the Tab key to move to the field you want to change and type the new value for the field.

To delete a record, move to the record you want to delete and choose the Record⇨Delete Record command. This will work in both list and form view.

Working with Calculated Values

Much like the Works Spreadsheet, Database lets you create fields that show the results of calculations based on other fields. For example, you could add a field named *Average* to the "Batting Stats" database we've been working on, which would calculate each batter's batting average. Here is a procedure for adding this batting average calculated field, which also serves as a general procedure for adding any calculated field. This procedure works in list view.

1. Put the cursor in the column next to where you want the new column to appear.

Remember that in list view, adding a new database field results in a new column being added to the database.

2. Use the Record⇨Insert Field command to insert a new field.

You'll be prompted to create the new field before or after the current field; your response depends on whether you want the new column to appear to the left (before) or to the right (after) of the column you selected in Step 1.

Then, an Insert Field dialog box will appear. This dialog box bears a striking resemblance to the Create Database dialog box shown back in Figure 4-1, so I won't repeat it here.

3. Type a name for your new field.

For this example, type the name "Average" just to stay with our baseball fantasy.

4. Select a Format for the new field.

Batting averages are usually shown with three decimal places, so click Number, select 1234.56 in the Appearance list, then set the Decimal Places setting to 3.

5. Click Add.

The field will be added, but the Insert Field dialog box will remain on the screen.

6. Click Done.

Now the Insert Field dialog box disappears, returning you to the database in list view, with the new field intact.

7. Click the column heading for the new Average field to select the entire column.

8. Type the formula for the field.

In this case, type the following formula:

```
=Hits/At Bats
```

The formula must begin with an equal sign so that Works knows you are entering a formula rather than a value.

Within the formula, you can use arithmetic symbols (+, -, * for multiplication, and / for division) as well as functions such as those used in the Spreadsheet. (For more information about functions, refer to Chapter 3.)

When you press the Enter key, the formula is calculated for each record in the database, as shown in Figure 4-4.

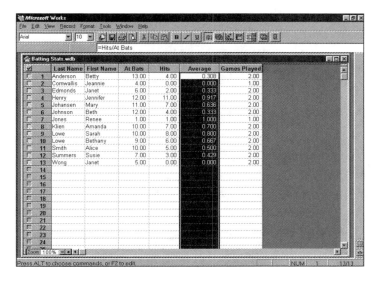

Figure 4-4
A database with a calculated field.

Sorting Records

You can sort the records in a database into order based on any of the fields in the database by choosing the Record⇨Sort Records command. The Sort Records dialog box appears, as shown in Figure 4-5.

The very first time you call up the Sort Records command, a first-timers dialog box appears. You can opt to take a brief tour of sorting, or you can click "To sort a database" to skip the tour.

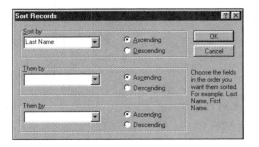

Figure 4-5
The Sort Records dialog box.

The Sort Records dialog box allows you to specify up to three fields on which the database will be sorted. By default, Works suggests sorting the database into ascending sequence on the first field of the database (in this example, Last Name). You can change the field used for the sort, or you can specify that the field should be sorted into descending sequence instead.

You can also specify up to two additional sort fields. For example, you may want to sort on First Name in addition to Last Name. That way, if you have two people with the same Last Name, they will be shown in order based on their first name.

When you have all your sort fields set up the way you want them, click OK to sort the database.

Marking Records

Notice the little check box that appears to the left of each record in list view? This check box can be used to *mark* a record. To mark a record, simply click the record's checkbox. To unmark a marked record, click the checkbox again.

There are several things you can do with marked records:

■ You can show all marked records by choosing the Record⇨Show⇨ Marked Records command. This temporarily removes all unmarked records from view, leaving only marked records visible.

■ You can show all unmarked records by choosing the Record⇨Show⇨ Unmarked Records command. As you might guess, this temporarily removes all marked records from view, leaving only unmarked records visible.

■ You can unmark all records by choosing the Record⇨Unmark All Records.

Marking records is useful when you have some function you wish to perform on an arbitrary group of records. For example, suppose you have an elementary school PTA membership list, and you want to print up a list of everyone who signed up to work on the Carnival Committee. Just open the database, switch to list view, mark each person who is on the committee, show marked records, and print your list.

Or suppose you want to delete everyone whose kid has finally moved on to middle school. Switch to list view, mark each record you want to delete, show marked records, then delete them all by choosing the Edit⇨Select All command, then choosing the Record⇨Delete Record command.

You can also hide an individual record without marking it first. Just select the record, then choose the Record⇨Hide command. To make the record visible again, choose Record⇨Show⇨All Records.

Working with Filters

A *filter* allows you to select only those database records that meet a criteria you set up. For example, in the Batting Stats database, you may want to see a list of all the players who have a batting average above .500. A filter lets you do just that.

Creating a filter

To create a filter, follow these steps:

1. Choose the <u>T</u>ools⇨<u>F</u>ilters command.
 Or, click the Filters button. Either way, the little dialog box shown in Figure 4-6 appears. (Unless this is the first time you've used the Filters command, in which case you will see a first-timers dialog box allowing you to take a tour of filtering. To skip the tour, click the "To create and apply a new filter" button.)

Figure 4-6
Creating a new filter.

2. Type a name for your filter.
Use something creative, like **Over .500 Hitters** or **Sluggers**.
3. Click OK.
The Filter dialog box appears, as shown in Figure 4-7.

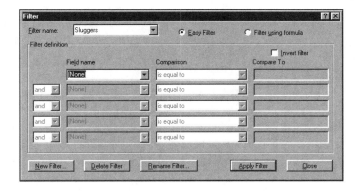

Figure 4-7
The Filter dialog box.

4. Select the field on which you want to base the filter in the Fie<u>l</u>d name list.
For example, to filter batters with an average above .500, select the Average field from the drop-down list.
5. Select a comparison type.
The comparison type determines how Works will filter out records based on the field you selected in Step 4 and a value you will enter in Step 6. For this example, select "is greater than."
6. Type the comparison value in the Compare To field.
This is the value that will be compared with the field you selected in Step

4, using the type of comparison you selected in Step 5. For this example, type .500. This causes Works to include only those records whose Average field is greater than .500.

Figure 4-8 shows how the Filters dialog box should appear after you set it up to filter batters with an average above .500.

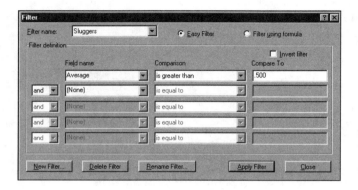

Figure 4-8
The Filter dialog box with a filter all dressed up and ready to go.

7. Click the Apply Filter button.

You are returned to the database, but only those records that meet the filter criteria you set up are shown. For example, Figure 4-9 shows how the Batting Stats database appears after you apply the Sluggers filter. As you can see, only those records whose Average field is greater than .500 are shown.

Clicking the Apply Filter not only applies the filter, but also saves it so you can recall it later by name.

It's important to understand that applying a filter does not remove records from your database. Instead, it simply hides from view all the records that do not meet the filter criteria. Thus, in Figure 4-8, the seven records that do not have a batting average of over .500 are still in the database. These records are just temporarily hidden from view.

You can create more than one filter for a database. To create additional filters beyond the first, choose the Tools⇨Filters command. This time, because you already have at least one filter, the Filters dialog box appears. Click the New Filter button to create a new filter. Then, proceed with steps 2 through 6 of the above procedure.

If your database has more than one filter, you can apply any of the filters by calling up the Tools⇨Filters command and selecting the filter from the Filter Name list before clicking Apply Filter.

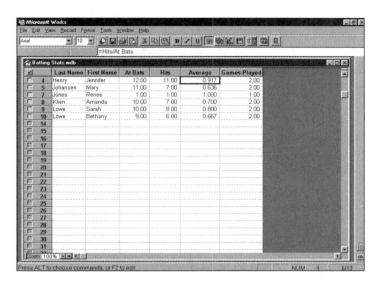

Figure 4-9
The Batting Stats database after you apply the Sluggers filter.

Undoing a filter

To remove a filter so that all the records in the database are visible again, choose the Record⇨Show⇨All Records command.

A filter with more complicated criteria

You may have noticed in Figure 4-7 that one of the batters was included in the Sluggers filter even though she had only had one hit. Because she also had only one time at bat, her season batting average is 1.000. Still, you can hardly consider a batter who has but one hit to be a slugger. This type of problem often occurs in filters; it is a sign that you need to tighten the filter's criteria.

The Filter dialog box lets you set up filtering criteria based on up to five fields in the database. Figure 4-10 shows how you could set up the Sluggers filter to list all your players who have better than a .500 average after having at least five at-bats.

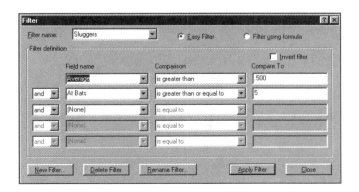

Figure 4-10
A tighter Sluggers filter that screens out batters who have fewer than five at-bats.

When you create filters based on more than one criteria, Works lets you specify that each criterion should be linked to the preceding criteria by an And or an Or operation. There's a big difference between the two. *And* means that both of the criteria must be met for a record to be included by the filter. *Or* means that if the first or second set of the criteria is met, the record will be included.

In Figure 4-10, I used And because I want the filter to select only those batters whose average is above .500 *and* who have had at least five at-bats. Suppose, however, that you want to change the filter so that it includes not only everyone who bats better than .500 after five at-bats, but also anyone whose last name is *Jones*, perhaps because Mr. Jones is an important client whom you don't want to lose. In that case, you could set up the filter, as shown in Figure 4-11.

Figure 4-11
The filter that plays favorites.

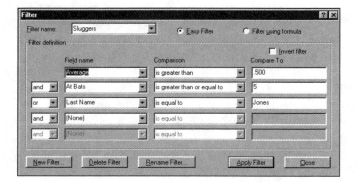

Be careful about how you use And in filters that specify two or more criteria on the same field. For example, switch streams for a moment and consider a database with name and address information. Suppose you want to create a filter that selects everyone who lives in San Francisco and Oakland. You may be tempted to set up this filter as follows:

```
      City  is equal to  San Francisco
  and City  is equal to  Oakland
```

However, this filter won't work; you'll end up with no records selected. What you want is this instead:

```
      City  is equal to  San Francisco
   or City  is equal to  Oakland
```

Working with Reports

The Works Database includes a powerful reporting feature that lets you create many different types of reports for your databases. The following sections show you how to work with simple and complex reports.

Creating a report

To create a report, open the database in which you want to create the report, then follow these steps:

1. Choose the Tools⇨ReportCreator command.

The Report Name dialog box appears, as shown in Figure 4-12. (If this is the first time you have created a report, you will see one of those first-timer dialog boxes, offering to let you take a brief tour of reporting. To skip the tour, click the "To create a report" button.)

Figure 4-12
The Report Name
dialog box.

2. Type in a report name and click OK.

Pick a meaningful name, such as *Team Roster.* When you click OK, the Report Creator dialog box appears, as shown in Figure 4-13.

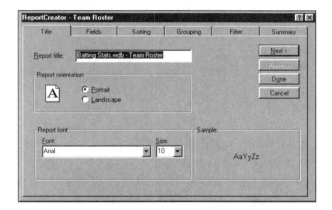

Figure 4-13
The Report Creator
dialog box.

3. Type a title for the report and click Next.

The title proposed by Report Creator will be a combination of the database name and the report name. You may prefer something simpler. For example, if the report is a simple listing of a softball team, type "Team Roster" for the report name. Also, note that you can change the report orientation (whether it prints in portrait or landscape) and the default font used for the report on this dialog box.

Make sure you don't click the Done button yet. Click the Next button to work your way through all of the tabs of this dialog box.

When you click Next, the Fields tab will be selected and you'll see the controls shown in Figure 4-14.

Figure 4-14
**Report Creator asks
what fields you want to
include in the report.**

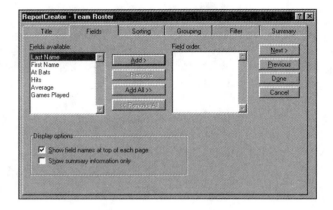

4. Select each field you want to include in the report and click Add. A report does not have to include all of the fields in a database. You can create a report that includes just the fields you are interested in for that report. In addition, you can list the fields in the report in any order you wish — the report fields don't have to be in the same order as the fields appear in the database in list view.

To add a field to the report, click the field you want to add in the Fields Available list, then click the Add button. You can repeat this process for as many fields as you'd like to include in the report.

If you change your mind about a field, you can remove it from the report by clicking the field in the Field order list, then clicking the Remove button.

For the Team Roster report, I selected just the Last Name and First Name fields. When I clicked Next, the dialog box shown in Figure 4-15 appeared.

Figure 4-15
**Report Creator lets you
select a sort order.**

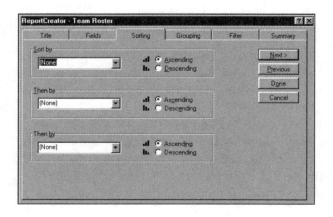

5. When you have selected all the fields you want, click Next.

6. Select the sort order for the report.

For the Team Roster report, sort first on Last Name, and then on First Name.

7. If the report requires grouping, click the Grouping tab and fill out the Grouping options.

Figure 4-16 shows the Grouping options. Grouping allows you to summarize records based on the value in a field. Although most reports don't require grouping, this book explains exactly how to set the grouping options for any reports that do.

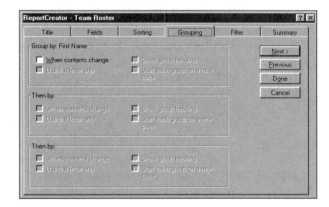

Figure 4-16
Grouping options.

8. If the report requires a filter, click Next or the Filter tab and fill out the filter criteria.

Figure 4-17 shows the Filter options. You can select an existing filter, or you can create a new filter. For more information, refer to the section, "Working with Filters."

Notice that the Filter tab lets you choose Current Records or All Records. If you choose Current Records (the default choice), you can exclude records from the report by hiding them (use the Record⇨Hide command) or by marking records you want to exclude, then choosing Record⇨Show⇨Unmarked records. Only those records that are visible at the time you print the report will be listed in the report.

If you choose All Records, all of the records in the database will be listed in the report, whether or not the records are visible or hidden.

Figure 4-17
Creating a report filter.

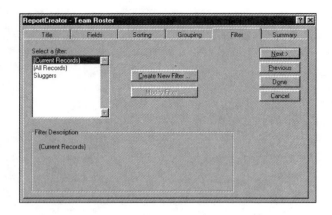

9. If you want the report to include a summary line, click the Next button or the Summary tab and select the summary option you want.

Figure 4-18 shows the Summary options. For each field, you can elect to print the Sum, Average, Count, Minimum value, Maximum value, Standard Deviation, and Variance to calculate these common summary values. For example, if you select Average, Works will add up all of the values for this field for the entire report, then divide the result by the number of records.

If your report includes grouping, you can select whether you want summary information for each group or for the entire report and how you want the summary information positioned.

For this report, we don't need any summary fields. Go ahead and click the Summary tab (or click Next) and gawk at the summary options, but don't touch any of them.

Figure 4-18
The summary options.

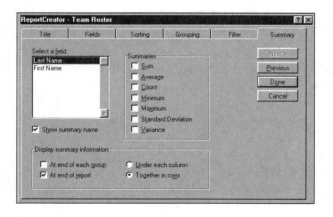

10. When you have set all the report options you want, click Done. The dialog box shown in Figure 4-19 appears.

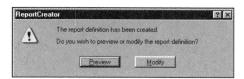

Figure 4-19
Report Creator asks if you want to preview the report or fiddle with the report's design.

11. Click Preview.

A preview of the report appears, as shown in Figure 4-20.

The mouse pointer becomes a little magnifying glass, which you can use to zoom in for a closer look at your report. Just click on the area where you'd like to see more detail. You can click once to get a medium close-up view and click again for a close-up. On the third click, you'll be returned to the wide-angle view that shows the entire page.

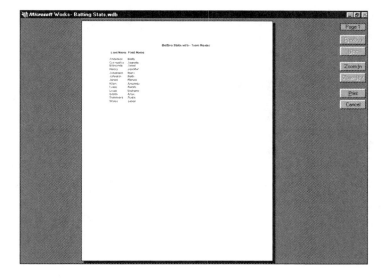

Figure 4-20
The report preview shows how the report will appear when printed.

12. If the preview looks good, click the Print button to print the report.

This step summons the Print dialog box, where you can change the number of copies or the range of pages to be printed. Click OK to print the report.

If you don't want to print the report, click the Cancel button instead of the Print button.

Modifying a report

To modify the report layout, click Modify when the Report Creator is finished. Or, you can choose the View⇨Reports command, select the report you want to modify, and click the Modify button. Or, if you selected Preview when you finished creating the report, but you don't like the looks of the preview, click Cancel. Whichever method you choose, a screen similar to the one in Figure 4-21 will appear. Of course, the appearance of this screen will vary greatly depending on the report you are modifying.

Figure 4-21
Modifying a report in Report Design view.

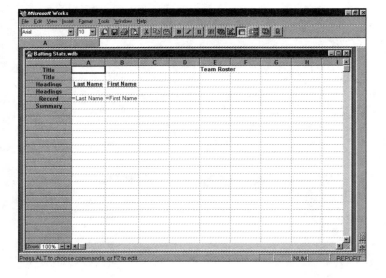

Report Design view looks remarkably like the Works spreadsheet. In fact, most of the formatting options that are available in Spreadsheet are also available here. You can use the Format menu to change the font, size, style, borders, shading, and number format of any "cell" in the report, just as if you were working with a spreadsheet.

Report Design has some extra features, however, that cannot be found in spreadsheets. For starters, the six rows in Report Design have special significance:

- **Title:** Title rows are printed only at the top of the report's first page.
- **Heading:** Heading rows appear at the top of each page of the report.
- **Record:** A set of record rows appear for each record printed by the report.
- **Intr:** If the report is grouped, each grouping can have one or more Intr rows. These rows are printed *before* the record rows for each group.
- **Summ:** If the report is grouped, each grouping can have one or more Summ rows. These rows are printed *after* the record rows for each group.
- **Summary:** Summary rows are printed after the last record in the report.

Note that Intr and Summ rows appear in Report Design only if you have specified grouping for the report. The Intr and Summ rows will also indicate the grouping field to which they apply. For example, if you group the report on Last Name, Report Design will include the Intr Last Name and Summ Last Name rows.

You can change the sorting, grouping, and filtering options for a report by calling up the Tools⇨Report Sorting, Tools⇨Report Grouping, and Tools⇨Report Filter commands. These commands bring up the same options that were available under the Sorting, Grouping, and Filter tabs in the Report Creator. When you're finished tweaking these options, click Done.

In addition to these Tools menu commands, several commands are available on the Insert menu for designing reports:

- **Insert⇨Insert Row:** Inserts a new row for the report. A dialog box asks you what type of row to insert (Title, Heading, Record, and so on). The new row is inserted immediately before the currently selected row.

- **Insert⇨Delete Row:** Deletes the current row.

- **Insert⇨Field Name:** Inserts the name of one of the database fields — not the value of the field, but the name. The database field names are presented in a list box so you can choose the field name you want to insert. This command is commonly used in Heading rows.

- **Insert⇨Field Entry:** Inserts the value of one of the database fields. This command is commonly used in Record rows, but is also sometimes used in Intr rows to include the value of the field on which records are grouped.

- **Insert⇨Field Summary:** Inserts a summary calculation for one of the fields in the database. A dialog box lets you choose which field to summarize and what type of calculation to perform for the field (Sum, Average, Median, and so on). This command is commonly used with Summ or Summary type rows.

Designing a Form

When you first build a database, Works creates a form for the database that lists all the database fields in a single column to make it easy to enter data into the fields. Although this default form is serviceable, it's not very attractive, and sometimes it has a downright cluttered appearance.

Fortunately, Works lets you modify the layout of the form. You can move fields around, add text to the form, and spruce up the form with fonts, colors, borders, shading, and even simple pictures. For example, Figure 4-22 shows a data-entry form I created for the Batting Stats database. I embellished the basic form by adding the gray rectangles to serve as borders for related fields, adding a title to the form, and changing the font used for the labels.

Figure 4-22
A customized database form.

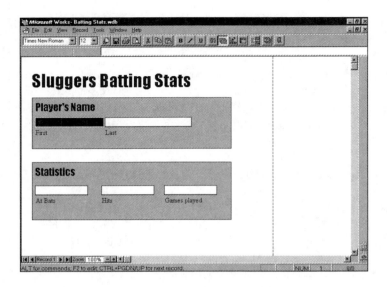

To switch to Form Design view so you can modify a database form, choose the View⇨Form Design command, press Ctrl+F9, or click the Form Design button in the toolbar.

While in Form Design view, you can drag fields on the screen to any location you want. To add your own labels, choose the Insert⇨Label command, type the text for the label, and click OK. The label is added to the form, but probably not at the location you want it to appear. Drag it to the correct location. After you position the label, use the font and size controls in the toolbar to set the label's font and font size.

You can display database fields on a form with or without the name of the field attached as an automatic label. By default, the field names are shown. However, you'll have more design flexibility if you hide the automatic field names and then create a label for each field by using the Insert⇨Label command. That's what I did to create the field labels in Figure 4-21. To hide a field's name, first select the field, and then choose the Format⇨Show Field Name command.

To insert a rectangle, choose the Insert⇨Rectangle command. This inserts a rectangle in the center of the form, which you can then drag and resize as you want. Initially, the rectangle is transparent. However, you can add shading by calling up the Format⇨Shading command.

However, when you apply shading to a rectangle, it obscures any other labels or fields that fall behind the rectangle. To avoid that problem, select the rectangle and choose the Send to Back command. This brings any other objects on the form "in front" of the rectangle so they are visible.

To create the white database fields in Figure 4-21, I selected the database fields and chose the Format⇨Borders and Format Shading commands to apply a thin border and white shading to the fields. This provides contrast against the gray background provided by the rectangle, which helps the database fields stand out.

Use your imagination when designing forms. All sorts of interesting effects are possible. To get ideas for designing attractive forms, just check out the forms that are created by the various TaskWizards that come with Works.

PART II:

HOME LIFE
WITH
WORKS

CHAPTER FIVE

A PLACE FOR EVERYTHING
AND EVERYTHING
IN ITS PLACE

In This Chapter

- Creating a home inventory
- Creating video tape lists for prerecorded films and home movies
- Cataloging your library of books and your CD collection

If you're a neat freak, you'll love this chapter. It contains three projects that let you keep track of the things you keep at home: video tapes, CDs, books, and so on. These projects are adapted from the Home Inventory template that comes with Works, so much of the work required to get these projects started has already been done for you courtesy of the good folks at Microsoft.

Project 1: A Home Inventory

A home inventory is a detailed record of all your valuable possessions, from your TV set to your dining room set to your croquet set. A home inventory serves several purposes:

■ If you need to file an insurance claim for loss due to fire or flood, a home inventory can help back up your claim.

■ If you want to figure your net worth, the home inventory can help you determine the value of your many possessions.

■ If something breaks down, you can check your home inventory to quickly determine if the object in question is still under warranty.

The following sections describe several procedures related to creating and using a household inventory database.

FAST TRACK

HOME INVENTORY

1. **Create the Home Inventory database by using the supplied Home Inventory TaskWizard.**

2. **Make up a list of locations and categories for your Home Inventory database. Make sure you spell the locations and categories the same each time you use them.**

3. **Gather information about your valuables one room at a time, and then enter the data into the Home Inventory database.**

4. **Print a copy of each record's form, attach a photograph of the item to the form, and gather the forms in a binder which is stored at another location (such as a safe deposit box or at your office) or in a fireproof safe.**

5. **Whenever you purchase a new goodie for the home, add it to the Home Inventory database. When you toss something or donate it to the Salvation Army, delete the item from the database.**

6. **Whenever you have something repaired, record the repair in the database.**

Creating a Home Inventory database

To create a Home Inventory database, start Microsoft Works. When the Works Task Launcher dialog box appears, click on Household Management to reveal the list of household management templates. Then select the Home Inventory template and click OK. You are asked whether to run the TaskWizard or display a list of existing documents. Click the "Yes, run the TaskWizard" button to start the Home Inventory TaskWizard, shown in Figure 5-1.

As you can see, this TaskWizard allows you to create three types of databases: a general Home Inventory database to keep track of your valuables, a Library database to keep track of books, and a CDs and Tapes database for your audio and video collections. The Home Inventory button should already be selected (as it is in Figure 5-1); if it isn't selected, select it. Then click the Create It! button.

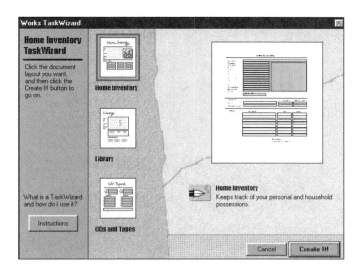

Figure 5-1
The Home Inventory
TaskWizard.

Your computer will grind and churn for a moment, and then a blank form for the first record in your Home Inventory database will appear, as shown in Figure 5-2. (I clicked the Shrink Help button here so more of the database is visible.)

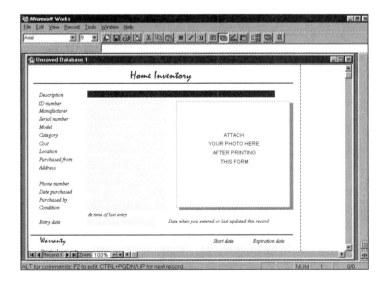

Figure 5-2
The Home Inventory
database.

As soon as you have run the TaskWizard, use the File⇨Save command to save the database. Choose a meaningful name such as *Home Inventory* for the database.

For more information about creating a database, see the section "Creating a New Database" in Chapter 4.

CROSS
REFERENCE

Customizing the Home Inventory database

The Home Inventory database lets you record three categories of information about each of your valuables:

■ General descriptive information such as a description, manufacturer, serial number, model number, purchase price, and so on.

■ Warranty information, including the date and duration of both the standard warranty and any extended warranty you may have purchased.

■ Repair information, listing a description, date, and cost of up to eight repairs.

You may find that some of the fields that Microsoft has included in the Home Inventory database do not suit your fancy, and that some information you want to record is missing. No problem; just select the View➪Form Design command and add, remove, or rearrange the database fields in any way you want. Here are some suggestions:

■ The ID number field may come in handy if you've engraved identification numbers on your valuables. If you haven't, and don't plan to, you can safely remove this field. Just click the field to select it, then press the Delete key.

■ The Home Inventory database wants to store more detail about where items were purchased than is necessary. Consider removing the Address and Phone Number fields if you don't want to enter this information.

■ If you don't want to track warranty or repair information, you can drop those fields as well.

■ Consider adding a field titled "Bequeath to." Then you can record any items that you would like to leave to specific individuals after your death. For example, you may want to leave the rocking chair in the den to your nephew, your china set to your eldest daughter, and your fine jewelry collection to your favorite computer book author.

Creating a location and category list

Before you begin to record information in your Home Inventory database, make a list of valuables you will type into the Location and Category fields. Use the Word Processor to create these lists, and keep a printed copy handy whenever you enter information into the Home Inventory database.

Use short words or abbreviations for the Location and Category lists. For example, here are some suggestions for the Location list:

```
living room
den
kitchen
dining room
bath 1
bath 2
master bath
master bedroom
bedroom 1
bedroom 2
bedroom 3
utility
pantry
garage
patio
pool
```

You could opt for shorter names (such as LR for Living Room), but the more cryptic your codes, the harder it is to remember them later.

For the Category list, provide meaningful categories but avoid overcategorizing. Here are some suggestions:

```
furniture
clothing
appliances
office equipment
electronic
computer
tools
camping
sports
```

For both the Category and Location list, spell each category or location exactly the same whenever you use it. This way, the database can properly group your inventory by category or location.

Recording your inventory

Recording a home inventory can be an enormous task. Here are some suggestions to make the job easier:

- Tackle the inventory one room at a time, and make sure you record every item of value in the room before moving on to the next room.
- One approach is to record all the information for each item in a room on a notepad. Then later sit down at the computer with the notepad and type in all the information.

TIP

- Another approach is to print several copies of a blank form, and then use the form to hand write information about each item. You can then later transfer the information from the handwritten forms to the computer.
- You can dispense with the computerized Home Inventory database altogether. Just print out a copy of a blank form, have about 200 copies made, and then hand write information on the forms, gather the forms into a binder, and store the binder in a safe place.

For more information about entering data into a Works database, see the section "Entering and Editing Data" in Chapter 4.

Storing the home inventory in a safe place

After you've completed the monumental task of inventorying your entire household and entering all the data into the computer, print out a copy of the database forms. This will result in one page for each item you've cataloged in your inventory. Place all these pages into a binder, and store the binder in a safe place: a fireproof safe, a safe deposit box, or at a friend or relative's house.

Note that the Home Inventory database form includes an area where you can attach a picture of each item. It's a good idea to include pictures for your more valuable items for insurance purposes and to provide identification if your goods are stolen.

Keeping the home inventory up to date

The hardest part about keeping a home inventory is creating the initial database. However, all your hard work will go for naught if you neglect the database after you've created it. Here are just some of the routine maintenance chores you must do to keep your database current:

- Whenever you purchase a new item for the home, be sure to add it to the Home Inventory database. After you've added the new item, print a copy of its form (use the File⇨Print command, and choose the "Current record only" option). Attach a picture of the item to the printed form and add the form to your Home Inventory binder.
- When you get rid of a household item, either by selling it, giving it away, or tossing it in the dumpster, be sure to delete the item from the database. Open the Home Inventory database, locate the item by working the navigation buttons at the bottom of the form window, and then choose the Record⇨Delete Record command.
- Whenever you have something repaired, call up your Home Inventory database, locate the item that was repaired, and record a description of the repair, the date, and the cost of the repair.
- If you're obsessive about the accuracy of your database, don't forget to record any location changes. For example, if you purchase a new phone and move the old phone from your den into your teenage

daughter's bedroom (something my daughter has been begging me to do for years), make sure you update the database to reflect the new location for the old phone.

Reports you can print

The Home Inventory database includes several reports that you can print. To access these reports, open the database and chooose the Print⇨Report command. A dialog box listing three reports will appear:

- **Location list:** This report prints a listing of all your items grouped by location. For example, all the kitchen items will be grouped together. This report is the reason you should use consistent spelling when you enter the locations for each database item.
- **Category list:** This report prints a listing of all your items grouped by category: furniture, appliances, electronics, or whatever other categories you used.
- **Supplier list:** This report lists your household inventory grouped according to where the items were purchased. Of the three reports, this one is the least useful.

Double-click the report you want to print. The report will appear in preview mode. You can either print the report by clicking Print, or click Cancel to switch to report design view.

Creating a warranty list

One report that the Home Inventory TaskWizard doesn't create for you is a listing of the items in your home inventory that are still under warranty. Here are the steps needed to create a warranty list for your Home Inventory database.

EXTRA CREDIT

1. Open the Home Inventory database (if it isn't already opened) and choose the Tools⇨ReportCreator command. Works will display a dialog box asking for a name for your report.

2. Type Warranty List for the report name, then click OK. The ReportCreator dialog box will appear.

3. Fill in the fields on the ReportCreator dialog box as follows:

- In the Title tab of the ReportCreator dialog box, type "Items Still Under Warranty for the Report Title" field and check the Landscape checkbox.
- In the Fields tab, select the Description, Manufacturer, Orig. End, and Ext. End fields to include on the report.
- In the Filter tab, click Create New Filter to create a new filter for the report. Specify Warranty as the name for the new filter, and then provide the following criteria for the Warranty filter:

```
Orig. End is greater than or equal to =now()
or Ext. End is greater than or equal to =now()
```

The now() function provides the current date. Thus, this filter selects all records in which the Orig. End or Ext. End fields have a date that is greater than today's date, indicating that the warranty is still in effect. Figure 5-3 shows how the Filter dialog box should appear after you have entered the criteria.

Figure 5-3
The filter criteria for the Warranty List report.

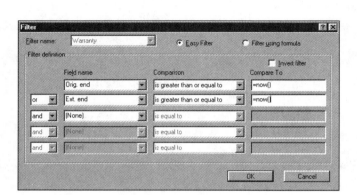

4. Click Done.

That's all there is to it! When Works asks whether you want to preview or modify the report, click Preview to view the Warranty List report.

For more information about creating reports, refer to the "Creating a Report" section in Chapter 4.

Project 2: A Library

Microsoft's Home Inventory TaskWizard includes an option that lets you create a database for your library. This option is especially useful if you have a large library of books from which you frequently borrow and have trouble remembering what you've loaned out and to whom.

Unfortunately, the good folks at Microsoft, who are usually quite sensible about such matters, really went overboard when they designed the Library database. They assumed that not only would you want to loan out your books, but also video tapes, CDs, stereo equipment, pictures, old newspapers, computer software, and who knows what else. In this project, I'll give you some suggestions for simplifying the Library database to make it easier to keep track of your books.

1. Create the Library database by using the supplied Home Inventory TaskWizard.
2. Modify the Library database to remove any fields you don't plan to use.
3. Create a record in the Library database for each book in your library.
4. Whenever you loan out a book, update the database so you'll know who has the book.
5. Whenever someone returns a book (which probably happens rarely), update the database so you won't forget and keep bugging that person to return the book.
6. Use the Report Creator to create a report that lists all your books that are currently loaned out.

FAST TRACK

LIBRARY

Creating a Library database

The Library database is created from the Home Inventory TaskWizard. To begin, start up Works. When the Works Task Launcher dialog box appears, click Household Management to reveal the list of Household Management templates. Then choose Home Inventory and click OK. Works asks whether you want to run the TaskWizard or display a list of existing documents. Click the "Yes, run the TaskWizard" button to start the Home Inventory TaskWizard. (Refer to Figure 5-1 if you need a reminder of what this TaskWizard looks like.)

When the TaskWizard fires up, click the Library button. Then click the Create It! button to create the Library database. The computer will work for a moment and then display the blank form for the Library database, as shown in Figure 5-4.

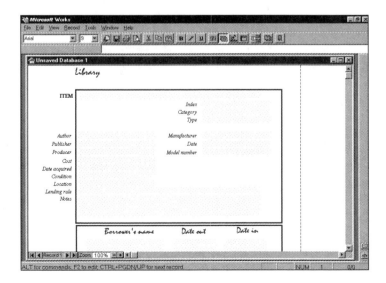

Figure 5-4
The Library database.

When you have run the TaskWizard, use the File⇨Save command to save the database by using a memorable name such as *Library*.

For more information about creating a database, see the section "Creating a New Database" in Chapter 4.

Customizing the Library database

The Library database has, frankly, too many fields that aren't needed to keep track of your books. "Manufacturer" and "Model Number" are useful if you want to loan out your stereo equipment, but important information such as the publication date and ISBN are missing.

To modify the Library database to make it easier for keeping track of a library of books, choose the View⇨Form Design command. Then make the following suggested changes to the database form (remember to save frequently as you work):

■ Delete the fields that aren't related to books: Index, Category, Type, Manufacturer, Model Number, and Producer. (To delete a field, click the field and press the Delete key. Works asks for your confirmation before deleting database fields; click OK to delete the field. Also, don't forget to delete the labels that are next to the fields themselves.)

■ Change the name of the Item field to Title. To change the field name, click the Item field, choose the Format⇨Field command, type the new name, and click OK. To change the name of the label next to the Item field, click the label to select it, press F2 to edit it, type the new label (**TITLE**), and press Enter.

■ Rearrange the remaining fields to eliminate the gaps left when the unnecessary fields were deleted. To align the fields with greater precision, use the zoom control to increase the zoom factor.

■ Add a new field named *ISBN*. To add the field, choose the Insert⇨Field command, type the name of the new field (**ISBN**), and select Text as the field type. Click OK to add the field. Then, choose the Format⇨Show Field Name command to remove the field name that Works automatically inserts. Now position the field where you want it, and add a label by using the Insert⇨Label command.

Finally, eliminate three of the four sets of fields used to record who has borrowed the book. You don't have much reason to keep track of four different borrowers; all you're really interested in is who has the book at the moment. By eliminating the extraneous borrower fields, you'll be able to create a report that lists all your books that are currently loaned out.

To remove the extra rows, switch to List view and delete the following fields:

```
Name 2
Date Out 2
Date In 2
Name 3
Date Out 3
Date In 3
Name 4
Date Out 4
Date In 4
```

Next, delete the Date In 1 field and rename the Name 1 field to *Name* and the Date Out 1 field to *Date Out*. Finally, rearrange the Name and Date Out fields and their labels and resize the box that contains them.

Figure 5-5 shows the Library database form after all these changes have been made.

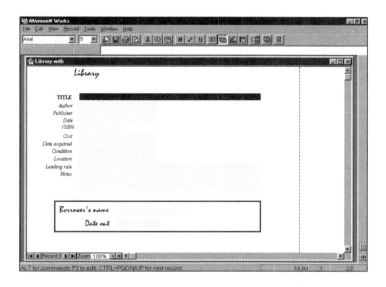

Figure 5-5
The Library database after it has been customized.

For more information about working with forms, see the section "Designing a Form" in Chapter 4.

CROSS REFERENCE

Using the Library database

The first phase of using your Library database is creating a new database record for each one of the books in your collection. Obviously, the difficulty of this task depends on the size of your library.

When you have completed the initial data entry for your Library database, you can maintain it simply by creating records for new books and removing records for books you sell, give away, or discard.

In addition, you should also update the database whenever a friend borrows one of your books. Just call up the database, look up the book being borrowed, and record the borrower's name and the current date in the appropriate fields. When the book is returned, call up the record again and remove the borrower's name and the date.

You can search for a book by any word that appears in its title, by the name of the author, or even by the name of someone who has borrowed books simply by calling up Edit⇨Find command (or use the keyboard shortcut Ctrl+F). Type a word from the title or the author's or borrower's name and click OK. Works will find any record that has the word you typed anywhere in the record.

Creating a report listing borrowed books

The Library database includes several reports, the most useful of which is a simple listing of books by title. However, one report that the Library database doesn't include is a listing of which books have been loaned out, showing who has borrowed the books and when they borrowed them.

Fortunately, you can easily create such a list. Follow the procedure "Creating a Report," found in Chapter 4, with the following variations:

- Type **Borrowed Books** for the report name.
- In the Title tab of the ReportCreator dialog box, type **Borrowed Books** for the <u>R</u>eport Title field and check the <u>P</u>ortrait checkbox.
- In the Fields tab, add the Title, Author, Name, and Date Out fields.
- In the Sorting tab, specify that the report should be sorted on the Name field.
- In the Grouping tab, check the "<u>W</u>hen contents change" setting under "Group by Name."
- In the Filter tab, click <u>C</u>reate New Filter to create a new filter. Specify *Borrowed Books* for the filter name, and then specify the following criteria:

```
Name is not blank
```

Figure 5-6 shows how the Filter dialog box should appear when you have entered the criteria.

For more information about creating reports, refer to the "Creating a Report" section in Chapter 4.

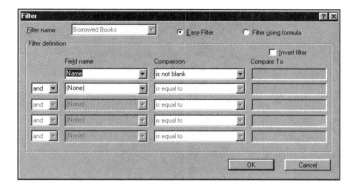

Figure 5-6
The filter criteria for the Borrowed Books report.

Project 3: A CD or Video Tape List

The last project derived from the Home Inventory TaskWizard is a CD and Video Tape library. If you have a large collection of CDs or videos, cataloging them on your computer opens up all sorts of possibilities. For example, if you remember the name of a song but can't remember which CD the song is on, you can quickly search your database to find out. For home videos, you can even record individual segments so that you can quickly locate your daughter's fourth birthday or the family trip to the Grand Canyon.

FAST TRACK

CD AND VIDEO LIBRARY

1. **Create the CD and Video database by using the supplied Home Inventory TaskWizard.**
2. **Create a record in the CD and Video database for each disk or tape in your collection. This creation will take awhile if you opt to record the individual tracks on each disk.**
3. **Keep the database current when you acquire new disks or tapes or when you discard old ones.**

Creating a CD and Video database

To create a CD and Video database, use the Home Inventory TaskWizard. You'll find it located in the Works Task Launcher dialog box lurking under Household Management. When the Home Inventory TaskWizard starts up, select CDs and Tapes, and then click the Create It! button. You'll hear your computer's gears grind for a moment, and then the CD and Tapes database will spring to life, as shown in Figure 5-7.

Figure 5-7
The CD and Video
database.

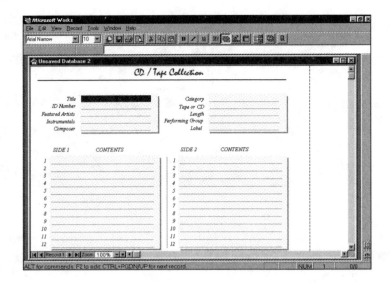

When the CDs and Tapes database appears, choose the File⇨Save command to save the database. Pick a meaningful name such as *CDs and Tapes*.

Customizing the CDs and Tapes database

Fortunately, the CDs and Tapes database is designed well: It doesn't include a bunch of fields you aren't likely to use, nor is it missing any important fields. As a result, you probably won't need to modify it significantly before you begin to use it. Here are two variations to consider:

- You can safely drop the ID Number field.
- The CDs and Tapes database contains both a Featured Artist field and a Performing Group field. If you want, you can drop the Performing Group field. Then just type **Beatles** in the Featured Artist field for your Beatles albums.

Using the CDs and Tapes database

The hardest part about the initial data entry for the CDs and Tapes database is recording all the individual tracks for each of your CDs. Depending on how many CDs you have, this can take a lifetime.

Of course, no law says you have to actually record the name of each song for each CD. To save time, start by recording just the basic information for each CD: Title and Featured Artist. Then you can return later to fill in the additional details for selected CDs.

When cataloging your home videos, consider listing the major sequences on each video in the Contents fields. If possible, include the index time for each sequence so you can quickly locate the sequence on the tape.

For movies, you can list the actors and actresses in the Contents field. That way, you can later search for movies staring your favorite performers.

When all your CDs and videos are cataloged, you can use the Edit⇨Find command to quickly find information in your database. You can search for any information you have entered into the database, such as some or all of a title, an artist's name, or the name of a song.

For more information about entering data into a Works database, see the section "Entering and Editing Data" in Chapter 4.

CHAPTER SIX

HOUSEHOLD CHORES AND
OTHER STUFF YOU HATE
TO DO

In This Chapter

- Tracking auto maintenance
- Figuring out how much mulch to buy
- Scheduling chores fo the kids

This chapter contains several projects for routine maintenance items that have to be done around the house, such as changing the oil in your car and fertilizing your lawn. As an added bonus, there's a project that will help you delegate household chores to your kids and keep track of whose week it is to clean up after Rover.

Project 4: Tracking Auto Maintenance

The favorite saying of most auto mechanics is, "You can pay me now, or you can pay me later." Personal experience has convinced me that this cliché is oh-so-true. Fortunately, you can easily use Works to create an automobile maintenance record that will help you stay on top of your oil changes, tire rotations, and other scheduled maintenance.

Creating an auto maintenance schedule

Works doesn't come with a TaskWizard to create an automobile maintenance schedule, but you can create a simple schedule yourself by using the Spreadsheet tool. Grab the maintenance book that came with your car so you'll know what maintenance items should be included in the schedule. Then fire up Works and create a new Spreadsheet document.

FAST TRACK

AUTO MAINTNANCE

1. **Use the Spreadsheet to create a schedule of maintenance required for your car.**
2. **Update the spreadsheet whenever you perform maintenance.**
3. **Keep receipts for your auto maintenance together in a file folder.**

Figure 6-1 shows what the maintenance schedule will look like when it's finished. As you can see, this spreadsheet includes one row for each scheduled maintenance interval, with columns devoted to the actual mileage the maintenance was performed, the cost of the maintenance, and a separate column for each maintenance item that needs to be performed. The greyed-out boxes indicate when the various maintenance items need to be done. For example, oil changes should be done every 3,000 miles, tire rotations every 6,000 miles, and the transmission fluid should be changed every 15,000 miles.

Figure 6-1
An auto maintenance spreadsheet.

Of course, the actual services and maintenance intervals will vary depending on your car. That's why you need to have your car's maintenance book handy when you create this spreadsheet.

If you're not familiar with spreadsheets, refer to Chapter 3 for more information.

To create an auto maintenance schedule, start a blank spreadsheet. Then, follow these steps:

1. Create a heading in cell A1 that identifies the year and make of your car.

For example, "Maintenance Schedule for 1996 Dodge Caravan." To center the heading over the entire spreadsheet, highlight cells A1 through J1, choose the Format⇨Alignment command, and select the Center Across Selection option to center the heading over the entire spreadsheet. Click OK to center the heading. (If you end up adding additional columns beyond column J, you can always come back and recenter the heading.)

2. Create column headings in Row 2.

In Figure 6-1, I used the following column headings:

A2:   Mileage
B2:   Date Service Performed
C2:   Actual Mileage
D2:   Oil/Lube
E2:   Rotate Tires
F2:   Change Xmission Fluid
G2:   Replace Air Filter
H2:   Change Engine Coolant
I2:   Tune Up
J2:   Replace Timing Belt

You may need to use different headings, depending on the maintenance requirements for your car. However you create your headings, I suggest you combine oil changes, lubrication, and all the inspections that go along with every oil change under a single column titled, "Oil/Lube." And all the tune-up-related items that typically occur at 30,000 mile intervals, such as changing spark plugs and replacing the PCV filter, can be combined under one heading, "Tune Up."

Once you've typed in the headings, select all of the columns you typed and click the Bold button or press Ctrl+B to make the headings boldface. Then, summon the Format⇨Alignment command to summon the Alignment tab of the Format Cells dialog box. Check the Wrap text option, then click OK.

For more information about formatting cells, see the section "Formatting Cells" in Chapter 4.

3. Save the file.

Use the File⇨Save command, and choose a meaningful name such as *Auto Maintenance*.

4. Create the maintenance intervals in Column 1.

This step is actually easier than it looks. Just type the first two maintenance intervals in cells A3 and A4. For example, if your maintenance is performed every 3,000 miles, type **3,000** in cell A3 and **6,000** in cell A4. Then use the mouse to highlight both cells. A small rectangle appears at the bottom-right corner of the selection; this rectangle is called the *fill handle.* Just drag the fill handle down the column, as far as you want to go. When you release the mouse, the cells you highlighted will be filled based on the interval you entered into the first two cells. Drag the fill handle down to cell A37 to create maintenance intervals to go up to 99,000 miles.

For more information about using the Fill feature, refer to the section "Using the Fill Feature" in Chapter 4.

5. Save the file again.

6. Mark out the cells that don't correspond to a required maintenance interval by shading them dark gray.

For example, since tire rotations are called for every 6,000 miles, I shaded out every other cell in the tire rotation column. And since transmission fluid needs to be changed only every 15,000 miles, I shaded all the cells except the cells for 15,000, 30,000, 45,000, 60,000, 75,000, and 90,000 for column F.

To shade a cell or range of cells, select the cell and call up the Format⇨Shading command. Select the shading you want to use in the Pattern list, and then click OK.

You can simplify the shading of large blocks of adjacent cells by creative use of cut and paste. For example, to shade the Change Xmission fluid column, I first shaded cells F3, F4, F5, and F6. Next, I selected cells F3 through F6 and pressed Ctrl+C to copy these cells to the clipboard. Then I selected cell F8 and pressed Ctrl+V to paste the contents of the clipboard. This option shaded cells F8 through F11, leaving cell F7 unshaded. I also pasted the clipboard into cells F13, F18, F23, F28, and F33.

7. Adjust the cell alignment.

To center the column headings, select all of Row 2 and choose the Format⇨Alignment command. Choose Center from the Horizontal alignment options, and then click OK. (Be sure you don't choose Center across selection by mistake; that's an entirely different type of alignment.)

Next, select the entire range of columns used for maintenance items — in Figure 6-1, columns D through J — not just the heading rows, but the entire columns. Then choose the Format⇨Alignment command, select Center from the Horizontal alignment options, and click OK.

8. Save the file once more.

You can never save your work too often.

9. Add a section for unscheduled maintenance items.

Scroll down to the end of the maintenance schedule, and type **Unscheduled maintenance** into column A a row or two below the last row of the maintenance schedule. Then skip a row and type headings for **Mileage, Date, Cost,** and **Description** in columns A through D. Figure 6-2 shows how this unscheduled maintenance section should appear. Use this section to record items such as brake jobs, new tires, and other repairs that don't fall at predictable intervals.

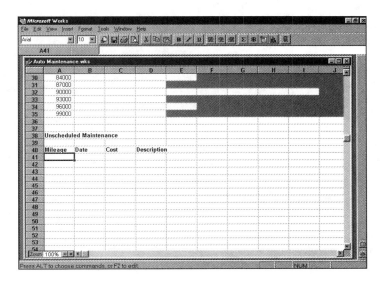

Figure 6-2
An area for unscheduled maintenance.

10. Save the file one last time.

Recording your maintenance

Whenever you take your car in for service, call up the auto maintenance spreadsheet and record the service that was performed. For routine maintenance, type in the date and actual mileage the service was performed, and type an X in the appropriate cells to indicate what service you had done. Record any unscheduled maintenance — brake jobs, new tires, and so on — in the unscheduled maintenance section of the spreadsheet.

Make sure you keep the receipts for all your maintenance. That way, you'll have proof that the car was maintained when it comes time to sell the car.

If you want, you can print out a copy of the spreadsheet and keep it in the car's glove box. Then you can write maintenance information on the spreadsheet printout until you can get back to the computer.

Figure 6-3 shows how the spreadsheet will appear after the car has been driven awhile.

For more information about entering data into a spreadsheet, see the section "Entering Spreadsheet Data" in Chapter 4.

Figure 6-3
I wish my car were as
well maintained as
this one.

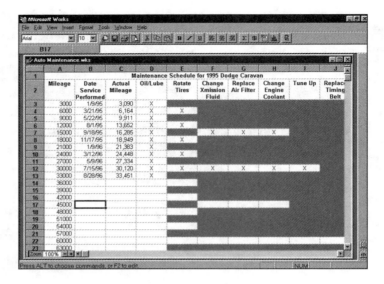

FAST
TRACK

Project 5: A Cubic Yardage Calculator

CUBIC
YARDAGE   Create a spreadsheet document that automatically calculates the cubic yards of material
CALCULATOR required to cover a given square footage to a given depth.

If you're one of those people who likes to spread decorative bark or mulch about your yard, or if you're undertaking a landscaping project and need to know how much topsoil, sand, or concrete to order, this simple little project will come in handy. It performs a simple little calculation that tells you how much material you will need in cubic yards to cover a given amount of square footage to a depth of 1, 2, 3, or 4 inches. And, if you type in the cost per yard, it will calculate the total cost for you.

Figure 6-4 shows how the Cubic Yardage Calculator will appear when it is completed. Just type the number of square yards of material you need in cell D3 and the price per cubic yard in cell D5. When you do, the spreadsheet will automatically calculate the number of yards needed and the cost for covering the area in depths of 1, 2, 3, or 4 inches. For example, Figure 6-5 shows the spreadsheet after I entered 1,000 square feet at $17.50 per cubic yard.

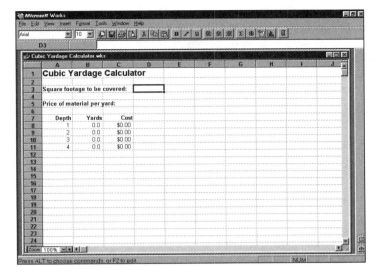

Figure 6-4
A cubic yardage calculator.

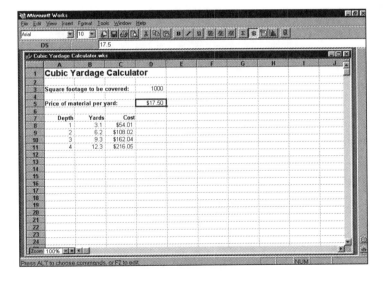

Figure 6-5
See, it works!

To create the Cubic Yardage Calculator, start Works and go to the Spreadsheet tool to create a new, blank spreadsheet. Then enter the values and formats into the cells as specified in Table 6-1.

TABLE 6-1: CELL ENTRIES FOR THE CUBIC YARDAGE CALCULATOR

CELL	VALUE TO ENTER	FORMAT TO APPLY
A1	Cubic Yardage Calculator	Arial, 14 pt, Bold
A3	Square footage to be covered	Bold
A5	Price of material per yard	Bold
D5	(no value)	Format⇨Number: Currency
A7	Depth	Bold, Right Align
B7	Yards	Bold, Right Align
C7	Cost	Bold, Right Align
A8	1	
A9	2	
A10	3	
A11	4	
B8	=D3/324	Format⇨Number: Fixed: 1
B9	=B8*2	Format⇨Number: Fixed: 1
B10	=B8*3	Format⇨Number: Fixed: 1
B11	=B8*4	Format⇨Number: Fixed: 1
C8	=B8*D5	Format⇨Number: Currency
C9	=B9*D5	Format⇨Number: Currency
C10	=B10*D5	Format⇨Number: Currency
C11	=B11*D5	Format⇨Number: Currency

When you have entered these cell values, type 1000 into cell D3, then type 17.50 into cell D5 and see if you get the same results in cells C8, C9, C10, and C11 as are shown in Figure 6-5. If not, carefully recheck the entries you made in each cell.

If the spreadsheet checks out, select the entire spreadsheet. Then choose the Format⇨Protection command, check the Locked option, and click OK. This will lock all the cells in the spreadsheet. Next, click on cell D3 to select it, choose the Format⇨Protection command, uncheck the Locked option, and click OK. Then do the same for cell D5.

Finally, choose the Format⇨Protection command, check the Protect Data option, and click OK. This prevents you from modifying the contents of any cell in the spreadsheet except cells D3 and D5. That way, you won't inadvertently type over one of the cell formulas. In addition, cell D3 will automatically be selected when you open the spreadsheet, and you can use the tab key to move the selection between cells D3 and D5.

Project 6: Scheduling Chores for the Kids

FAST TRACK

CHORE SCHEDULER

> **Create a spreadsheet document that prints a calendar of chores that are rotated among two or more kids on a weekly basis.**

If you have kids beyond the toddler stage, you probably know that keeping track of their household chores is sometimes not as easy as it should be. I know; I have three girls ranging in age from 9 to 14, and the past few years have seen many "discussions" concerning whose week it is to fold towels, who feeds the dogs, and who vacuums the carpets.

The solution is at hand with this simple spreadsheet project. With the Works spreadsheet, it's easy to create a rotating schedule of chores. This project creates a schedule of chores that rotates on a weekly basis among three children (who, coincidentally, just happen to have the same names as my three daughters), as shown in Figure 6-6. You can easily adapt the spreadsheet to any number of children or a different set of chores.

To create a schedule similar to the one in Figure 6-6, start by creating a blank spreadsheet. Type a heading such as "Weekly Chores for 1997" into cell A1. Then type a column heading such as "Week Of" in cell A3, and type a column heading for each of the chores you want to assign in subsequent columns of row 3. For example, I typed "Fold Towels" in cell B3, "Set Table" in cell C3, "Vacuum" in cell D3, and so on. The exact values you type in these cells will vary depending on the chores you want to assign to your kids.

Don't worry about the cell formats yet. You'll doctor up the spreadsheet's appearance once you get the basic data entered.

Figure 6-6
A rotating schedule of chores.

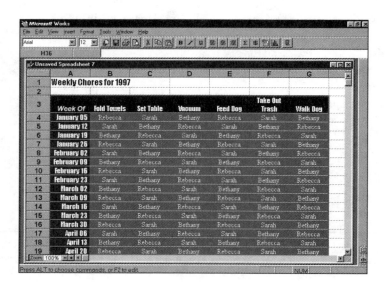

Next, set up the dates for the weeks you want your schedule to apply to. To set up the dates, start by typing the date of the first week in cell A4 and the date of the second week in cell A5. For example, I typed 1/5/97 in cell A4 and 1/12/97 in cell A5. (I later changed the date format for these cells, which is why they appear as January 05 and January 12 in the figure.) Now, select both of these cells, then drag the fill handle (the little rectangle that appears at the bottom-right corner of the selection box) down to cover as many weeks as you want. To do a schedule for an entire year, drag the fill handle all the way down to cell A54.

When you release the mouse, Works automatically fills all the cells you included in the fill with dates at one week increments. At this point, your spreadsheet should resemble the one in Figure 6-7.

For more information about fills, see the section "Using the Fill Feature" in Chapter 4.

In the first column of chores, type in the names of the people responsible for doing the chore for the first few weeks. Just type in enough names for one complete rotation of the chore. For example, if you have three kids and this chore rotates on a weekly basis, type the names for the first three weeks. Then select all three weeks and drag the fill handle down to the bottom of the schedule. The name rotation you typed for the first three weeks will be duplicated for the rest of the year.

Repeat this process for the remaining chore columns until all the chores have been assigned on a rotating basis. Make sure you get the chores for the first few weeks parceled out properly.

Figure 6-7
The chores schedule after the headings and dates have been entered.

When you have set up the chore rotation, you can "pretty up" the spreadsheet. Select all of Column 1 (click on the header above the column) and choose the Format⇨Number command. Click Date, and then choose the date format you would like to use and click OK.

Next, highlight the entire table starting with the heading row and ending with the last week in the schedule. For this example, the selection would be the range C1:G55. Then choose the Format⇨Autoformat command. This summons the AutoFormat dialog box, which lists several predefined formatting options you can apply to ranges of spreadsheet cells. Pick the format you like best. For this example, I chose the Colorful Bold format. Uncheck the "Format last row and/or column as total" option, and then click OK. (Because the spreadsheet cells you applied the AutoFormat to are still selected, the colors applied to those cells are inverted. Click somewhere outside of the selected cells to see the true colors applied by the AutoFormat.)

For more information about AutoFormats, see the section "Using Auto-Format" in Chapter 3.

You may want to apply additional formatting to improve the appearance of the schedule. For this example, I increased the point size of the entire file to 12 point, and I centered the data in columns 2 through 7. I also formatted the headings in row 3 so the longer headings would be shown on two lines if necessary by choosing the Format⇨Alignment command and checking the Wrap text option. Finally, I changed the font of the heading in cell A1 to use Impact, the font that was selected for the rest of the spreadsheet by the Autoformat.

For information about how to apply these formats, refer to the section "Formatting Cells" in Chapter 3.

CHAPTER SEVEN

SLAVING OVER A HOT OVEN

In This Chapter

- Creating a recipe book
- Planning meals
- Making a grocery list

No matter what you do, you can't coax your computer to cook your dinner or do the dishes after you've eaten. However, you can put your computer to good use by helping you simplify your kitchen chores. This chapter will show you how to set up a simple recipe book that will store your favorite recipes in a form that is suitable for distribution to your friends and enemies; plan your meals a week at a time so you don't always end up with take-out on Tuesday; make up a grocery list for your next major shopping trip; and keep track of those valuable coupons.

Project 7: Creating a Recipe Book

1. **Use the word processor to create a recipe book in which your favorite recipes are neatly kept.**
2. **Use easy formats to simplify formatting for the recipes.**
3. **Print your recipes on 5.25 x 8.5 stationary.**

You might think at first that the ideal way to put your recipe box on the computer would be as a database. After all, a recipe book is a type of database. And the sorting and filtering tools available in the database would make it easy to print lists such as deserts that don't have walnuts or casseroles that use leftover turkey.

Unfortunately, the Works database just isn't cut out for such tasks. However, you can use the Word Processor to create a simple recipe book which includes your favorite recipes, attractively formatted so you can print out a single recipe or the entire book to give to your friends (or enemies, depending on how good the recipes are).

Figure 7-1 shows a sample page from my own recipe book.

Figure 7-1
Use fresh clams if you can get them.

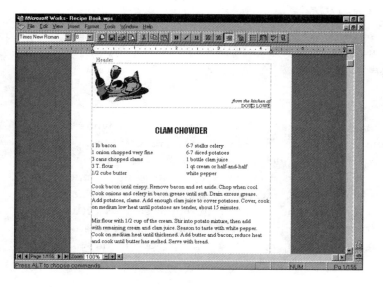

Setting up a recipe book
To create your own recipe book, follow these steps:

1. Fire up Works and start the Word Processor.

In the Task Launcher dialog box, click the Works Tools tab, then click Word Processor.

2. Call up the File⇨Page Setup command.

The Page Setup dialog box will appear, as shown in Figure 7-2.

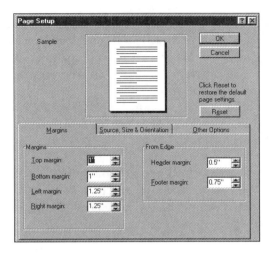

Figure 7-2
The Page Setup dialog box.

3. Set the left and right margins to 0.5". Then click the Source, Size and Orientation tab. Set the Width to 5.25" and the Height to 8.5". Then click OK.

4. Click in the header area of the page to begin creating the header which will appear for each recipe.

5. Choose the Format⇨Tabs command to call up the Format Tabs dialog box.

See Figure 7-3.

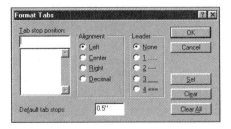

Figure 7-3
The Format Tabs dialog box.

6. Type 4.25 in the Tab Stop Position text field, click the Right option button, then click Set to create a right-justified tab stop at 4.25".

For more information about working with tabs, refer to the section "Using Tabs" in Chapter 2.

7. Click OK.

8. Choose the Insert⇨ClipArt command.

The ClipArt Gallery will appear.

9. Select a clip art picture you'd like to appear on each page of your recipe book, then click Insert.

The clip art picture you selected will be inserted into the header area of the document. It will probably be too large, so you should resize it by dragging one of its corner handles to a smaller size.

10. Press the Tab key, then type whatever text you want to appear at the top of each recipe.

For my recipe book, I typed "*from the kitchen of*" on one line, then pressed the Enter key to start a new paragraph, pressed the Tab key and typed "DOUG LOWE."

Creating the Easy Formats

The Recipe Book uses two Easy Formats so that you can easily type in your recipes without having to manually format each one. These Easy Formats are:

■ **Recipe Title:** Used for the title of each recipe. This Easy Format displays the recipe title centered on the page in 14-point Impact and adds one blank line before and after the title.

■ **Recipe Text:** This Easy Format is used for all other text in a recipe, formatted in 10-point Times New Roman. It includes a tab stop at 2.25", which lets you set up a two-column ingredients list, and a right-justified tab stop at 4.25" in case you want to add flush-right text (for example, to list the person who gave you a particular recipe).

To create these Easy Formats, follow these steps:

1. Choose the Format⇨Easy Formats command.

The Easy Formats dialog box will appear.

2. Click the New button.

The New Easy Format dialog box will appear, as shown in Figure 7-4.

3. Type "Recipe Title" as the name for the Easy Format.

4. Click the Font button and set the font to 14-point Impact.

Click OK to return to the New Easy Format dialog box.

5. Click the Paragraph button to summon the Paragraph dialog box.

Click Center, then click the Spacing tab and set both the Before spacing and the After spacing to 1 line.

Click OK to return to the New Easy Format dialog box.

6. Click Done to create the Easy Format.

7. Repeat steps 2 through 6 to create the Recipe Text Easy Format.

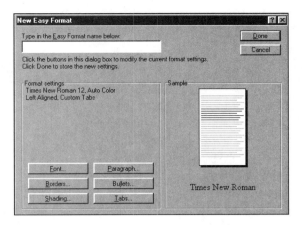

Figure 7-4
The New Easy Format
dialog box.

This time, type "Recipe Text" for the Easy Format name. Use the Font button to set the font to 10-point Times New Roman. Then, use the Tabs button to create a left tab at 2.25" and a right tab at 4.25".

8. Click the Close button to dismiss the Easy Formats dialog box.

The Easy Formats are now ready for you to use.

You'll find more information about using Easy Formats in the section "Using Easy Formats" found in Chapter 2.

Adding a recipe

To add a recipe to the recipe book, follow these steps:

1. Create a blank page for the recipe.

If you are adding the first recipe for the book, you are already on a blank page. To add subsequent recipes, move the insertion point to the end of the recipe you want to insert the new recipe after and press Ctrl+Enter.

2. Type the title of the recipe, then choose the Format⇨Easy Formats command, select "Recipe Title," and click OK.

The title will be formatted in 14-point Impact, centered, with a line of spacing before and after.

3. Press Enter to start a new paragraph, then choose the Format⇨Easy Formats command, select "Recipe Text," and click Apply.

4. Type the ingredients list in two columns.

Use the Tab key to separate columns. If you need to create a heading within the ingredients list (for example, to type a separate list for a sauce or dressing), press Enter twice to create a blank line before the heading, then format the heading with boldface type.

5. Type the recipe's instructions.

6. Choose the File⇨Save command to save the new recipe.

That's all there is to it!

Printing a recipe

Because each recipe is on its own page, you can print up a single recipe by scrolling to the recipe and noting which page the recipe is on. Then, call up the File⇨Print command and set the from and to fields in the Print range portion of the dialog box to the page number for the recipe. For example, if your favorite chili recipe is on page 17, call up the File⇨Print command, set both from and to to 17, and click OK.

    If you don't have a supply of 5.25" × 8.5" paper handy, you can always print the recipe on normal 8.5" × 11" paper. However, the page will look funny because the recipe won't be centered on the page — you'll have to use the File⇨Page Setup command to twiddle with the margin settings to get the recipe centered on 8.5" × 11" paper. You can also experiment with other paper sizes, such as 3" × 5"cards, but you'll have to make further adjustments to the margins and other layout elements if you do.

Project 8: Making a Meal Planner

1. **Use the Word Processor to create a simple table which allows you to plan meals for each day of the week.**
2. **Add a legend that lists short codes for all of your cookbooks so you can quickly find the recipes listed in your meal plan.**
3. **If desired, expand the table to include dietary exchange information.**

If you're family is like most, you find yourself ordering out for pizza and Chinese food more often than you should. Often, resorting to fast food for dinner is simply due to lack of planning. If you sit down early in the week and plan out each of the meals for the week, you'll be less likely to make that last-minute run to the pizza parlor on Tuesday night because you have nothing planned for dinner.

Creating a meal plan

A basic meal plan can be created with the Word Processor using a simple table. The table will have two rows and seven columns: the first row will hold headings for each day of the week, and the second row will hold the menu for your planned meals for that day. See Figure 7-5.

    Although this meal planner shows dinners only, you can easily adapt it to provide space for planning breakfast and lunch as well. Just add additional rows for the other meals you want to plan.

    To create a meal planner such as the one shown in Figure 7-5, just follow these steps:

1. Fire up the Word Processor to create a new, blank document.

2. Type a heading such as "Weekly Meal Planner" and format it however you wish.

For Figure 7-5, I formatted the heading in 12-point Impact.

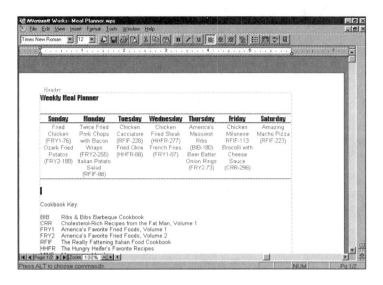

Figure 7-5
A simple meal planner.

3. Place the insertion point on the blank line below the heading you typed in Step 2, then choose the Insert⇨Table command.

The Insert Table dialog box will appear, as shown in Figure 7-6.

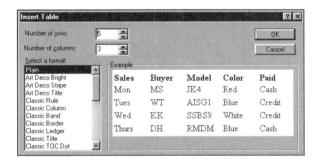

Figure 7-6
Inserting a table.

4. Set the Number of rows to 2 and the Number of columns to 7.

5. Pick a format for the table.

My favorite is "Art Deco Bright."

6. Click OK.

The table will be inserted into the document.

7. Type headings for the weekdays in the cells of the first row of the table.

8. Select one of the cells in the second table row, then call up the Format⇨Row Height command.

The Row Height dialog box will appear, as pictured in Figure 7-7.

Figure 7-7
The Format Row Height
dialog box.

9. Set the Row height field to 75, then click OK.

This will open up the second row of the table so it is large enough to contain your meal plan. (Don't worry; the table will automatically expand if still more room is necessary.)

10. You've already gone too far without saving your document.

Choose the File⇨Save command and save the file. Use a creative name such as "Meal Planner," "What We're Gonna Eat," or "If You Don't Like It, YOU Cook!"

11. Click to the right of the table to move the Insertion Point out of the table, then press the Enter key a few times to add some space.

12. Type a list of your favorite cookbooks with a three- or four-character code assigned to each.

You can see that I listed only health-oriented cookbooks in Figure 7-5 because I wanted to impress everybody.

13. Type your meal plan into the cells in the second table row.

For each item, be sure to list the cookbook and page number. For example, the recipe for Wednesday's main course (Chicken Fried Steak) can be found on page 277 of *The Hungry Heifer's Favorite Recipe*.

14. Save the file again.

15. Print the Meal Planner and stick it on the refrigerator.

Expanding the meal planner to include exchange counts

If you're really into healthy eating, you may want to expand the meal planner project so that single-serving exchange counts are included for each day. Many health-oriented cookbooks include such exchange counts for all their recipes.

To add exchange counts, create the meal planner table with 8 rows and 8 columns instead of 2 rows and 7 columns. The last six rows will be used to indicate how many exchanges of the six recognized exchange groups a single serving of each course will provide, as shown in Figure 7-8. (If you want to create a meal planner that adds up total exchanges for a day or for a week, you might want to consider using the Spreadsheet program instead of the Word Processor.)

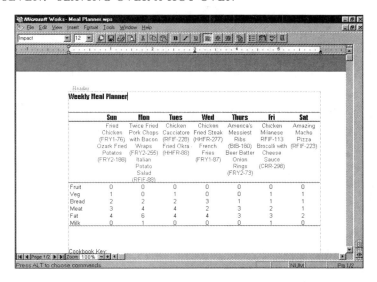

Figure 7-8
Adding exchange counts to the Meal Planner.

Project 9: Making a Grocery List

FAST TRACK

1. Create a database that contains all of the items you normally purchase while grocery shopping.
2. Before you go shopping, work your way through the database and mark the quantity of each item to be purchased. Then print a list of purchases to be made.

GROCERY LIST

It would be great if you could coax your computer into doing your grocery shopping for you. While that may not be realistic, you *can* use your computer to simplify your shopping chores by creating a grocery list. You can expect to spend a few hours setting up the grocery list but, once you get it set up, you can print out lists that are sorted into the order in which the products appear in the store, allowing you to race through your shopping chores in record time.

Setting up your grocery database

The first step in setting up a grocery list is to create a grocery database and enter information about every type of grocery item you routinely purchase. Here's the procedure:

1. Fire up Works and create a new database by choosing the <u>D</u>atabase program from the Works <u>T</u>ools tab.

The familiar Create Database dialog box will appear, unless this is the first time you've used the database. In that case, you may get a first-timer help dialog box, which offers to take you on a tour of creating a database. Click "To create a database" to skip the tour.

2. Create the database fields for the grocery database.

The database should include the following four fields:

> Item
> Location
> Quantity
> Store

To create each field, type the name of the field into Field name text box and click Add.

When you create the Quantity field, check the "Automatically enter a default value" checkbox and type 1 into the text box. That will set the default value for the Quantity field so you'll have to change the quantity only when you want to purchase more than one of a given item.

Also check the "Automatically enter a default value" checkbox when you create the Store field. Then, type the name of the store you do most of your shopping at in the text field. That way, you'll only have to type a value into the Store field for those few items which you don't regularly purchase from your usual store.

When you have created all four fields, click Done.

3. Save the file.

Use the File⇨Save command and pick a meaningful name such as "Grocery List."

4. Working in list view, enter information for as many grocery items as you can.

This is the hardest part of setting up the grocery database. You don't have to enter your local grocery store's entire inventory into the database, but you should create a record for every item you routinely purchase. To get started, try working from a few weeks' worth of saved grocery receipts.

For each grocery item, enter a description of the item ("Peaches" or "Oatmeal") and the location within the store where the item can be found (for example, "Produce" or "Dairy"). Change the Store field only if the item is one that is not purchased at your usual grocery store. And leave the Quantity field blank for now.

5. Save the file frequently.

Get into the habit of pressing Ctrl+S (the shortcut for the File⇨Save command) every four or five records to save your work.

6. When you're done, click any cell in the Location column, choose the Record⇨Sort Records command, and press Enter.

This will sort the records into sequence based on their store location.

Figure 7-9 shows how the Grocery database should appear when it is finished.

Figure 7-9
The Grocery database.

If you really want to streamline your grocery shopping expeditions, print out a copy of the grocery list (just choose File⇨Print; don't worry about setting up a report). Take the printed copy to the grocery store and wander the aisles, writing down the isle number for each item on the list. Then, when you print a shopping list, the grocery items will be listed in the same sequence in which the goods are found on the store shelves. Or, ask the store manager if he or she can give you a map of how the store is laid out and what is kept in each aisle.

For more information about creating a database, see the section "Creating a New Database" in Chapter 4.

Creating the grocery list report

To create a report that will be used to print your grocery list, follow this procedure:

1. Call up the Tools⇨ReportCreator command.

If this is the first time you've created a report, you may get a first-timer dialog box offering to take you on a tour. You can skip the tour for now.

2. When Works asks for a report name, type "Grocery List" and click OK.

The Report Creator dialog box will appear. For details about using this dialog box, refer to the procedure "Creating a Report" in Chapter 5.

3. Type "Grocery List" for the Report Title.

4. Click the Fields tab then click the <u>A</u>dd All button to add all four database fields to the report.

5. Set the Sorting options.

Click the Sorting tab, then select Store for the first sort field, Location for the second sort field, and Item for the third sort field.

6. Set the Grouping options.

Click the Grouping tab, then select the following options in the Group by: Store section:

<u>W</u>hen contents change
Show group heading

Start <u>e</u>ach group on a new page (if you want the report printed that way; this is a matter of personal taste).

For the Then by: Location section, choose the following options:

<u>W</u>hen contents change
Show group heading

7. Set the report filter.

Click the Filter tab, then select (Current Records) and click D<u>o</u>ne.

8. When Works asks if you want to Preview the new report or Modify it, click Modify.

You will be dropped into report view.

9. Delete the information in Heading columns C and D and Record columns C and D.

To delete these items, click the cell you want to delete and press the Delete key. You can safely delete these items from the record rows of the report because they also appear in the group heading rows (Intr Store and Intr Location).

10. Click anywhere in the first column, then choose the <u>I</u>nsert➪Insert <u>C</u>olumn command.

A new column A will be inserted.

11. Select the cell in Column A of the Intr Store row then choose the F<u>o</u>rmat➪<u>B</u>order command. Click Botto<u>m</u>, then click OK.

12. Do the same for the cell in Column A of the Intr Location row.

13. Select the cell at Column A of the Record row and type the letter "o."

14. Choose the F<u>o</u>rmat➪<u>F</u>ont and Style command, select the Wingdings font, and click OK.

The "o" will change into a box character.

15. Choose the F<u>o</u>rmat➪Column <u>W</u>idth command, change the column width setting to "2" and click OK.

At this point, the report definition should resemble Figure 7-10.

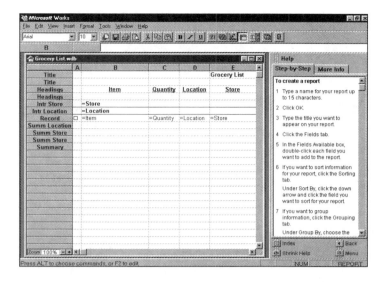

Figure 7-10
Report definition for
the Grocery List.

16. Choose File⭢Save to save your report definition in the database file. Then return to List view by choosing the View⭢List command.

If you want to see how the report will look when printed, click the Preview button on the toolbar. Click Cancel when you've seen enough, or click Print to actually print the report.

Making a shopping list

When it's time to prepare for a shopping expedition, work your way through the grocery list database, marking any records you want to include in the list for this particular shopping spree.

For more information about marking database records, see the section "Marking Records" in Chapter 4.

Here are the steps to create a customized grocery list:

1. If the entire database isn't visible, choose the Record⭢Show⭢All Records command.

2. In List view, click the Check mark button in the top left corner of the database window to clear check marks in all database records.

3. Work your way through the entire database, clicking the checkbox to the left of the row number for those items which you wish to purchase. Change the quantity setting if you wish.

4. For any items that do not appear on the list, go to the end of the list and choose Record⭢Insert Record and type the information for your list.

If you wish, you can then re-sort the list by Location or Item.

5. When the list is ready, choose the Record⭢Show⭢Marked Records command.

All records except those you've marked will disappear.

CROSS
REFERENCE

6. Choose the <u>V</u>iew⇨<u>R</u>eport command. When the View Report dialog box appears, click the <u>P</u>review button.

The report preview will appear, as shown in Figure 7-11.

Figure 7-11
The grocery list, ready for printing.

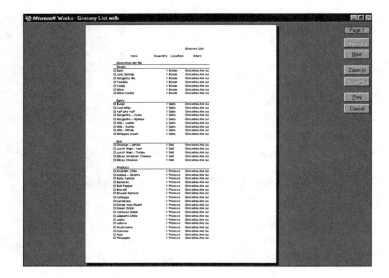

7. Click <u>P</u>rint to print the grocery list.

PART III:

LETS GET
PERSONAL

CHAPTER EIGHT

GETTING CONTROL OF YOUR LIFE

In This Chapter

- Making a To Do list
- Creating a Family Calendar

E ver feel like your life is out of control?

The two projects in this chapter will help you get control of your daily life. The To Do list project will show you how to make a list of the things that just *have* to be done, and how to prioritize the list so that you make sure the most important things are at the top of the list. The Family Calendar project will help you make sure you remember the PTA meeting next Tuesday, lunch with your sister next Wednesday, and your daughter's softball game on Thursday.

Project 10: Creating a To Do List

1. **Use the Spreadsheet to set up a simple To Do list with columns for Status, Priority, Date, and Description.**
2. **Create reports sorted by Priority or Date.**
3. **Periodically add new items and remove completed items.**

A To Do list is one of those things that everyone needs now and then. Some people swear by To Do lists and keep them all the time. These people often have $100 organizers that they use to chart every aspect of their lives. They don't even use the restroom unless such a task appears on their To Do list.

Others, such as myself, wait until life becomes really hectic to create a To Do list. Unfortunately, by then it's often too late to regain control.

A good To Do list not only helps you keep track of what you need to do, but it also helps you prioritize tasks in order of importance and urgency. Note the difference between importance and urgency: Some tasks are important, but not urgent. For example, buying your spouse an anniversary present when your anniversary is still nine months away. This is important, but not urgent — yet. Other tasks are urgent but not important. Mowing the lawn can be an example: You know you've got to do it Saturday morning, but at the same time the world won't end if you don't.

Of course, urgent but unimportant items often become both urgent *and* important if you put them off. After two or three weeks of not mowing the lawn, your yard will start to look bad and your spouse may threaten to leave. Thus, mowing the lawn becomes both urgent *and* important. Likewise, buying an anniversary present is not urgent while the anniversary is still nine months away. But the day before the anniversary, buying a present becomes not only important but urgent as well.

By computerizing your To Do list, you can categorize tasks in terms of urgency and importance. When you categorize by urgency, you assign each task a completion date. The closer you are to the completion date, the more urgent the task. To categorize tasks by importance, assign each task a priority rating of A, B, or C, with the most important tasks being assigned an A. It then becomes a simple matter to sort the list in order by date or priority.

You could use any of the three Works tools to create a To Do list. You could create the list as a simple Word Processor document, using tabs to align columns such as priority, date, and a description of each task. However, the Works Word Processor does not have a sorting feature, so you wouldn't be able to sort the list by priority or date.

Another alternative is to create the list in a spreadsheet, using columns to record each task's priority, date, and description, with one spreadsheet row for each task on the list. Because the Spreadsheet does have a sorting feature, you could sort the rows into any sequence you want.

However, I recommend you use the Works Database program for your To Do list. The Database allows you to not only sort the list, but it also allows you to easily create printed reports of high-priority or urgent items. As a bonus, the Database allows you to hide tasks that you have marked as completed. This feature prevents your list from getting cluttered with old tasks that you have completed months ago.

Figure 8-1 shows how the To Do list will appear when you finish.

Figure 8-1
A To Do list.

If you have purchased your copy of Microsoft Works recently, you may be lucky enough to have the newer version 4.0a instead of the older version 4.0. For version 4.0a, Microsoft added several new templates, including a To Do List template. If a To Do List appears in the list of Works templates in the Works Task Launcher dialog box, you may prefer to use the template rather than create a To Do list from scratch as described in this project.

Creating the To Do List database

To create the To Do List database, follow these steps:

1. From the Works Task Launcher, click the Works Tools tab, and then click the Database button. The Database comes to life, displaying the screen shown in Figure 8-2.

Figure 8-2
Creating the To Do list.

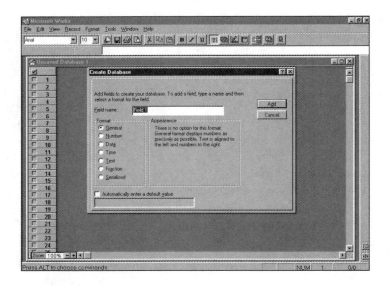

2. Create the database fields. For each field, type the field name, optionally select a format for the field, and click Add. The To Do List database requires four fields:

FIELD NAME	FORMAT
Status	General
Priority	General
Date	Date (select your favorite date format)
Description	General

3. Click Done to create the database. The empty database appears in list view.

4. Change the width of each field to a more suitable setting. To change a field width, click anywhere in the field's column and choose the Format⇨ Field W command. Then type the appropriate field width and click OK. Use the following widths for each of the To Do List database fields:

FIELD NAME	WIDTH
Status	7
Priority	7
Date	8
Description	50

5. Center the Status, Priority, and Date fields. First, click anywhere in the Status column. Then, hold down the shift key and click anywhere in the Date column. This step selects the Status, Priority, and Date fields. Now choose the Format⇨Alignment command to summon the Alignment settings tab in the Format dialog box. Click Center, and then click OK.

The database should now resemble Figure 8-3.

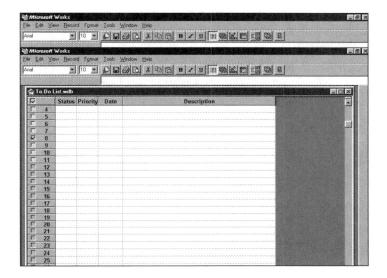

Figure 8-3
The To Do List
database.

6. Choose the File⇨Save command to save the database. Type a reasonable name for the database, such as **My To Do List**, and then click the Save button.

For more information about creating a database, see the section "Creating a New Database" in Chapter 4.

Creating the To Do List filters

Next, create the filters that allow you to select only those To Do list items that have not yet been completed or those items that are still uncompleted. Here's the procedure:

1. Choose the Tools⇨Filters command.

The Filter Name dialog box appears, as shown in Figure 8-4. (If this is the first time you've ever used the Tools⇨Filters command, a first-timer help dialog box will appear, offering to take you on a tour of filters. Click "To create and apply a new filter" to skip the tour and proceed directly to the Filter Name dialog box.)

Figure 8-4
The Filter Name dialog
box.

2. Type "Inactive Tasks" for the filter name, and then click OK.
The Filter dialog box appears.

3. Choose Status from the Field Name drop-down list, make sure the Comparison field is set to "is Equal to," and then type "Done" in the Compare To field. Figure 8-5 shows how the Filter dialog box should now appear.

If your Filter dialog box has just one big text field rather than neatly arranged columns of text boxes as shown in Figure 8-5, the Filter using formula option button has been selected. Click the Easy Filter option button to straighten things out.

Figure 8-5
The Inactive Tasks filter.

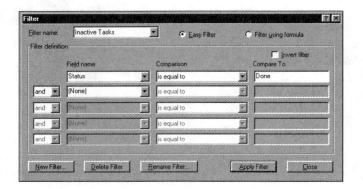

4. Click New Filter, and then click Yes when Works asks if you want to save the changes to the filter.

The Filter Name dialog box appears again (it was shown back in Figure 8-4).

5. Type "Active Tasks" for the filter name, and then click OK.
The Filter dialog box appears again.

6. Choose Status from the Field Name drop-down list, choose "is not equal to" from the Comparison drop-down list, and type "Done" in the Compare To field.

Figure 8-6 shows how the Filter dialog box should appear for the Active Tasks filter.

7. Click Close, and then click Yes when Works asks if you want to save the changes to the Active Tasks filter.

The Filter dialog box disappears.

8. Choose the File⇨Save command to save your work.

For more information about filters, see the section "Working with Filters" in Chapter 4.

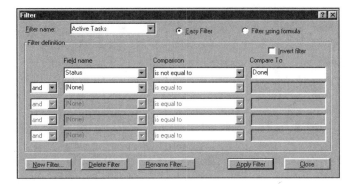

Figure 8-6
The Active Tasks filter.

Creating the To Do List reports

Finally, to create the reports for the To Do List database, follow these steps:

1. Choose the Tools⇨ReportCreator command.

The Report Name dialog box appears, as shown in Figure 8-7. (If this is your first time creating a report, you may see a first time help dialog box offering to take you on a brief tour of reporting. To skip the tour, click "To create a report.")

Figure 8-7
The Report Name
dialog box.

2. Type "Priority List" for the Report Name and click OK. Then, type "Priority List" for the report title.

See Figure 8-8.

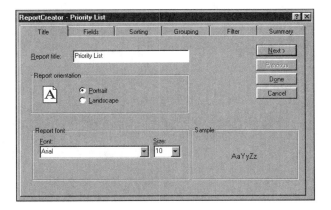

Figure 8-8
Creating the Priority
List report.

3. Click <u>N</u>ext, or click the Fields tab.

4. Add the Priority, Date, and Description fields to the report.

To add a field to the report, click on the field name in the <u>F</u>ields Available box, and then click <u>A</u>dd.

5. Click <u>N</u>ext or click the Sorting tab to display the sorting options.

6. Choose Priority from the drop-down list for the <u>S</u>ort by field.

7. Click the Filter tab, or click <u>N</u>ext twice, to display the filter options.

8. Select the Active Tasks filter from the list of filters.

9. Click D<u>o</u>ne to complete the report.

The following steps may be required to correct a glitch in Works, which causes the report title to be placed incorrectly on the report.

10. When Works asks if you want to Preview or Modify the report, click Modify.

You are now in report view, as shown in Figure 8-9.

Figure 8-9
Modifying the Priority List report.

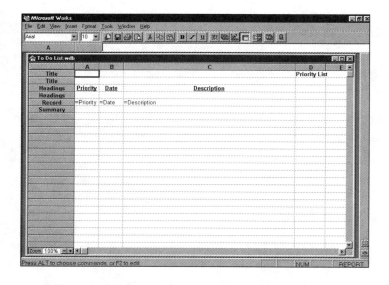

11. Click in column D of the first Title row.

The report title ("Priority List") is selected.

12. Choose the <u>E</u>dit⇨Cu<u>t</u> command.

13. Click in column A of the first Title row.

14. Choose the <u>E</u>dit⇨<u>P</u>aste command.

15. Choose the <u>F</u>ile⇨Print Pre<u>v</u>iew command.

A preview of the report is displayed so you can make sure it is formatted correctly. Figure 8-10 shows how the report should appear (I zoomed in so the report would be more readable).

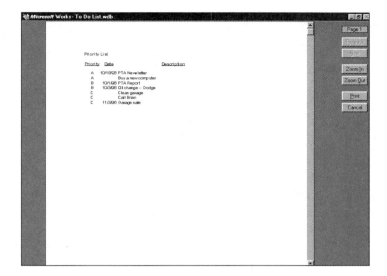

Figure 8-10
The Priority List report.

16. Click Cancel to leave Print Preview mode.

17. Save your work.

You have completed the first report. Now, we're going to create a second report, similar to the Priority List report, but that sorts by date rather than by priority.

18. Choose the Tools⇨Duplicate Report command.

The Duplicate Report dialog box appears.

19. Type "Date List" in the text box. See Figure 8-11.

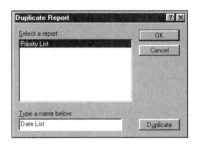

Figure 8-11
The Date List report.

20. Click OK. You are taken back to Report Design mode.

21. Click column A in the first Title row and type "Things to Do — by Date."

22. Choose the Tools⇨Report Sorting command. Your sorting options appear.

23. Change the Sort by field from Priority to Date.

24. Click Done.

25. Use the <u>F</u>ilePrint Pre<u>v</u>iew command to preview the new report.

The report should appear similar to the Priority List report, but any tasks you have entered will be listed in Date sequence rather than in Priority sequence.

26. Click Cancel.

27. Choose the <u>F</u>ile<u>S</u>ave command to save your work.

For more information about creating reports, refer to the "Creating a Report" section in Chapter 4.

Using the To Do List

The easiest way to work with the To Do List database is to work in list view, entering each task you need to complete as a separate row.

Whenever you complete a task, type **Done** in the task's Status column. The task will be excluded by the Active Tasks filter used to print the reports.

To remove tasks that you have completed from the To Do list, follow these steps:

1. Open the To Do List database. You can find it by selecting the Existing Documents tab in the Works task launcher and double-clicking it in the list of Works documents that appears.

2. Switch to list view if you are not already there. Use the <u>V</u>iew<u>L</u>ist command to switch to list view.

3. Call up the <u>T</u>ools<u>F</u>ilters command. The Filter dialog box appears.

4. Select the Inactive Tasks filter, and then click <u>A</u>pply Filter. You are returned to list view, but any tasks that do not have "Done" in the Status field will be hidden from view.

5. Choose the <u>E</u>ditSelect A<u>l</u>l command. Or, use the keyboard shortcut Ctrl+A. Either way, all of the visible records will be selected.

6. Choose the <u>R</u>ecordD<u>e</u>lete Record command. All inactive records are deleted.

7. Choose the <u>R</u>ecordSh<u>o</u>wAll Records command. The active records magically reappear.

For more information about filters, see the section "Working with Filters" in Chapter 4.

Project 11: Creating a Family Calendar

> 1. Create a model calendar as a Works word processing document.
> 2. Modify the model calendar each month to create a monthly calendar of family events.

A calendar is one of the basic type of documents many people want to create with their computers. Basic enough that you'd think Works would come with a Calendar TaskWizard. Unfortunately, there is no such TaskWizard. So you're on your own to create your own calendar using the Works Word Processor. Figure 8-12 shows an example of a calendar created with the Works Word Processor.

**Figure 8-12
A calendar created in
Works.**

The trouble is, creating a good looking calendar isn't as easy as it would first seem. The obvious approach is to use a table to represent the grid of days and weeks. That works well, except that Works tables have an annoying limitation: All the text within a table cell must be formatted exactly the same. Most calendars include the date in the upper corner of each day. For example, September 1 should be identified by a large "1." Then information you want to record for that date should be shown in a smaller font so you can get more information into each cell. Unfortunately, Works won't let you do that. You must format all the text — the date as well as the tasks to do on that day — in the same font size.

So how did I create the calendar in Figure 8-12, in which the date numbers are obviously much larger than the text associated with each day? The secret is that each date on the calendar is represented by two cells in a table: a narrow cell to hold the date number, and a wider cell that accommodates reminders or other text you want to provide for a particular date.

If you're lucky enough to have the newer 4.0a version of Works, you'll find a TaskWizard specifically devoted to creating calendars. If you have this TaskWizard, by all means use it. But if you're stuck with the older 4.0 version of Works, follow the procedure described in this section.

Here is the procedure for creating a calendar:

1. From the Task Launcher, choose the Word Processor to create a new word processing document.

2. Choose the File⇨Page Setup command.

The Page Setup dialog box appears, as shown in Figure 8-13.

Figure 8-13
The Page Setup
dialog box.

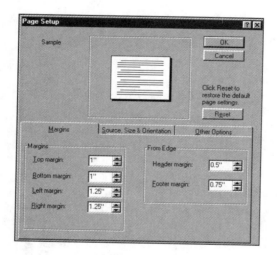

3. Change the margin settings.

The default margin settings leave too much space around the edge of the page. To fit a larger calendar on the page, specify smaller margins, as follows:

MARGIN	SETTING
Top	1.0
Bottom	0.4
Left	0.5
Right	0.5
Header	0.2
Footer	0.2

4. Click the Source, Size & Orientation tab, click the Landscape option, and then click OK.

Your document is now set up to work in Landscape mode to accommodate a wide calendar.

5. Click the Zoom number in the Zoom control, then select Whole Page from the menu that appears.

This setting enables you to see the entire page. (The Zoom number appears adjacent to the word Zoom at the bottom of the Works window.)

6. Set the Font to Times New Roman and the Size to 48. Then, type the month and year (for example, "September 1996"), and then click the Center button to center the title. Finally, press Enter to start a new line.

Use the Font and Size controls in the toolbar to set the font and size.

7. Choose the Insert⇨Table command.

The Insert Table dialog box appears, as shown in Figure 8-14.

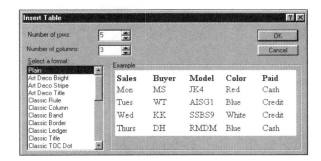

Figure 8-14
The Insert Table dialog box.

8. Change the number of rows to 1 and the number of columns to 7, and then click OK.

9. If the table appears too small to work with, zoom in until you can comfortably work with the table.

The best zoom setting for the following steps in this procedure will depend on the size of your computer's monitor. The larger your monitor, the larger the zoom setting you can get away with. (Feel free to adjust the zoom setting at any time in this procedure; changing the zoom setting in no way affects the appearance of your calendar when printed.)

10. Click the row selector to the left of the table row to select the entire row. Then use the toolbar controls to set the text format to Times New Roman, 14 point, Bold, Italic, and Centered.

11. Type the days of the week into each cell in the table, starting with Sunday. Then click outside and below the table to deselect the table and move the cursor back to the document.

At this point, the calendar should look like Figure 8-15.

Figure 8-15
The calendar so far.

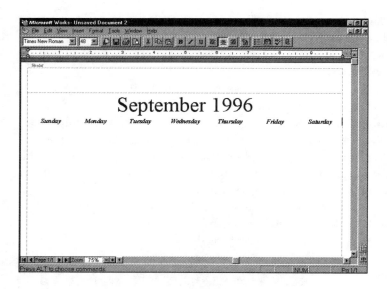

12. Choose the Insert⇨Table command again. This time, specify 5 for the number of rows and 14 for the number of columns, then click OK.

That's right, 14 columns — not 7. Because all the text in a table cell must be formatted the same, you're going to use two columns for each day of the week. The first column will be narrow — just wide enough for the day number, which will be formatted in 14-point Times New Roman. The second column will be for any notes you want to make. These notes will be formatted in 8-point Arial, so you'll be able to cram plenty of text into each day.

13. Format the odd numbered columns to display the date.

First, click the column selector for the first column. Then use the toolbar controls to format the column as Times New Roman, 14-point, Bold, Left aligned. Next, choose the Format⇨Alignment command, click the Top option for Vertical Alignment, and then click OK. Finally, choose the Format⇨Column Width command, set the width to 4, and click OK. Repeat this process for the 3rd, 5th, 7th, 9th, 11th, and 13th columns.

14. Format the even numbered columns to display any notes typed for the date.

First, click the column selector for the second column. Then use the toolbar controls to format the column as Arial, 8-point, Left aligned. Choose the Format⇨Column Width command and set the column width to 15. Then repeat these formatting steps for the 4th, 6th, 8th, 10th, 12th, and 14th columns.

15. Set the row height for all the table rows to 84.

Select the entire table by clicking the table selector button (located at the top-left corner of the table), and then choose the Format⇨Row Height command. Type **84** for the row height and click OK.

16. Apply borders to the entire table.

Select the entire table again if it is still not selected. Then choose the For-mat⇨Border command and click Outline, Top, Botto_m, and Left. (Do *not* click Right.) Click OK to apply the borders.

17. Remove the left border from the even-numbered columns.

First, click the column selector for the second column. Choose the For-mat⇨Border command and click Left three times to remove the border, and then click OK. Repeat for columns 4, 6, 8, 10, 12, and 14.

18. Type dates into the narrow columns according to the calendar month.

For example, September 1996 starts on a Sunday, so type **1** in column 1 of the first row, **2** in column 3, **3** in column 5, and so on. Hint: Use the Tab key to move from cell to cell.

19. Remove borders from any unused cells.

Select any unused cells at the beginning of the first row. For example, if the month begins on Wednesday, select the cells for Sunday, Monday, and Tuesday. Then choose the Format⇨Borders command and remove borders on the top and left. (You may have to click the Top and Left controls several times to make the borders go away.) Then click OK.

Then repeat the process for any unused cells at the end of the last row, but remove the bottom and right borders rather than the top and left bor-ders. You will also need to remove the left border from all but the left-most unused column in the last row.

After all this work, the calendar should resemble Figure 8-16. (To make the entire calendar visible for Figure 8-16, I reduced the zoom factor to 50%. You may need to choose a different zoom setting, depending on your monitor.)

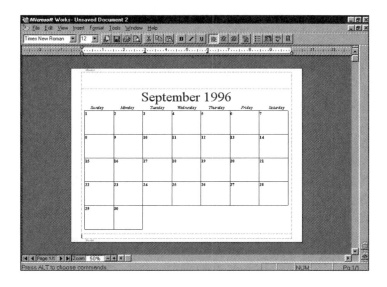

Figure 8-16
The finished calendar.

20. Save your work.

Choose the File⇨Save command and save your file, using a file name such as **Calendar**.

21. Use the File⇨Save As command, this time using a specific name for the month represented by the calendar.

For example, **September 1996**.

22. Add any reminders you want to the calendar.

For example, if you have to remember to have lunch with Mom on the 14th, click the wide cell for that date and type something like **Lunch with Mom**.

23. When you've typed in all your reminders, save the file again. Then print the calendar by choosing the File⇨Print command.

Because you saved the model calendar using a generic name (*Calendar*), you can easily create a new calendar for a different month by calling up the model calendar and immediately saving it under a new file name. Then, make any necessary changes and save the modified calendar under the new file name.

CROSS REFERENCE

For more information about using any of the word processing features described in this project, refer to Chapter 2.

CHAPTER NINE

SO MANY PEOPLE:
COMPUTERIZING YOUR
ADDRESS BOOK

In This Chapter

- Computerizing your personal address book
- Creating a list of baby-sitters
- Printing a list of emergency numbers

If you're an isolationist, living alone in an 11'x14' cabin four miles from the nearest road, with no phone or mail service, you can skip this chapter. Otherwise, read on. This chapter will show you how to computerize your address book and how to get the most from it. It will also show you how to create a specialized address book for baby-sitters — very useful if you have young ones in the house. Finally, it wraps up with a simple project that shows you how to create a cleanly formatted list of emergency contact numbers, such as the police and fire departments, neighbors, relatives, and so on.

Project 12: Computerizing Your Personal Address Book

My wife and I have kept the same tattered book for more than a decade, and it is a mess. It has pages falling out, some pages are filled, many names and addresses are crossed out, and the listings for our friends who move every two years have become all but unreadable.

If we had any sense, we'd computerize it. A computerized address list has many advantages over a handwritten one. When someone moves, you don't have to cross out the old address and find space to write in a new one; you just update the person's record to indicate the new address. For example, if you have a friend named Melissa, but you just can't remember her last name, the computerized address book lets you quickly display all the "Melissas" in your address book so you can find out.

The personal address book lets you print out your address information in various ways. And, if you have a modem, it can even dial phone numbers for you.

FAST
TRACK

ADDRESS
BOOK

1. **Create your address book using the Address Book Wizard.**
2. **Transfer all the information from your personal address book into the computerized address book.**
3. **Create reports to print directories and lists of upcoming birthdays and anniversaries.**

About address books and the Address Book Wizard

An address book is a fairly complicated database that contains many different types of fields that enable you to store information about your friends and enemies. Fortunately, Works comes with a sophisticated Address Book Wizard that can set up an address book for you. All you have to do is answer a few questions and let the Wizard do the work.

The Address Book Wizard can create six types of address books:

■ **Personal:** Designed to record phone numbers and addresses of your personal friends and relatives.

■ **Business:** Lists businesses you work with. You could create a separate business address book to record information about your plumber and gardener, but these people can just as easily go in your personal address book.

■ **Customers or Clients:** Keeps track of the people who are the lifeblood of your business.

■ **Suppliers and Vendors:** Keeps track of the companies that provide goods or services for your business.

■ **Sales Contacts:** If you're in sales, this one is vital.

■ **Employees:** If you own a small business, this database will help keep track of your employees.

Although six types of address books are possible, only the first one is for personal use; the other five are designed for business use. So this project will use the Address Book Wizard's Personal Address Book option.

Every Works program has a toolbar button that can instantly summon your default address book. If you want your personal address book to appear when the Address Book button is clicked, you can have the personal address book become your default address book. If you don't make the personal address book your default address book, you can still access it from the Works Task Launcher's Existing Documents tab. And you can make it your default address book later by choosing the Tools➪Address book command, which allows you to designate any Works database as your default address book.

Creating the personal address book

Here is the procedure best followed to create a personal address book:

1. Summon the Address Book Wizard.

From the Works Task Launcher, click the TaskWizards tab, and then click Common Tasks. Click Address Book, and then click OK. When Works asks if you want to use the Task Wizard, click Yes. The Address Book Task Wizard will make a grand entrance, as shown in Figure 9-1.

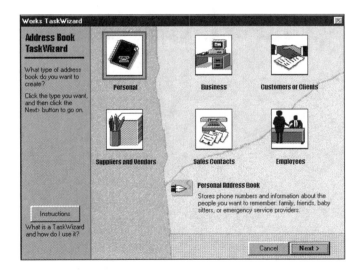

Figure 9-1
The Address Book Wizard.

2. Click Personal Address Book, and then click Next.

The Address Book Wizard displays information about creating a personal address book, as shown in Figure 9-2. Review this information to get an idea of the type of information that you can store in the personal address book.

Figure 9-2
Address Book Wizard
prepares to create a
personal address book.

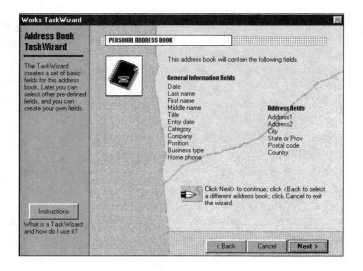

3. Click Next.

The dialog box shown in Figure 9-3 appears. Here you have the option of adding additional information to your database by clicking one of the three buttons (Additional Fields, Your Own Fields, and Reports).

Figure 9-3
The Address Book
Wizard offers some
options.

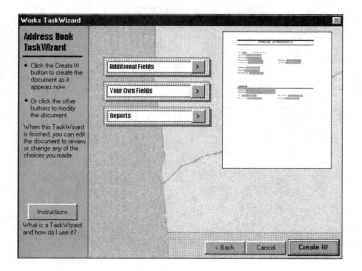

4. Click Additional Fields to summon the Additional Fields dialog box. See Figure 9-4.

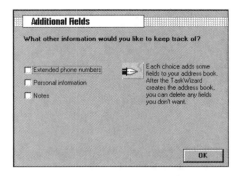

Figure 9-4
The Additional Fields
dialog box.

5. Click the options for the additional fields you want to include, and then click OK.

For a personal address book, select the Personal Information fields. These fields include family information such as the name of spouses and children, as well as birthday and anniversary dates.

If you want to record more than a home phone number — for example, a business phone, mobile phone, pager number, or e-mail address, check the Extended Phone Numbers option.

Finally, if you want a general note-taking field for each listing, so you can record notes such as "Big 49er Fan" or "Loves Chocolate," select the Notes option.

Check all three options.

6. Click the Reports button or choose the View⇨Report command to summon the Reports dialog box.

See Figure 9-5.

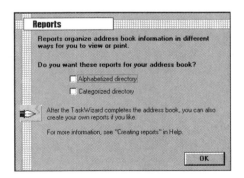

Figure 9-5
The Reports dialog
box.

7. Select the report options you want, and then click OK.

The Alphabetized Directory report is the basic address book listing, with names sorted into alphabetical order by last name. You almost certainly want the Alphabetized Directory report.

The Categorized Directory prints an address book grouped by category. Because you get to create your own categories, this can mean anything you want. It doesn't hurt to select the Categorized Directory even if you end up not using it.

When you've selected the reports you want, click OK.

8. Click Create It.

The dialog box shown in Figure 9-6 appears.

Figure 9-6
The Address Wizard's
final screen.

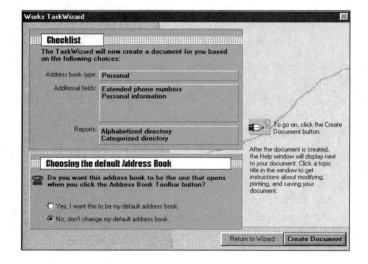

9. If you want the personal address book to be your default address book, click the "Yes, I want this to be my default address book" option.

10. Click Create Document.

Works whirls and spins a few moments, grunts a few times, and then presents the beautifully crafted address book shown in Figure 9-7.

11. Choose the File⇨Save command to save your address book.

Use a meaningful name such as "My Address Book," "Friends and Enemies," or "Kith and Kin." Then click Save to save the file.

Modifying the form

The personal address book form is attractive and, for the most part, well laid out. However, it has one irritating layout problem you need to correct before you start entering names: It places the spouse's name way down at the bottom of the form, as if you may not want to enter it. I prefer to place the spouse's name at the top of the form.

If you agree, modify the form accordingly. Open the Personal Address Book database, and then choose the View⇨Form Design command to switch to form design view. Start by dragging down the Business Type, Position, Company, and Home Phone fields to make some room beneath the

Middle Name field. Then drag the Spouse's Name field up where it belongs. When everything is lined up properly, choose the <u>V</u>iew⇨<u>F</u>rom command to return to form view, and then use <u>F</u>ile⇨<u>S</u>ave to save the file.

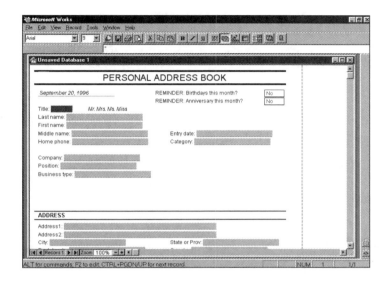

Figure 9-7
The personal address book ready to use.

Figure 9-8 shows how the modified form layout should appear.

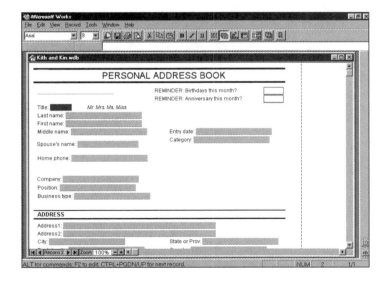

Figure 9-8
The personal address book with the form modified.

Here are a few pointers to assist you when making this modification:

■ Work in an enlarged view when you move things around on the form. Try zooming to 150% or 200%.

■ Use the Format⇨Snap To Grid command to force alignment of fields as you move them. Unfortunately, the grid spacing differs from the vertical spacing that the Address Book Wizard uses to create the form. As a result, if you turn on Snap To Grid, you won't be able to space the fields on the form properly. Sigh.

■ Dragging the Spouse's Name field from the bottom of the form to the top may seem impossible, since you can't see the entire form in the window — especially if you have zoomed in to 150% or 200%. No problem. Just drag the field up to the top of the window. The window will automatically begin to scroll up. When the top of the form comes into view, drag the field down a bit to stop the scrolling. Then drag it into its proper position between the Middle Name and Home Phone fields.

Creating a category list

Before you start typing names into your database, you should first decide what categories you are going to use in the Category field. Here is a suggested list:

■ Friend
■ Family
■ Business
■ Clinton's Half Brother
■ Other

You could make a much more detailed list, but you'd probably end up wishing you hadn't. After you create a few detailed categories, you'll end up creating dozens of categories that serve little purpose. It's best to stick to just a few broad categories.

Here are a few other tips for creating categories:

■ Try to keep the category names short. You'll have to type the category name for each entry in your address book. "Friend" is much easier to type than "acquaintance." If you want, use single-letter categories like "F" for Friend, "B" for Business, and so on.

■ Make sure you spell the categories the same each time. Works is smart enough to ignore capitalization when grouping categories. Thus, "Friend" is the same as "friend." However, "Friend" and "Friends" will be treated as two separate categories.

■ Consider creating a separate category for your kid's friends. For example, if you have two kids — say, Bert and Ernie — consider creating "Bert" and "Ernie" categories for their friends.

■ Create a simple word processing document with a list of your categories. Then print out the list and keep it handy when you're entering names into your address book.

Keep in mind that Works doesn't know anything about the categories you use in this field. As a result, you can type anything you want in the Category field. The whole point of creating a list of categories before you start entering names and addresses into your address book is so that you'll be consistent when you enter the category for each record in the address book.

Typing in the names and addresses

Now comes the hard part. An empty address book is good to no one. Although it may take hours, you'll have to sit down with your old, tattered, hard-copy address book and type all the names into the computer. Bother.

After you have entered all the names and addresses into the computer, sort the records by choosing the Record⇨Sort Records command. Select Last Name for the Sort By field, and then click OK. Any time you add additional records, you should use the database.

Here are some thoughts to keep in mind when you type in your names and addresses:

- When you enter names and addresses, don't worry about the information you don't know. The Address Book will work fine even if most of the fields are left blank.
- Always enter the name by which you want an entry to be sorted in the Last Name field, even if you are creating an entry for which you do not have a person's name (such as the name of your kid's school or your local video store). Also, be sure to drop the first word of the name if it's a common word such as "The" or "A." For example, enter "The Video Store" as "Video Store," unless you want to look up The Video Store under Ts instead of V.
- If the idea of typing your whole address book into the database in one sitting gives you hives, break the task down into more tolerable goals. For example, consider doing one letter of the alphabet each day.

Adding report fields

The Personal Address Book database that is created by the Address Book Wizard can create two simple reports: a sorted Addresses directory and a Categories listing that lists names grouped by category. However, these listings have a few minor problems. In particular, they don't list spouse names or work phone numbers. To add this information, you need to modify the report designs for these reports.

Before you modify these designs, however, add three fields to the database, named *Report Name*, *Report Home*, and *Report Work*. These fields are set up with formulas that automatically create text that you can use in the reports. The Report Name field combines the First Name and Spouse's Name field so that both names are listed. If no Spouse's Name is given, the Report Name will be identical to the First Name field. If a Spouse's Name is given, the Report Name will combine the First Name and Spouse's Name fields with "and," as in, "Fred and Wilma."

The Report Home and Report Work fields create text that lists home and work phone numbers if you have entered them; if you have not, these fields will be blank. As a result, you can eliminate orphaned "Home:" and "Work:" headings from addresses that have no home or work phone numbers.

Unfortunately, the address book database provides no easy method to print an address directory that lists spouses names properly, as in "Clinton, Bill and Hillary." To do that, you must add an additional field to the database, and then create a formula that automatically combines first names when necessary. You can then use this new First Names field in reports to print a useful directory.

You don't have to enter any information into these three fields; they are formulated automatically using the information you type into the First Name, Spouse's Name, Home Phone, and Work Phone fields.

To add the three fields, follow these steps:

1. Choose the View⇨List command to switch to List View.
2. Select the right-most column in the database.
3. Choose the Record⇨Insert Field⇨After command.

An Insert Field dialog box appears, as shown in Figure 9-9.

Figure 9-9
The Insert Field dialog box.

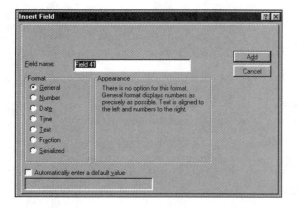

4. Type Report Name for the field name, and then click Add.
5. Type Report Home for the field name, and then click Add.
6. Type Report Work for the field name, and then click Add.
7. Click Done.

Three columns are added to the database, as shown in Figure 9-10.

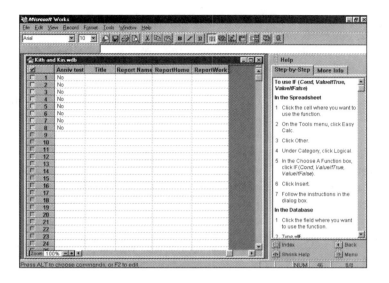

Figure 9-10
The address book database with three new columns added.

8. Select the first cell in the Report Name column.
9. Type the following formula into the field:

```
=First name&IF(Spouse's name="",""," and
"&Spouse's name)
```

Make sure you type it exactly as shown, with all the ampersands, parentheses, commas, and quotation marks in place.

10. Select the first cell in the Report Home column.
11. Type the following formula:

```
=IF(Home phone="","","Home: "&Home phone)
```

12. Select the first cell in the Report Work column.
13. Type the following formula:

```
=IF(Work phone="","","Work: "&Work phone)
```

You're done!

Well, almost. Unfortunately, the three new fields you added in Steps 4, 5, and 6 will mess up the database's form — they'll be added to the upper left corner of the form without regard to the information that is already laid out there on the form. To clean up the form, choose the View➪Form Design command, then one by one drag the superfluous fields to the very bottom of the form, where they will be hidden from view.

Modifying the directory reports

The Personal Address Book database includes two reports that you can print. To access these reports, choose the View➪Report command. A dialog box listing the two reports appears.

The Addresses report is a simple listing of names, addresses, and phone numbers. It does not list spouses, work phone numbers, cell-phone numbers, e-mail addresses, or any other information. It also does not sort the database, so you should make sure the database is sorted *first* if you want the listing to appear in alphabetical order.

The Categories report lists the same information as the Addresses report, but it groups the output by category.

You added the three fields — Report Name, Report Home, and Report Work — in the previous section to modify the Addresses and Categories report to include properly formatted names and phone numbers. Start by modifying the Addresses report. Choose the View⇨Reports command, click Addresses, and then click Modify. You are taken to report view, where you can make the following modifications:

- Column A in the first Record row contains the following formula:

```
=Last name&", "&First name&" "&Middle name&"
Home phone:"&Home phone
```

Select this cell. Then press F2 and change the formula to the following:

```
=Last name&", "&Report Name
```

- Column A in the second Record row contains this formula:

```
=Address1&", "&Address2&", "&City&" "&State or
Prov
```

Add **&" "&Postal code** to the end of this formula, so it looks like this:

```
=Address1&", "&Address2&", "&City&" "&State or
Prov&" "&Postal code
```

- Delete the entries in columns D and E of the second Record row.
- Add the following formula to column E of the first Record row:

```
=Report Home
```

- Add the following formula to column E of the second Record row:

```
=Report Work
```

- Select the E column in both Record rows, call up the Format⇨Alignment command, set the Horizontal Alignment to Right, and then click OK. Then use the Size control in the toolbar to set the font size to 10 point.

Figure 9-11 shows an example of how the Addresses report will appear after these changes have been made.

ADDRESS / PHONE DIRECTORY

Date report printed: 9/21/96 PERSONAL ADDRESS BOOK

Adams, Gomez and Morticia	
1234 Gouhle Lane, , Spooksville CA94733	
Banks, George and Winnefred	Home: 555-8483
#7 Cherry Tree Lane, , London TX89392	
Clampet, Jed	Home: 555-3811
#7 Mansion Drive, , Beverly Hills CA90210	Work: 555-3884
Clinton, Bill and Hillary	Home: 555-3748
1700 Pennsylvania Ave, , Washington DC10001	
Doe, John and Jane	Home: 555-2134
123 Fourth Street, , Somewhere PA19293	
Smith, Jake	Home: 555-9872
8584 N. 38 Street SE, , Seattle WA12345	Work: 555-3722
Robinson, Will	Home: 555-1234
Jupiter 2, , Outer Space00000	

Figure 9-11
The Address/Phone Directory report.

When you have made the changes to the Addresses report, save the database (choose the File⇨Save command). Then call up the Categories report and make the same changes.

For more information about creating reports, refer to the "Creating a Report" section in Chapter 4.

Creating an anniversary list

Did you notice that the address book has fields for birthdays and anniversaries, and that the form has a special field that displays "Yes" or "No" to indicate whether someone is celebrating a birthday or anniversary this month? This feature is quite useful, but it would be even more useful if you could print out a report of everyone in your address book who will be celebrating a birthday or anniversary in the coming month. You can, by creating a report of your own design.

Start with the Anniversary list; it's the easiest to create. Here is the procedure for creating it:

1. Choose the Tools⇨ReportCreator command.
ReportCreator asks for the name of the report you want to create.
2. Type "Anniversaries" for the report name, and then click OK.
The ReportCreator comes to life.
3. In the Title tab, type "Anniversaries This Month" for the Report Title, and then click Next.
4. In the Fields tab, select the Last Name and Anniversary fields, and then click Next.
5. In the Sorting tab, choose Anniversary for the Sort By field, and then click Next.
6. Click Next to skip the Grouping tab.
7. In the Filter tab, click Create New Filter.
Works asks for the name of the new filter.
8. Type "Anniversaries" for the Filter Name, and then click OK.
The Filter dialog box appears.

9. Choose "Anniv Test" for the Field Name, "contains" for the Comparison, and "Yes" for the Compare To field.

Figure 9-12 shows how the filter should look.

Figure 9-12
The anniversaries filter.

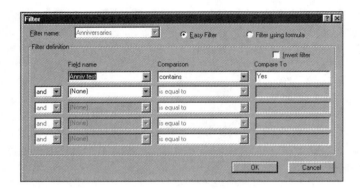

10. Click OK, and then click Done.

Works asks if you want to preview or modify the report.

11. Click Modify.

You are now in report view.

12. Select the A column in the Record row, and then choose the Format⇨Number command.

The Number tab of the Format dialog box appears.

13. Choose the General format option, and then click OK.

14. Press F2 to edit the A column of the Record row, and then change the field contents to:

```
=Report Name&" "&Last name
```

Press Enter.

15. Select the E column of the first Title row, and then choose the Edit⇨Cut command. Select the A column of the first Title row, and then choose the Edit⇨Paste command.

The report heading moves from the center of the page to the left edge.

16. Choose the Format⇨Column Width command, and then change the column width setting to 50.

Click OK to dismiss the Column Width dialog box.

17. Select the B column in the Record row, and then choose the Format⇨Number command. Change the number format to Date.

Click OK to dismiss the Format dialog box.

18. Select the entire first Heading row, and then press the Delete key.

The column headings (which are not necessary for this simple report) are deleted.

When you finish creating the report, be sure to save your work by choosing the File⇨Save command.

Figure 9-13 shows a sample of output created by the Anniversaries report.

Anniversaries This Month

George and Winnefred Banks	9/1/80
Archie and Edith Bunker	9/5/76
Bill and Hillary Clinton	9/22/57
John and Jane Doe	9/6/88

Figure 9-13
The Anniversaries report.

If no one in the database has an anniversary in this month, you'll get a dialog box displaying the following message:

```
No records matched the criteria.
Check the filter formula for accuracy.
```

Click OK to dismiss the dialog box, then try again next month.

Creating a birthday list

Creating a birthday list is a little more difficult; each record in the address book can have as many as seven birthdays: the birthday for the main person listed for the entry, plus birthdays for a spouse and up to five children.

Fortunately, the Address Book Wizard automatically creates a field named *Test* that tells you how many birthdays in each record occur in the current month. As a result, you can easily create a query that lists only those records in which at least one family member has a birthday in the current month. Unfortunately, you have no easy way to go a step further and list only those individuals whose birthdays are in the current month. The best you can do is list the names and birthdays of everyone in the family. At least one of the birthdays listed will be in the current month, but you'll have to look at the listing to find out which birthday.

Figure 9-14 shows how the Birthday List report should look. Because the step-by-step procedure for creating this report would run into dozens of steps, I won't list the details here. Instead, I'll just suggest the general procedure. If you've created a few database reports, you should be able to fill in the gaps. If not, I suggest you create a few simpler reports before taking on this one.

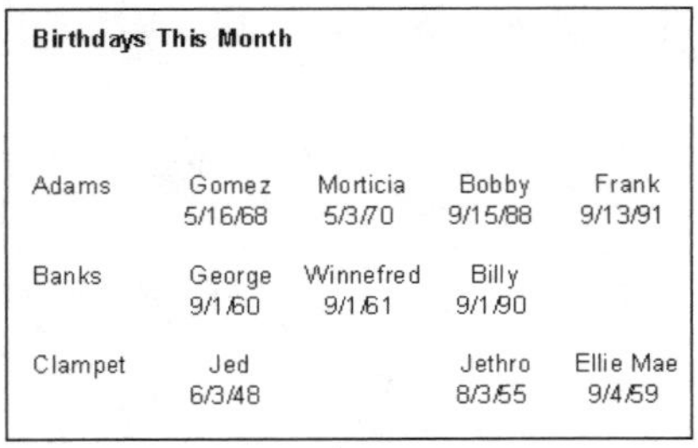
Birthdays This Month

Adams	Gomez 5/16/68	Morticia 5/3/70	Bobby 9/15/88	Frank 9/13/91
Banks	George 9/1/60	Winnefred 9/1/61	Billy 9/1/90	
Clampet	Jed 6/3/48		Jethro 8/3/55	Ellie Mae 9/4/59

Figure 9-14
A listing of families in which at least one member has a birthday in the current month.

Figure 9-15 shows the finished design for this report. Listed here are the highlights of the design:

- The design was created with the ReportCreator, selecting the Last Name, First Name, Spouse's Name, and all five Child Name fields. Birthday fields were *not* included — they were manually added later.
- The report is sorted on the Last Name field.
- The report is based on a filter that specifies "Test is greater than 0" as the filter criteria. The filter is named *Birthdays*.
- The birthdays are shown on a separate line beneath the family member names. To insert the second record row, select the Summary row, choose the Insert⇨Row command, and then choose Record as the row type and click the Insert button. Use the Insert⇨Field Entry command to insert the Birthday, Spouse bday, and B1 through B5 fields in the columns beneath the First Name, Spouse's Name, and Child Name fields.
- Delete the first heading row.
- Center columns B through H.
- Increase the row height of the first Record row to 24 so that extra space is inserted between each group of record lines when the report is printed.

Project 13: Creating an Emergency Contact List

It's good to have a list of emergency numbers posted in a prominent area where you, your kids, or a baby-sitter can find it. My wife and I keep our list taped to the inside of a cupboard door right next to the phone in the kitchen.

Hopefully, you'll never need to use such a list. If, however, you're unlucky enough to need it, lucky Project 13 will ensure that your list is current — very important in an emergency — and legible.

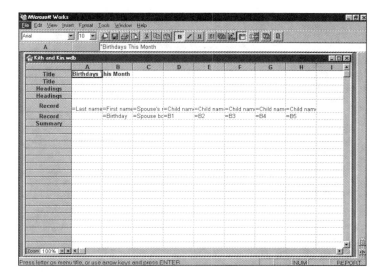

Figure 9-15
The finished report design.

FAST TRACK

EMERGENCY CONTACT LIST

1. Create a simple word processing document that lists emergency contact numbers.
2. Post the list near the telephone.

The previous project was so big that I decided it was time for a small project to wrap up this chapter. The Emergency Numbers List is nothing more than a simple word processing document that contains the phone numbers you think you may need in an emergency. Here are some ideas for phone numbers to include on the list:

- Obviously, 911.
- Immediate family members: your parents, spouse's parents, siblings, children, or any other family you think you may need to contact quickly in an emergency.
- Neighbors.
- Your children's schools.
- You and your spouse's work numbers. Also include cell phone numbers, pagers, etc.
- Medical numbers, including your doctor, dentist, and — if you have pets — veterinarian.

Figure 9-16 shows an example of a document with such numbers.

Figure 9-16
An emergency contact
list.

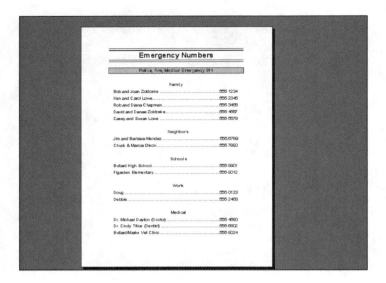

Here are some pointers to help you create a document similar to the one in Figure 9-16:

■ It's easier to come back and apply formatting to text you've already typed than it is to fuss with the formatting as you type the document. So I suggest you type the entire document first, then apply the formatting.

■ Use the "Contemporary Masthead" Easy Format to create the "Emergency Numbers" heading. To apply the Easy Format, type the text for the heading. Then choose the Format⇨Easy Formats command, select "Contemporary Masthead," and click Apply.

■ Format the 911 line centered with 14-point Arial. Then choose the Format⇨Borders and Shading command. In the Borders tab, apply a thin outline to the paragraph. In the Shading tab, select the solid pattern and set the foreground color to Light Gray.

■ Format the heading lines in 14-point Bold Arial and center them.

■ Format the phone number lines in 14-point Bold Arial. To create the leader tab, choose the Format⇨Tab command. Type **5.75** in the Tab Stop Position field, select Right Alignment and Leader Style 1, and then choose Set. Type the name of the person or persons. Then press the Tab key and type the phone number.

Be sure to save the document so you can update and reprint it if necessary. Use a name such as *Emergency Numbers*.

PART IV:

FUN

STUFF

CHAPTER TEN

LET'S HAVE A PARTY!

In This Chapter

- Printing up party invitations
- Making name tags

All work and no play makes for a boring time with your computer. Face it, you didn't buy your home computer just to pay the bills and balance your checkbook. Fun and games are a part of the reason most people want a computer in the home.

This chapter shows you how to put your computer to good use when you get the urge to put on a party. The first project shows you how to use Works to create cool computer-printed invitations. Your friends will think you're a computer genius when they get theirs in the mail. If you're throwing a really BIG party, and you want everyone to wear name tags so that everyone will know who is who, the second project will help guide you through the process.

Project 14: Printing Party Invitations

Desktop publishing programs (such as Microsoft Publisher) excel at creating greeting cards and invitations that can be folded over to create cards that contain text on the outside and on the inside. Unfortunately, creating such a card requires that the text (which ultimately appears on the outside of the card) be printed upside down, so that when you fold the paper over, then fold it in half, the text will be flipped to an upright position. You can hunt all you want, but you won't find an "upside down" option for text in the Works Word Processor.

However, you can use WordArt — one of the lesser-known features of Works — to create upside-down text. WordArt is a fancy text manipulation program that was originally designed to work with Works' bigger brother, Microsoft Word. Bill Gates was in a generous mood the day they decided what freebies to include with Works, so he decided to throw WordArt in just for good measure. This project exploits the upside-down text capability of Works to create invitations that can be folded twice to create a slick greetingcard appearance.

FAST TRACK

PARTY INVITATIONS

1. Use the Word Processor to create fancy party invitations.
2. Print the invitations on standard 8.5"x11" paper, but fold the paper twice to create a card with text on the front and on the inside.
3. Use WordArt to create upside-down text to be printed on the front of the invitation. When the card is folded, the text will appear right-side up.

Figure 10-1
Printing an invitation that can be folded over to make a card.

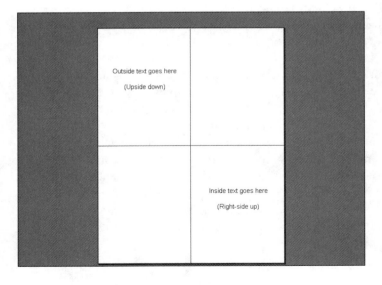

A little computer origami

The trick to creating invitations or other types of greeting cards is understanding how to lay out the page. You must divide a standard 8.5"x11" paper into quadrants, as shown in Figure 10-1. Whatever text you want to appear on the outside of your invitation must appear in the upper-left quadrant of the paper, upside down. Text you want to appear on the inside of the card must appear in the lower-right quadrant.

To fold the printed invitation to make a card, start by folding the invitation down along the horizontal line. Then fold on the vertical line so that the text from the top-left corner appears in front. Figure 10-2 shows how to make these folds.

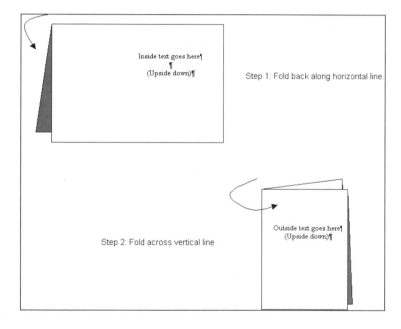

Inside text goes here¶
¶
(Upside down)¶

Step 1: Fold back along horizontal line.

Step 2: Fold across vertical line

Outside text goes here¶
(Upside down)¶

Figure 10-2
Folding the invitation to make a card.

Creating the invitations

The procedure that follows shows you how to create an invitation that can be folded over to create a card as described in the preceding section. For this particular procedure, the invitation says "It's a Party and…You're Invited!" on the outside, and "So Come and Join the Action" plus information about the time and location of the party on the inside. As you follow this procedure, feel free to substitute your own text where appropriate.

For more information about using the Word Processor, consult Chapter 2. Here's the procedure:

1. Fire up the Word Processor.

CROSS
REFERENCE

From the Works Task Launcher, click the Works Tools tab, and then click Word Processor.

2. Summon the File⇨Page Setup command.

The Page Setup dialog box appears.

3. Set all of the margins to .5" and reduce the header and footer margins to 0".

Figure 10-3 shows how the Page Setup dialog box should appear after you make these settings.

Figure 10-3
Setting the margins.

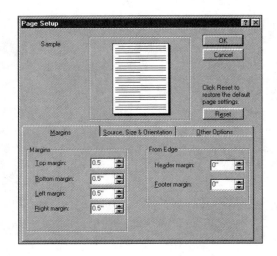

4. Click OK.

The Page Setup dialog box disappears.

5. If necessary, use the Zoom control at the bottom of the Works screen to reduce the zoom factor so that you can see the entire width of the page.

The exact zoom factor required to do this depends on the size and resolution of your computer's monitor. If you have a 17" monitor, odds are you can already see the entire width of the page, so you can skip this step. If you have a smaller monitor, you'll need to reduce the zoom factor to 75% or perhaps even 70% to see the width of the page.

6. Choose the Format⇨Paragraph command.

The Format Paragraph dialog box appears.

7. Change the Right indentation setting to 4.25" and change the alignment to Center.

Figure 10-4 shows how the dialog box should appear after you set the indentation and alignment.

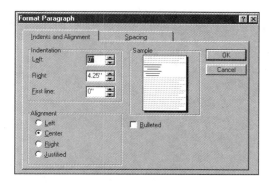

Figure 10-4
Setting the margins.

8. Click OK.

The Format Paragraph dialog box disappears.

9. Save your work!

Use the File⤳Save command to save the work you've done so far. Choose a meaningful filename for the document.

10. Press the Enter key eight times to move the cursor down the page a bit.

11. Choose the Insert⤳WordArt command.

WordArt, the magic text-decorating program that comes with Works, takes over the Works screen, as shown in Figure 10-5.

As you work with WordArt in Steps 12 through 23, avoid clicking anywhere outside of the WordArt object. If you do, and the WordArt toolbar disappears, double-click the WordArt object to get going again.

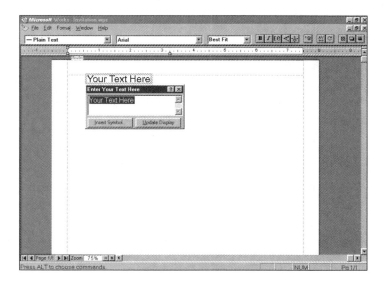

Figure 10-5
WordArt takes over.

12. Type the text for the last line of text that will appear on the outside of the card.

You must create a separate WordArt object for each line of text that appears on the outside of the card. In this example, the outside of the card will have two lines: "It's a Party and..." and "You're Invited!" Thus, you should type You're Invited! for this WordArt object.

13. Click the Update Display button.

14. Pick a shape for the text.

To pick a shape, click the down-button in the first drop-down list on the toolbar to reveal a palette of WordArt shapes, as shown in Figure 10-6. Click the shape you want to use. For this example, I chose the Wave 1 shape, which is the fifth shape in the fourth row. This squishes the "You're Invited" text into an almost unreadable form, but we'll fix that soon.

Figure 10-6
Picking a shape.

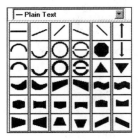

15. Change the font to Impact.

You can use the second drop-down list in the toolbar to change the font. If you don't like Impact, you can use any other font you may have installed on your computer.

16. Choose the Format⇨Stretch to Frame command.

Or, click the Stretch to Frame button in the toolbar.

17. Choose the Format⇨Shading command.

Or, click the Shading button in the standard toolbar. The Shading dialog box appears, as shown in Figure 10-7.

18. Pick a color for the foreground setting.

For this invitation, I picked Red. If you're really ambitious, try experimenting with different combinations of patterns, and foreground and background colors. You'll probably get your best results by using a solid pattern and a bright foreground color.

19. Click OK.

The Shading dialog box disappears.

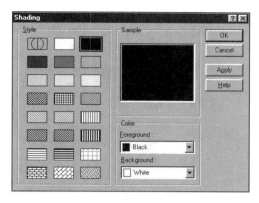

Figure 10-7
The Shading dialog
box.

20. Choose the Format⇨Shadow command.

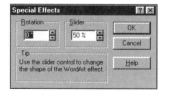 Or, click the Shadow button. The Shadow dialog box shown in Figure 10-8 appears.

Figure 10-8
The Shadow dialog
box.

21. Choose a shadow style and color, and then click OK.

For this example, I chose the third shadow style and Dark Violet for the shadow color.

22. Choose the Format⇨Rotation and Effects command.

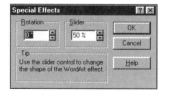 Or, click the Rotate button in the toolbar. The Special Effects dialog box shown in Figure 10-9 appears.

Figure 10-9
The Special Effects
dialog box.

23. Change the Rotation setting to 180, and then click OK.

The text is flipped upside down.

24. Click anywhere outside the WordArt object to return to the document.

The WordArt object is inserted in your document, but it is too small.

25. To adjust the size of the object, choose the Format⇨Picture command. The Format Picture dialog box appears, as shown in Figure 10-10.

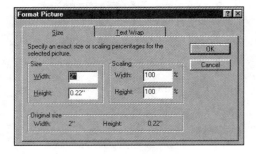

26. Set the width to 3.25 and the height to 1.5, and then click OK.

The size of the WordArt object is adjusted. The page should resemble Figure 10-11.

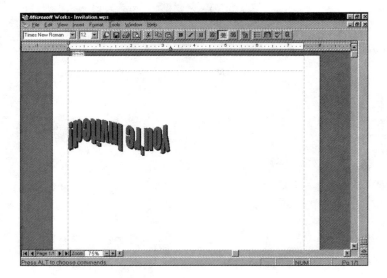

27. Save your work!

Choose File⇨Save before you go any further.

28. Press the right arrow key, and then press Enter three times.

Some added space appears below the WordArt object.

29. Repeat Steps 11-27 to create a second WordArt object.

This time, type It's a Party And... for the WordArt text, and skip Step 14 — that is, leave the WordArt shape set to Plain Text. In Step 26, set the width to 2.75 and the height to 0.375. The invitation should now resemble Figure 10-12.

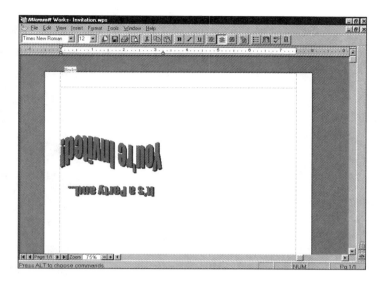

Figure 10-12
The invitation with
both WordArt objects
in place.

30. Place the insertion point immediately after the WordArt object, then press the Enter key 14 times.

The cursor moves to about the middle of the page.

31. Choose the Format⇨Paragraph command, set the left indent to 4.25 and the right indent to 0, and then click OK.

32. Change the font to 16-point Impact and specify a color if you want.

Choose the Format⇨Font and Style command to make these settings. You can set the font and size from the toolbar, but you must go through the Format⇨Font and Style command to set the color.

33. Type the text for the inside of the invitation.

Be sure to include the basic information such as what, when, where, what to bring, and how to RSVP.

Figure 10-13 shows a completed invitation.

34. Save your work!

Use the File⇨Save command.

35. Print the invitation and test fold it.

Fold the invitation to make sure everything lines up. If you have a vertical alignment problem, add or remove blank lines. If you have a horizontal alignment problem, double-check your margins and alignment settings for the paragraphs that are out of alignment.

**Figure 10-13
A completed invitation.**

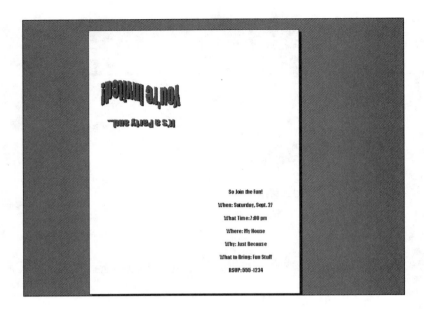

**Figure 10-13
A completed invitation.**

Adding clip art

If you want to spice up the invitation further, you can add a clip-art picture on the inside. The easiest way to add clip art is to place the picture on the left side of the page. To do so, follow these steps:

1. Select all the inside invitation text (but not the text inside the WordArt object).
2. Choose the Format⇨Paragraph command.
   The Format Paragraph dialog box appears.
3. Change the left indentation to 0 and the alignment to Left.
4. Click OK.
5. Choose the Format⇨Tabs command.
   The Format Tabs dialog box appears.
6. Type "1.625" in the Tab stop position field, click Center, and then click Set.
7. Type "5.875" in the Tab stop position field and click Set again.
   The Format Tabs dialog box should look like Figure 10-14.

**Figure 10-14
The Format Tabs dialog box.**

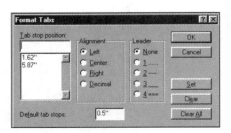

8. Click OK.

The Tabs dialog box disappears, and all the text that was previously centered on the right half of the page appears flush left.

9. Position the cursor at the beginning of each line of text inside the invitation. Then press the Tab key twice.

The text should return to its proper position, centered on the right side of the page.

10. Place the cursor over the first tab stop of one of the inside lines.

Preferably, select one of the lines near the middle of the text. For this example, place the insertion point on the "Where: My House" line.

11. Choose the Insert⇨ClipArt command.

The ClipArt Gallery dialog box appears as shown in Figure 10-15.

12. Choose a picture from the ClipArt Gallery, and then click Insert.

The picture is inserted.

13. Choose the Format⇨Text Wrap command. Click the Absolute button, and then click OK.

Figure 10-16 shows the Text Wrap dialog box.

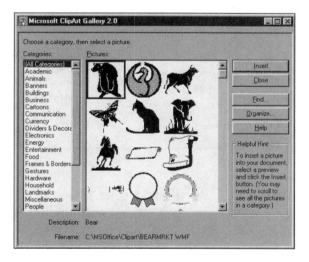

Figure 10-15
The ClipArt Gallery dialog box.

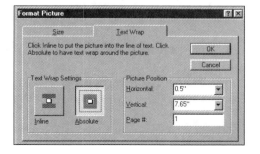

Figure 10-16
Setting the Text Wrap to Absolute.

14. If the picture messes up the alignment of your text, adjust the tab position of the lines that were affected.

Depending on the size of your picture, Works may adjust the margin and tab stop settings for one or more lines of your text. By adjusting these settings to bring the tab stops back to the correct position, you can realign the disturbed text lines with the rest of your text.

15. Save your work!

Use the File⇨Save command.

Figure 10-17 shows a finished invitation with clip art in place.

Figure 10-17
A finished invitation.

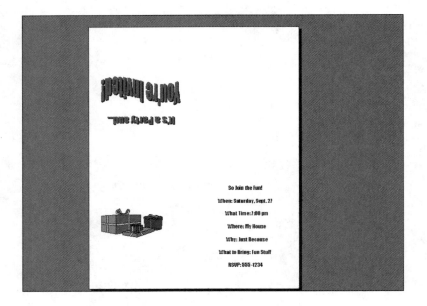

Project 15: Name Tags

Works includes a Labels feature that, although designed to print mailing labels from a database of names and addresses, you can easily use to create name tags. If you're in charge of a gathering (large or small) for which you want to provide name tags, this project will show you how to coerce the Labels feature into printing the name tags for you.

FAST TRACK

NAME TAGS

1. **Create a simple database containing the names of the people for whom you want to print name tags.**
2. **Use the Label TaskWizard to create a Word Processing document for your labels.**
3. **If you want, add a splashy graphic to add spice to your name tags.**

Creating the Names database

To print name tags, you must first create a simple database to hold the names you want printed. You could use the Address Book TaskWizard to create the database, but the databases created by the Address Book TaskWizard are overkill for your tasks. All you need is a database with just a few fields: First Name and Last Name will usually do. Depending on your objectives, you may need additional information (such as a company name or home town).

To create the Names database, follow these steps:

1. From the Works Tools tab of the Works Task Launcher, choose the Database.

The Create Database dialog box appears, as shown in Figure 10-18.

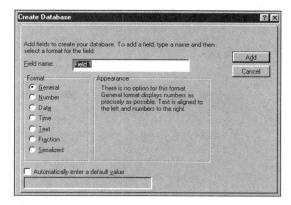

Figure 10-18
The Create Database dialog box.

2. Type "First Name" in the Field Name text box, and then click Add.

3. Type "Last Name" in the Field Name text box, and then click Add.

4. If you want to include any other information on the name tags, create fields for the additional information as well.

5. Click Done when you have added all the fields you need.

The database is displayed in list view, as shown in Figure 10-19.

6. Save the file.

Choose the File⇨Save command, type a meaningful name for the file (such as Name Tags), and then click OK.

7. Type the names.

Because the database contains only a few fields, it's easiest to just type the names in List View. If you prefer to work with a proper database form, choose the Form⇨View command to switch to Form View.

Figure 10-20 shows how the database should appear after you enter some names.

Figure 10-19
An empty Name Tags
database.

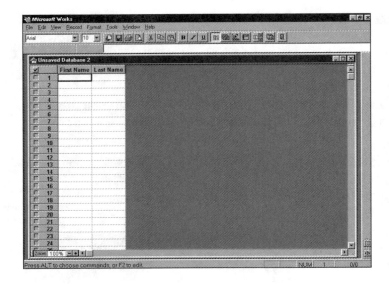

Figure 10-19
An empty Name Tags
database.

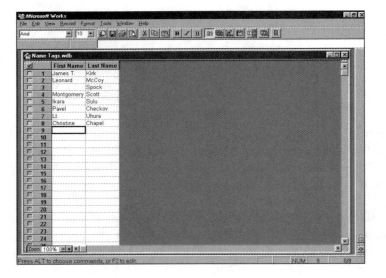

Figure 10-20
The Name Tags data-
base with the names of
a Motley Crew.

8. Close the database.

If Works asks whether you want to save changes, click Yes.

For more information about creating a database, see the section "Creating a New Database" in Chapter 4.

Printing name tags

After you have your Name Tags database in place, you can use the Word
Processor to print name tags. Before you do so, you should purchase blank

name tags from your local office supply store. Name tags generally come in two sizes. Standard name tags are 2-1/8" x 3-1/2". You can also get them in a larger size — sometimes referred to as *Convention Size* — which are 3"x4".

Here is the procedure for printing name tags in either format:

1. From the Works Tools tab of the Works Task Launcher, choose the Word Processor.

The Word Processor starts up with a blank document.

2. Choose the Tools⇨Labels command.

Works displays the dialog box shown in Figure 10-21.

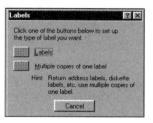

Figure 10-21
Works asks if you want to print a bunch of different labels or a bunch of the same label.

3. Click Labels.

The Labels dialog box appears, as pictured in Figure 10-22. As you can see, this dialog box contains eight tabs, one of which is devoted to providing instructions on how to use the other seven.

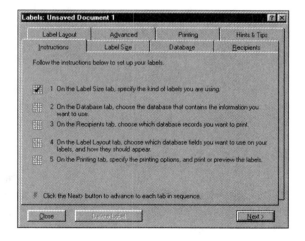

Figure 10-22
The most complicated dialog box in all of Works.

4. Click the Label Size tab.

The Label Size controls appears, as shown in Figure 10-23. Works comes preconfigured to work with about 50 types of Avery labels. (Avery is one of the largest suppliers of computer labels in the U.S.) Unfortunately, name tags are not among the options.

Figure 10-23
The Label Size controls.

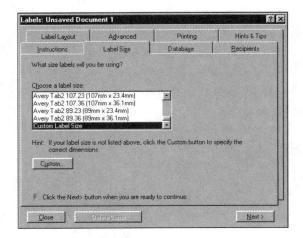

5. Click Custom.
The Custom Labels dialog box appears, as shown in Figure 10-24.

Figure 10-24
The Custom Labels
dialog box.

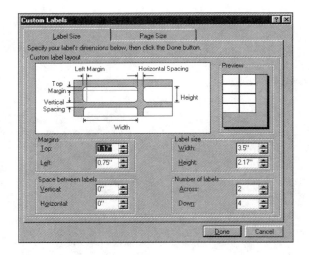

6. Set the custom label dimensions based on the name tags you are using.
The following table lists the appropriate settings for 2-1/8" × 3-1/2" and 3" × 4" name tags. If you are using a different size name tag, you will have to adjust the settings accordingly. Fortunately, most labels come with instructions on how to do that. If not, get out your ruler and start measuring.

SETTING	$2\frac{1}{8}$" x $3\frac{1}{5}$"	3" x 4"
Margin		
Top	1.17	1.13
Left	0.75	0.25
Space Between Labels		
Vertical	0	0
Horizontal	0	0
Label Size		
Width	3.5	4
Height	2.17	3
Number of Labels		
Across	2	2
Down	4	3

7. Click the Page Size tab and change the paper size to "Letter 8 1/2 by 11".

8. Click Done.

You are returned to the Labels dialog box, with the custom label settings you have provided in force.

9. Click the Database tab.

The Database settings appear, as shown in Figure 10-25.

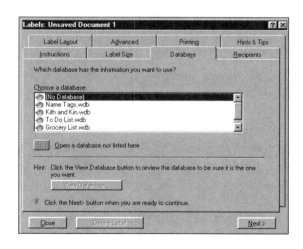

**Figure 10-25
Setting the database.**

10. Select the Name Tags database from the list of databases that appears.

If the Name Tags database doesn't appear in the list, click <u>O</u>pen to retrieve the database from another drive or folder.

11. Click the Label Layout tab.

The Label Layout controls appear, as shown in Figure 10-26.

Figure 10-26
Laying out the labels.

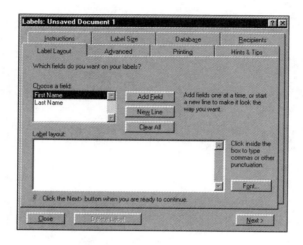

12. Click the F<u>o</u>nt button.

A familiar Format Font and Style dialog box appears.

13. Set the font and size you want to use for your labels.

For this example, I changed the font to Impact and the size to 24 point. If you have more information than just first and last name on your name tags, you may have to use a smaller point size.

14. Click OK to return to the Layout controls.

15. Add the database fields to the layout.

To add a field, click the field to select it, then click Add <u>F</u>ield. Or, you can just double-click the field. You can force a line break between fields by clicking Ne<u>w</u> Line, and you can type text that you want to appear on every label — such as "Hello, My Name is" — directly into the La<u>b</u>el Layout box.

To add the first and last names on separate lines, double-click First Name, click Ne<u>w</u> Line, and then double-click Last Name. Figure 10-27 shows how the Label Layout should appear.

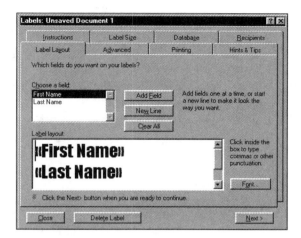

Figure 10-27
A simple label layout.

16. Click the Advanced tab.
The Advanced tab appears, as shown in Figure 10-28.

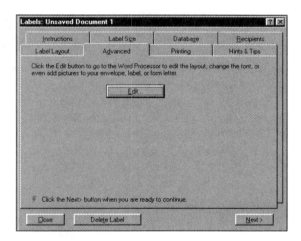

Figure 10-28
Advanced tab of the
Labels dialog box.

17. Click Edit.
The Word Processor magically appears so that you can edit the label layout, as shown in Figure 10-29.

Figure 10-29
Editing the label
layout.

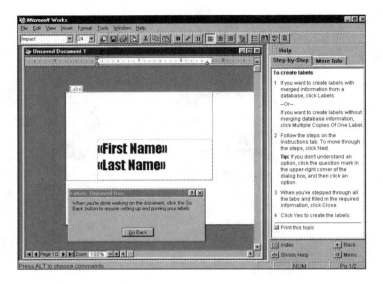

18. Center the two layout lines.

Select both lines and click the Center align button in the toolbar.

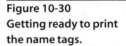

You can make any other changes you want to the label layout. For example, you can add clip art by choosing the Insert⇨ClipArt command. Or, you can use the Insert⇨WordArt command to add a WordArt logo. (Unfortunately, you can't use WordArt to format the first and last names inserted from the database. That would be cool, but it's not possible.)

19. Click Go Back when you finish tweaking the layout.

The Labels dialog box reappears.

20. Click the Printing tab.

The Printing controls appears, as shown in Figure 10-30.

Figure 10-30
Getting ready to print
the name tags.

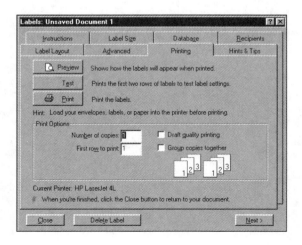

21. Click Preview.

22. When Works asks if you want to preview all records, click OK.

The Preview screen appears, as shown in Figure 10-31.

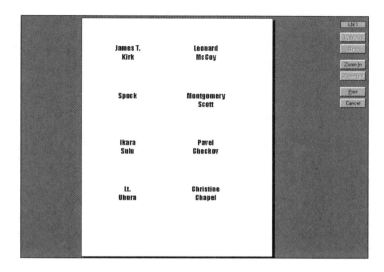

Figure 10-31
Previewing the name tags.

23. Test print one page of labels on plain paper.

To do that, click Cancel to return to the Printing tab of the Labels dialog box, and then click Test. A Test Printing dialog box will appear. Click Cancel to dismiss this dialog box when you are satisfied the labels print correctly.

24. Check that the name tags printed properly on plain paper.

Hold up a blank sheet of name tags against the test print and compare the alignment to make sure the name tags are aligned properly. If they are not, click the Label Layout tab and adjust the custom label settings.

25. When the name tags are aligned properly, load blank name tags into the printer. Then click the Print button to print the name tags.

The name tags are printed.

26. Click Close to dismiss the Labels dialog box.

27. Save the document if you want.

Use the File⇨Save command and assign a memorable name such as Name Tags. (You can use the same name here as you did for the database; Works uses different filename extensions to distinguish between database, word processing, and spreadsheet files.)

Saving the document allows you to reuse it, so you can print additional name tags without having to recreate all of the settings you established in this procedure.

28. Don't forget to put plain paper back in the printer!

Many a time I've forgotten this last step, only to print my next letter to my mom on a sheet of blank labels.

CHAPTER ELEVEN

GAMES PEOPLE PLAY

In This Chapter

- How to create your own crossword puzzles
- How to create a word scramble game

Project 16: Creating Your Own Crossword Puzzle

Almost everyone likes a good crossword puzzle now and then. But have you ever tried to create your own crossword puzzles? It can be loads of fun — and very challenging. Crossword puzzles can be not only fun, but also educational. Try putting together a crossword puzzle with the names of the planets, for example, or the names of presidents, or state capitals. You get the idea.

This project shows you how to create your very own crossword puzzle using simple tables in the Works Word Processor. Of course, the hard part is determining *how* to lay out your crossword puzzle. Unfortunately, I can't help you with that. But once you come up with a layout to rival the New York Times puzzles, this project will show you how to create it in Works.

Creating a grid

The first step in building a crossword puzzle is creating a grid within which the puzzle can be laid out. Here's the procedure:

1. Come up with the layout for a great crossword puzzle.

This is the part I can't help you with. It's the hard part — and the fun part, if you like that sort of thing.

2. From the Works Tools tab of the Works Task Launcher, start the Word Processor.

A new, blank document is created.

3. Choose the Insert⇨Table command.

The Insert Table dialog box appears, as shown in Figure 11-1.

FAST TRACK

CROSSWORD PUZZLE

1. **Devise a challenging crossword puzzle.**
2. **Create a word processing document with a table specially formatted to show the puzzle.**

Figure 11-1
The Insert Table dialog box.

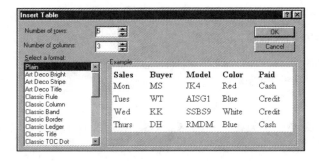

4. Set the number of rows and columns to match the dimensions of your crossword puzzle.

For example, if your puzzle fits into a 15x15 grid, set the Number of Rows and Number of Columns fields to 15.

5. Click OK.

A table is inserted into the document.

6. Select the entire table by clicking on the table selector, located at the upper-left corner of the table border.

7. Set the font to Arial and the size to 6.

Use the font and size controls in the toolbar to set the font and size.

8. Set the alignment to left top.

To do that, summon the Format⇨Alignment command. Choose Left for the Horizontal alignment and Top for the Vertical alignment, then click OK.

9. With the entire table still selected, choose the Format⟹Row Height command.

The Format Row Height dialog box appears, as shown in Figure 11-2.

Figure 11-2
The Format Row Height dialog box.

10. Set the row height to 25 and click OK.

The table expands to accommodate the extra height for its rows.

11. Choose the Format⟹Column Width command.

The Column Width dialog box appears, as shown in Figure 11-3.

Figure 11-3
The Column Width dialog box.

12. Set the column width to 10 and click OK.

The rows and columns of the table should now be approximately the same width, so each cell should be close to square. The entire table should still be selected.

13. Choose the Format⟹Border command.

The Format Cells dialog box appears with the Border options visible, as illustrated in Figure 11-4.

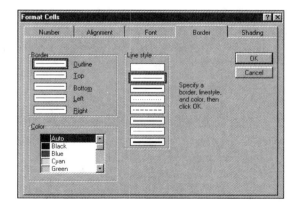

Figure 11-4
Setting the cell borders.

14. Click all five of the Border options: Outline, Top, Bottom, Left, and Right. Then click OK.

The borders give the table a grid-like appearance, as shown in Figure 11-5. (For this figure, I reduced the zoom factor to 75% so the entire table would be visible without scrolling. Unless you are working on a 17" monitor, you may want to reduce the zoom factor too.)

Figure 11-5
The table with borders to create a grid.

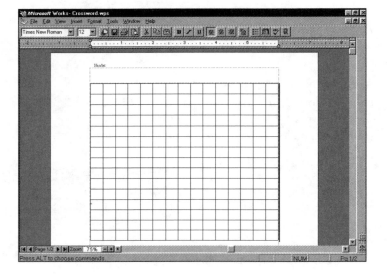

At this point, you can print out the grid if you want. Then you can fill in the answers to the puzzle and shade out any unused cells with a pencil. You can then use this marked up copy of your puzzle to help you with the next procedure.

Completing the puzzle

After you have set up a grid, you can shade out any unused cells and add numbers to mark where each word begins. This is a tricky and time-consuming chore, so prepare to squint. Here's the procedure:

1. Click anywhere inside the table, then select a block of unused cells to be shaded.

It's best to work your way from the upper-left part of the table, down the table, row by row. To save time, always select the largest possible rectangular range of cells to be shaded.

2. Choose the Format⇨Shading command.

The Shading options appear, as shown in Figure 11-6.

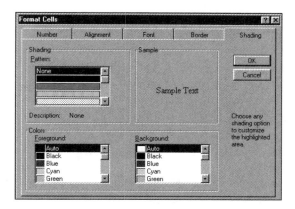

Figure 11-6
The Shading options dialog box.

3. Set the Pattern to the solid color. Then set the Foreground color to whatever color you want to use for the unused table cells.

Gray works well.

4. Click OK.

The shading is applied. You won't see it at first, because the rows which have received the shading are selected. Once you click anywhere else in the table, the shading will be visible.

5. Repeat steps 1–4 for all remaining unused cells that need to be shaded.

The tricky part of this whole process is keeping track of which cells need to be shaded and making sure you don't lose your place. When you finish, your table should resemble the table in Figure 11-7. (Of course, the pattern shown for your table will be different, depending on the particular puzzle you are trying to create.)

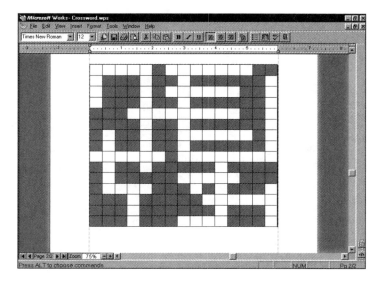

Figure 11-7
The puzzle begins to take shape.

6. Save your work.

Choose the File⇨Save command.

7. Type a number in the first cell of each word in the puzzle.

The numbers you type appear in small type in the upper-left corner of the cell. Words are customarily numbered across each row, and then down. For example, the first row in Figure 11-7 should receive four numbers: 1, 2, 3, and 4. The word that begins in the last column of the second row and runs down should be numbered 5. Then number 6 is assigned to the word that runs across row 3, starting in column 7, and so on.

Figure 11-8 shows how the table appears with numbers in place.

Figure 11-8
The puzzle after numbers have been assigned.

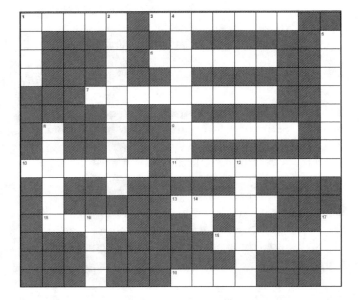

8. Save your work again!

This is too much work to lose because of a sudden power outage.

Adding the clues

No crossword puzzle is complete without a list of clues, arranged in two columns: one for words that go across, the other for words that go down. These columns are easy to create by using a simple two-column table with a row for each clue. Here is the procedure:

1. Click outside of the table, and then press the Enter key three times to add some space below the table.

2. Choose the Insert➪Table command again.

The Insert Table dialog box reappears.

3. This time, enter 2 columns in the Number of columns text box. For the number of rows, enter one more than the largest number of words that appear in the puzzle going across or down.

For example, if the puzzle has 11 words across and 8 words down, set the number of rows to 12 — one more than 11.

4. Make sure the Select a format list is set to "Plain," then click OK.

A table is inserted.

5. Type "Across" in the first column of the first row and "Down" in the second second column of the first row. Format these cells with bold type by clicking the Bold button before typing the heading for each cell.

6. Type the box numbers and the clues for the Across words in the first column.

7. Type the box numbers and the clues for the Down words in the second column.

Figure 11-9 shows the table with some clues.

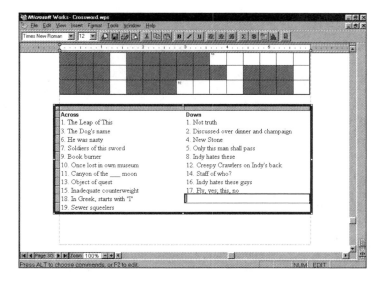

Figure 11-9
The clues are also typed in a table.

8. Save your work one last time.

Press Ctrl+S or choose the File➪Save command.

9. Print the crossword puzzle.

Press Ctrl+P or summon the File➪Print command. Figure 11-10 shows how the puzzle should appear when printed.

Figure 11-10
The finished crossword
puzzle.

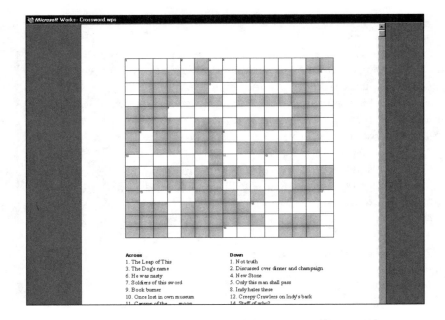

Project 17: Creating a Word Search Puzzle

Remember those word search puzzles you used to do as a kid — where you had to search through a grid of seemingly random letters to find a list of words? Kids still love these puzzles — and, as a result, so do parents, teachers, and baby-sitters. This project shows you how to create your own word search puzzles using the Works Spreadsheet program.

FAST
TRACK

WORD
SEARCH
PUZZLE

1. Make a list of words for a word search puzzle.
2. Create a spreadsheet grid.
3. Squeeze the words into the grid.
4. Add some partial words to make the puzzle fun.
5. Fill in the blanks with random letters.

Here is a procedure you can follow to create a word search puzzle:

1. Come up with a theme for the puzzle and a list of words.

For example, suppose you want to create a word search puzzle based on Indiana Jones, the famous archeologist. You might come up with the following list of words:

Indiana	Dr. Jones
Snakes	Rats
Lost Arc	Holy Grail

Whip   Junior
Archeology   Neolithic

2. Fire up the Works Spreadsheet program.

From the Works Task Launcher, click the Works Tools tab, and then click Spreadsheet.

3. Select a rectangular range of cells with an equal number of rows and columns.

Make the selection large enough to accommodate your puzzle. For the Indiana Jones puzzle, 15x15 should be enough.

At this point, make sure you don't click anywhere outside the table. The next seven steps will only work if the table remains selected. If you do accidentally click outside the table, just click anywhere in the table to reselect it.

4. Change the font to Arial and the font size to 14.

Use the font size control in the toolbar.

5. Choose the Format⇨Column Width command.

The Column Width dialog box appears.

6. Set the column width to 4, and then click OK.

7. Choose the Format⇨Row Height command.

The Format Row Height dialog box appears.

8. Set the row height to 20, and then click OK.

The cells in the selected range should now be close to square.

9. Choose the Format⇨Border command.

The Border tab of the Format Cells dialog box appears.

10. Click all five border options: Outline, Top, Bottom, Left, and Right. Then click OK.

A border is applied to the grid you have created. At this point, the spreadsheet should resemble Figure 11-11.

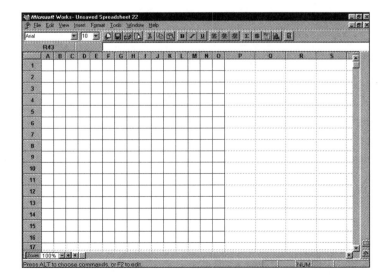

Figure 11-11
Start your word search puzzle by creating a simple grid.

11. Save your work.

Use the <u>File</u>⇨<u>S</u>ave command and assign a reasonable name for the spreadsheet.

12. Type the words from your list into the grid, one letter in each cell.

First, press the Caps Lock key so that all of the words will appear in capital letters. Work the words in both directions — horizontally and vertically. If you want to make the puzzle more challenging, make some of the words backwards. Figure 11-12 shows how the words for the Indy puzzle might be placed on the grid.

Figure 11-12
Add the words from
your list to the grid.

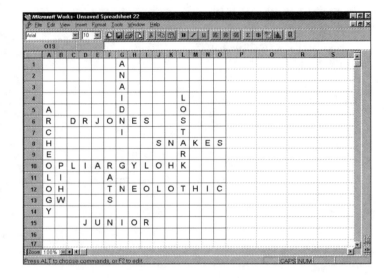

13. Save your work again.

14. Now add some false clues to frustrate your players.

Type some partial words or slightly misspelled words into the grid, as shown in Figure 11-13. (The false clues are highlighted in Figure 11-13 so you can see them easily; don't apply any shading to these partial or incorrect words when you create your puzzle!)

S		L				A	H		A					H
N		O				N	T		R					O
A		S				A	I		C					L
K		T				I	L		H		L			Y
A		A				D	O		E		O			G
R		D	R	J	O	N	E	S	O		S			
C						I	N		L		T			
H			W	H	A	P			S	N	A	K	E	S
E										R		J		
O	P	L	I	A	R	G	Y	L	O	H	K		U	
L	I				A							U		N
O	H			T	N	E	O	L	O	T	H	I	C	
G	W			S								O		
Y		D	R	J	O	N	S	E						
		J	U	N	I	O	R							
N	E	O	L									R	A	T

Figure 11-13
Add some partial words to send your players on wild goose chases.

15. Save the file once more.

The File⇨Save command is your friend.

16. Fill in any remaining blank squares with random letters.

Be careful not to accidentally complete any of the partial words you added in step 12! Figure 11-14 shows how the puzzle should now appear.

S	D	L	L	S	S	A	H	E	A	Q	J	G	K	H
N	G	M	O	D	Y	N	T	C	R	U	L	D	H	O
A	H	A	S	S	B	A	I	O	C	F	G	A	F	L
K	C	R	T	J	E	I	L	I	H	H	L	Z	S	Y
A	V	E	A	U	D	D	O	U	E	W	O	C	W	G
R	I	D	R	J	O	N	E	S	O	V	S	B	R	I
C	A	A	P	O	U	I	N	E	L	N	T	M	Y	P
H	E	I	W	H	A	P	X	D	S	N	A	K	E	S
E	G	L	W	Q	P	O	I	H	Y	T	R		J	K
O	P	L	I	A	R	G	Y	L	O	H	K		U	S
L	I	T	X	C	A	S	W	P	L	O	I	K	N	M
O	H	Y	U	T	T	N	E	O	L	O	T	H	I	C
G	W	U	E	R	S	Z	S	W	Y	H	N	U	O	J
Y	H	I	D	R	J	O	N	S	E	N	H	J	U	I
A	J	J	J	U	N	I	O	R	S	R	E	F	T	Y
N	E	O	L	Q	V	B	N	I	O	R	G	R	A	T

Figure 11-14
The puzzle after random letters have been added.

17. Save it again.

You can't save your work too often.

18. Now add a word list beneath the puzzle.

Skip a row or two, and then type each of the words into a separate cell, as shown in Figure 11-15.

Figure 11-15
Add a word list.

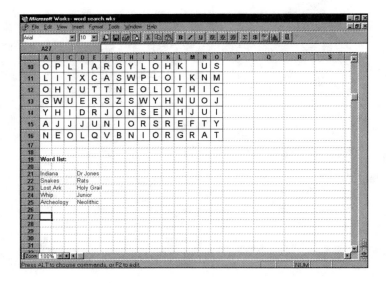

19. Save your file one last time.
20. Print the spreadsheet.

Use the File⇨Print command. Figure 11-16 shows how the puzzle looks when printed.

Figure 11-16
How the puzzle appears when printed.

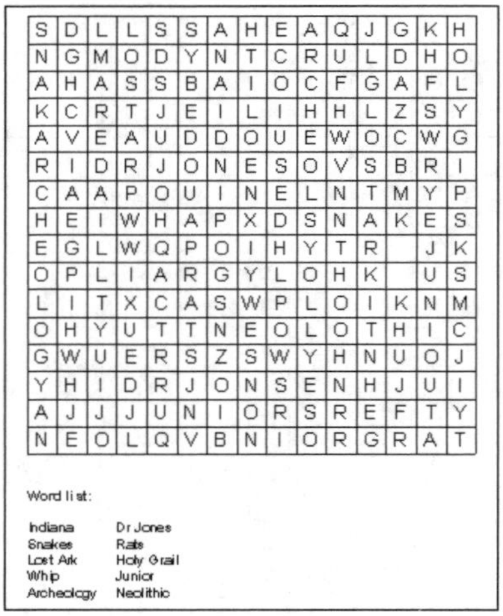

21. You're done!

CHAPTER TWELVE

TAKE ME OUT TO THE BALL
GAME

In This Chapter

- Creating a team roster and batting order
- Tracking batting averages

I f you're involved as a coach for any sport, youth or adult, you can greatly benefit from computerizing some of the record-keeping chores that go hand-in-hand with coaching. This chapter includes two projects designed especially for coaches of softball or baseball teams. The first project sets up a combined team roster and batting lineup. The second project tracks season-long batting averages for your players. These projects won't help your team win more games, but you will quickly develop a reputation as the most computer-savvy team in your league!

Although these projects are specifically designed for baseball and softball teams, they can be adapted for other sports as well. The Team Roster and Batting Order project can be easily adapted for any team sport and, with some work, the Batting Averages project could be adapted to track meaningful statistics for other sports as well.

Project 18: Creating a Team Roster and Batting Order

Every baseball or softball team needs a roster. This project will show you how to set up a database that lists your players' names, addresses, and phone numbers. It also doubles as a game lineup database. Before each game, call up the database and enter the batting order and playing position for each player on the team. Then you can print out a lineup report that lists your team lineup in batting order, with the substitutes listed at the end of the report.

Although this Team Roster database is designed for baseball or softball, it can easily be adapted for other team sports such as soccer, volleyball, or basketball.

FAST TRACK

TEAM ROSTER

1. **Create a database for your team roster with fields for the player's first and last names, address information, phone number, and the player's batting order and position.**
2. **Create two reports for the database: one to print a simple team roster, the other to print a batting order for a game.**
3. **Before each game, determine each player's position and batting order. Then print out several copies of the batting order report to take to the game.**

Creating the database

The following procedure shows how to create a Team Roster database:

1. Fire up the database.

From the Works Tools tab of the Works Task Launcher database, click the Database button. The familiar Create Database dialog box appears, as shown in Figure 12-1.

Figure 12-1
The Create Database dialog box.

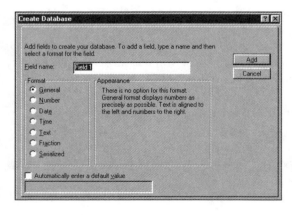

2. Create the database fields for the Team Roster database.

The database should include the following ten fields:

Last Name
First Name
Uniform #
Batting Order
Position
Address
City
State
Postal Code
Phone Number

To create each field, type the name of the field into Field Name text box. Set the format to Text, and then click Add.

When you have created all ten fields, click Done.

3. Save the file.

Use the File⇨Save command and pick a meaningful name such as *Team Roster*.

4. Choose the View⇨Form command to switch to Form View.

The database form shown in Figure 12-2 appears.

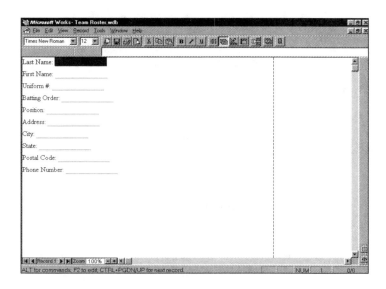

Figure 12-2
Form View of the Team Roster database.

5. Type in your players' names and addresses.

Don't worry about the batting order or position fields. You'll fill those in later. For now, just enter each player's name, address, phone number, and uniform number (if numbers have been assigned).

CROSS
REFERENCE

For more information about creating a database, see the section "Creating a New Database" in Chapter 4.

Create the Team Roster report

After you have entered all the names and addresses for your team, you can print out a simple team roster by opening the database and following this procedure:

1. Choose the Tools⇨ReportCreator command.

ReportCreator asks for the name of the report you want to create. (If this is the first time you have created a report, you will see one of those first-timer dialog boxes, offering to let you take a brief tour of reporting. To skip the tour, click the "To create a report" button.)

2. Type "Roster" for the report name, and then click OK.

The ReportCreator comes to life, as shown in Figure 12-3.

Figure 12-3
Use ReportCreator to create a team roster report.

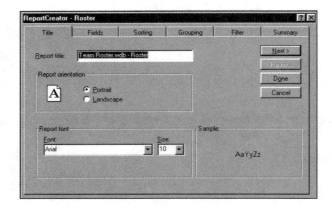

3. In the Title tab, type "Team Roster" for the report title, and then click Next.

If you prefer, type your team's name as part of the report title; for example, Mighty Ducks Team Roster.

4. In the Fields tab, add the Last Name, Address, and Phone Number fields to the report. Then click Next.

To add a field, click the field name, then click Add. Do *not* select the First Name, City, State, or Postal Codes fields. You'll add those fields in later.

5. In the Sorting tab, choose Last Name for the Sort By field, and then click Next.

6. Click Done.

Works asks if you want to preview or modify the report.

7. Choose Modify.

You are dumped into Report Design view. The report looks like the one in Figure 12-4.

8. Select the report title in the Title row, then choose the Edit⇨Cut command. Then select the A column of the Title row and choose the Edit⇨Paste command.

The report title moves to the A column so it will appear on the left of the report instead of centered.

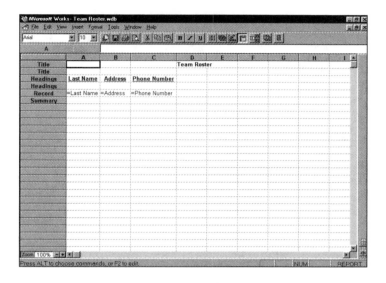

Figure 12-4
Modifying the Team
Roster report.

9. Select the A column of the Record row, press F2 to edit the cell, and then change the field contents to:

```
=Last Name&", "&First Name
```

Press Enter when you have finished typing the formula.

10. With the insertion point still in the A column, choose the Format⇨Column Width command, change the width of the A column to 25, and then click OK.

11. Select the B column of the Record row, and then choose the Format⇨Column Width command. Change the column width to 40, and then click OK.

12. Select any cell in the Summary row, and then choose the Insert⇨Row command. Select Record for the row type, and then click OK.

A new Record row is inserted above the Summary row.

13. Select the B column in the new Record row, and then type the following formula:

```
=City&" "&State&" "&Postal Code
```

When you finish, press Enter.

14. Save your work.

Use the File⇨Save command once again.

Figure 12-5 shows how the Team Roster report will appear when printed.

Team Roster

Last Name	Address	Phone Number
Anderson, Betty	3531 N. First Fresno CA 97311 `	555-1234
Cornwallis, Jeannie	3890 N. Feland Fresno CA 97311	55-2345
Edmonds, Janet	4107 N. Montreal Fresno CA 97311	555-3456
Henry, Jennifer	4780 N. Gentry Fresno CA 97311	555-4567
Johansen, Mary	3200 W. Ellery Fresno CA 97311	555-5678
Johnson, Beth	3890 N. Lincoln Fresno CA 97311	555-6789
Jones, Renee	2790 W. Washington Fresno CA 97311	555-7890
Klien, Amanda	3403 N. Sierra Fresno CA 97311	555--8901
Lowe, Bethany	5010 N. Cattleman Fresno CA 97311	555-9012
Lowe, Sarah	2988 W. Exeter Fresno CA 97311	555-0123
Smith, Alice	6010 N. Lexington Fresno CA 97311	555-4321
Summers, Susie	4293 W. Sierra Fresno CA 97311	555-5432
Wong, Janet	4567 W. Teneya Fresno CA 97311	555-6543

CROSS
REFERENCE

For more information about creating reports, refer to the "Creating a Report" section in Chapter 4.

Create the Team Lineup report

The Team Lineup report is similar to the Team Roster report, except that it is sorted into sequence based on each player's batting order; it shows each player's position in the field, and it does not include the address and phone number. The Team Lineup report is designed to be used on game day to determine the batting order and fielding positions for a particular game.

Open the Team Roster database, then follow these steps to create the Team Lineup report:

1. Choose the Tools⇨ReportCreator command.
ReportCreator asks for the name of the report you want to create.

2. Type "Lineup" for the report name, and then click OK.
The ReportCreator dialog box appears. Refer to Figure 12-3 if you've forgotten what it looks like.

3. In the Title tab, type "Team Lineup" for the report title, and then click Next.

4. In the Fields tab, add the Batting Order, Uniform #, Last Name, and Position fields to the report.

To add a field, click the field name, then click Add. Be sure to add the fields in the order indicated in this step so they appear in that order in the final report.

5. In the Sorting tab, choose Batting Order for the Sort By field, and then click Next.

6. Click Done.

Works asks if you want to preview or modify the report.

7. Choose Modify.

Report Design view comes to life, with a report that resembles the one shown in Figure 12-6.

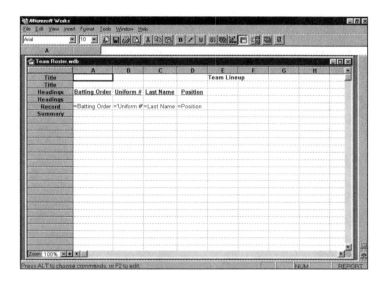

Figure 12-6
Modifying the Team Lineup report.

8. Select the report title in the Title row and choose the Edit⇨Cut command. Then select the A column of the Title row and choose the Edit⇨Paste command.

The report title is moved to the A column.

9. Select the C column of the Record row, press F2 to edit the cell, then change the field contents to:

```
=Last Name&", "&First Name
```

Press Enter.

10. Select the C column of the first Headings row, type "Name," and then press Enter.

11. Choose the Format⇨Alignment command to summon the alignment options. Click Left, and then click OK.

12. Choose the Format⇨Column Width command, change the width of the C column to 25, and then click OK.

13. Select any cell in the A column. Choose the Format⇨Column Width command and change the column width to 25. Then click OK.

Figure 12-7 shows how the report design should look.

Figure 12-7
The Team Lineup report after it has been modified.

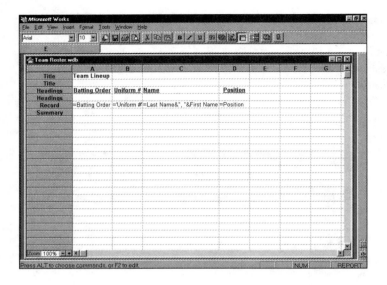

When you finish creating the report, be sure to save your work with the File➪Save command.

To create a team lineup, call up the Team Roster database in list view. Enter each player's batting order and position in the Batting Order and Position fields. Then choose the View➪Reports command to summon the Reports dialog box. Select the Lineup report, and then click Preview. When the report preview appears, click the Print button to print the lineup or click Cancel to bail out without actually printing the report.

Figure 12-8 shows how the Team Lineup report should appear when you print it.

Figure 12-8
The finished Team Lineup report.

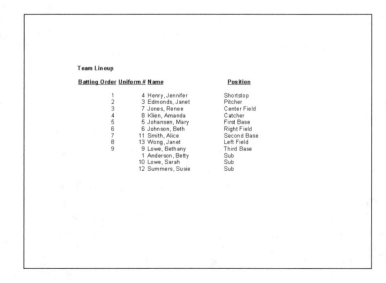

For more information about creating reports, refer to the "Creating a Report" section in Chapter 4.

Project 19: Tracking Batting Statistics

If you're both a coach and a statistician, you'll appreciate this project. It shows you how to set up a Works database that can track individual players' batting statistics over the course of a season. After each game, all you have to do is create a record for each player showing the number of times at bat and the number of hits. Then the database can print out a report listing each player's season batting average.

Even in a youth recreation league, this can be useful information. All too often coaches rely on impressions rather than facts about which players are batting well and which aren't. The actual statistics can sometimes be surprising.

One of the cool things about this project is that it uses a database CHOOSE function that automatically generates a player's name based on their uniform number. As a result, you don't have to type in all of your player's names after each game. All you have to enter is the uniform number, times at bat, and hits. The database determines the player name based on the uniform number you enter. This makes the database a little harder to set up at first, but saves you lots of time throughout the season.

Contrary to what you might expect, the Batting Statistics database will have more than one record for each of your players. In fact, the database will contain one record per player for each game you play. So, if you play 20 games in a season and you have 15 players, the Batting Statistics database will have a total of 300 records. After each game, you must enter the batting statistics for each player. The Batting Average report sorts and groups the records by player; then it calculates and prints the season batting average for each player.

Although it isn't absolutely necessary, I included a Games field in this database. This field allows you to keep track of which game each record belongs to by numbering the games. Whenever you enter a batch of records following a game, use the same game number for each record for that game. Thus, if you play 20 games and you have 15 players, you will have 15 records for game 1, 15 for game 2, and so on.

FAST TRACK

BATTING STATISTICS

---

1. **Create a database to track your team's batting averages. The database should include the following fields: Number, Game, Name, At Bats, Hits, and Walks.**
2. **After each game, enter the new data for each player. Then print out a new batting average report.**

Creating the database

The following procedure shows how to create a Batting Statistics database:

1. Fire up the database.

From the Works Tools tab of the Works Task Launcher, click the <u>D</u>atabase button. The familiar Create Database dialog box appears. Refer to Figure 12-1. (If this is the first time you've created a database, you'll see a special first-timer's help screen. Click on "Create a database" to get caught up.)

2. Create the database fields for the Batting Statistics database.

The database should include the following five fields:

Number
Game
At Bats
Hits
Name

To create each field, type the name of the field into the <u>F</u>ield Name text box and click A<u>d</u>d. Leave the format for each field set to <u>G</u>eneral.

When you have created all five fields, choose D<u>o</u>ne. The database appears in list view, as shown in Figure 12-9.

Figure 12-9
The Batting Statistics database after the fields have been created.

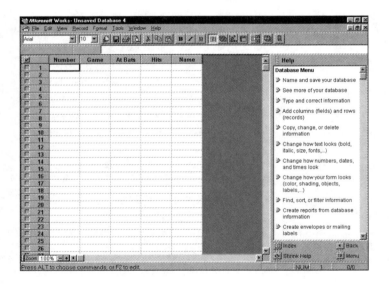

3. Select the Name column by clicking the Name field heading.

The entire column is selected.

4. Choose the Format⇨Field <u>W</u>idth command, change the width of the Name field to 16, and then click OK.

The width of the Name field is increased.

5. Type a CHOOSE function that will assign the correct player name based on the value typed into the Name field.

This step is tricky. The Works database allows you to use a special function called CHOOSE, which sets the value of a database field to one of several values, depending on the value of some other database field.

The CHOOSE function has this general form:

```
=choose(field-name,value-if-0,value-if-1,value-if-2,...)
```

The CHOOSE function assigns a value based on a number stored in another database field. The first argument of the CHOOSE function names the database field that will be used to determine the value. The remaining arguments provide values to be selected based on the value of the first argument. If the named field has a value of 0, *value-if-0* is used; if the field's value is 1, *value-if-1* is used; and so on. You can provide as many values as you want in the CHOOSE function.

What you want to do here is create a CHOOSE function that will set the Name field to a player's name based on the value you type into the Number field. For example, if you have 13 players on your team, with uniform numbers ranging from 1 to 13, you would create a CHOOSE function that resembles this:

```
=choose(Number,"","Betty Anderson","Jeannie
Cornwallis","Janet Edmonds","Jennifer
Henry","Mary Johansen","Beth Johnson","Renee
Jones","Amanda Klien","Bethany Lowe","Sarah
Lowe","Alice Smith","Susie Summers","Janet Wong")
```

Since there is no player with uniform number 0, I typed "" for the first argument after Number. Then I just typed the names of the players in quotation marks and separated by commas, in uniform number order. In other words, Betty Anderson is number 1; Jeannie Cornwallis is number 2; and so on. (Of course, you would use different player names, unless you happen to have the same players I do, which would be unlikely, since I made most of these names up.)

If you have other numbers that are unassigned, just leave a space for them marked by an empty pair of quotation marks. For example: "`Mary Johansen`","","`Renee Jones`".

The key to creating the CHOOSE function is to make sure you remember to enclose each name in quotation marks, separate the names with commas, list the names in uniform number order, and finish the entire list with a closing parenthesis. Then press Enter.

6. Test your CHOOSE function by typing various uniform numbers in the Number field.

When you type a 1 in the Number field, the name of player 1 should automatically appear in the Name field; likewise for other uniform numbers. If it doesn't, double-check your CHOOSE function to make sure you haven't made a mistake. The sidebar, "Trouble with the CHOOSE Function?" lists some of the more common mistakes you can make when creating the CHOOSE function.

Figure 12-10 shows how the database should appear after the CHOOSE function has been entered and the numbers 1-13 have been typed into the Number field.

Figure 12-10
The Batting Statistics database after the CHOOSE function has been created and tested.

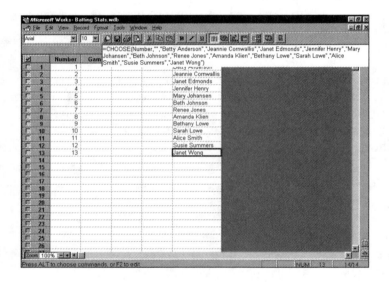

7. Save the file.

Use the File⇨Save command and pick a meaningful name such as *Batting Stats*.

8. Delete any records you created while testing the CHOOSE function.

To delete the records, highlight them by dragging the mouse over them and press the Delete key.

CROSS REFERENCE

For more information about creating a database, see the section "Creating a New Database" in Chapter 4.

The CHOOSE function is one of the more complicated functions that is used in this book. Even if you are very careful when you type it, you can still easily make a mistake. The following list points out some of the more common errors and how to correct them:

■ **Problem:** The text `"choose(Number,"",…"` appears in the Name field instead of the player's name.
Solution: You probably forgot to type an equal sign before the choose function.

■ **Problem:** I get the message `The formula contains an error` when trying to create the CHOOSE function.
Solution: The CHOOSE function contains what is technically known as a syntax error. The most common causes for this are (1) you forgot the closing parenthesis at the end of the function, (2) you forgot one of the commas required to separate the names, or (3) you left off a quotation mark at the beginning or end of a name.

■ **Problem:** The function seems to work, but the wrong player names are coming up.
Solution: You may have forgotten the first empty set of quotation marks following the Number argument. Or, if you have an unassigned uniform number (for example, if no one wears number 6), you may have forgotten to type an empty set of quotation marks between the players who wear numbers 5 and 7. Or, you may have simply typed the names in the wrong order.

TROUBLE WITH THE CHOOSE FUNCTION?

Creating the Batting Average report

After you set up the Batting Statistics database, you can create the Batting Average report, which will print each player's total batting average for the season. The Batting Average report is interesting because, unlike most reports, it does not include any record lines. Instead, the Batting Average report shows just a summary line for each group of records for each player.

Here's the step-by-step procedure for creating the Batting Average report:

1. Open the Batting Stats database if it isn't already open, then choose the Tools⇨ReportCreator command.
ReportCreator asks for the name of the report you want to create.

2. Type "Batting Average" for the report name, and then click OK.
The ReportCreator appears. (Refer to Figure 12-3.)

3. In the Title tab, type "Batting Average" for the report title, and then click Next.

4. In the Fields tab, select the Number, Name, At Bats, and Hits fields in that order, and then click Next.

5. In the Sorting tab, choose Number for the Sort By field, and then click Next.

6. In the Grouping tab, check the When Contents Change option for Group By: Number.

7. Choose Done.

Works asks if you want to preview or modify the report.

8. Choose Modify.

You are taken to report view. The report resembles the one shown in Figure 12-11.

Figure 12-11
Modifying the Batting
Average report.

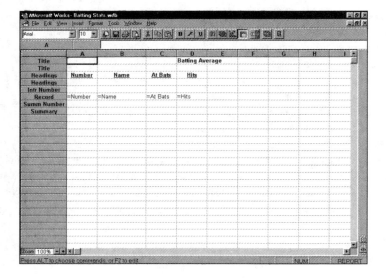

9. Select the report title in the Title row and choose the Edit⇨Cut command. Then select the A column of the Title row and choose the Edit⇨Paste command.

The report title is moved to the A column.

10. Select the A column of the Summ Number row, and then choose the Insert⇨Field Entry command.

The Insert Field Entry dialog box appears, as shown in Figure 12-12.

Figure 12-12
The Insert Field Entry
dialog box.

11. In the Select a Field list, select Number. Then click OK.

"=Number" is inserted in column A of the Summ Number row.

12. Select the B column of the Summ Number row, and then choose the Insert⇨Field Entry command again. This time choose the Name field and click OK.

"=Name" is inserted in column B of the Summ Number row.

13. Select the C column of the Summ Number row, and then choose the Insert⇨Field Summary command.

The Insert Field Summary dialog box appears, as shown in Figure 12-13.

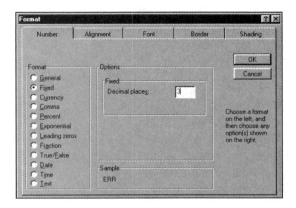

Figure 12-13
The Insert Field
Summary dialog box.

14. In the Select a Field list, click At Bats. Then click the SUM option button and click OK.

The formula =SUM(At Bats) is inserted in the C column of the Summ Number row.

15. Select the column D in the Summ Number row, and then choose the Insert⇨Field Summary command again.

Again, the Insert Field Summary dialog box appears.

16. From the Select a Field list, select Hits. Then choose the SUM option button and click OK.

The formula =SUM(Hits) is inserted in the D column of the Summ Number row.

17. Select column E in the Summ Number row, and then type the formula =SUM(Hits)/ SUM(At Bats).

This formula calculates the batting average.

18. Summon the Format⇨Number dialog box. Then pick Fixed for the number format and enter "3" in the Decimal Places text box. Click OK.

See Figure 12-14.

Figure 12-14
Setting the number for-
mat for the calculated
batting average.

19. Click column E in the first Headings row.

20. Type "Average."

21. Click the Bold and Underline button in the toolbar. Choose the Format⇨Alignment command, click Center when the Format dialog box appears, and then click OK.

The "Average" heading is now formatted like the other report headings: bold, underlined, and centered.

22. Select the Record row.

23. Choose the Insert⇨Delete Row command.

The Record row is deleted. The Batting Average report should now look like the one in Figure 12-15.

24. Save your work by choosing the File⇨Save command.

When you finish modifying the report, test it to make sure it works properly. To do that, enter some sample data into the database. All you need are ten or so rows, with two or three games of batting statistics for two or three players. Figure 12-16 shows some sample data I used to make sure the report was working properly, and Figure 12-17 shows how the report should appear with this data.

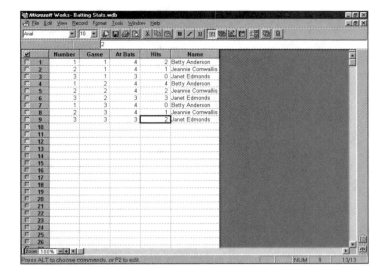

Figure 12-15
The Batting Average report after it has been modified.

Batting Average

Number	Name	At Bats	Hits	Average
1	Betty Anderson	12	6	0.500
2	Jeannie Cornwallis	12	4	0.333
3	Janet Edmonds	9	5	0.556

Figure 12-16
Some sample data used to test the Batting Average report.

Figure 12-17
The Batting Average report with the test data.

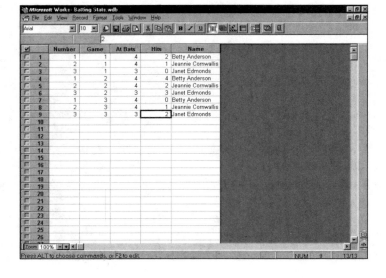

Don't forget to delete the sample data after you finish testing the report.

For more information about creating reports, refer to the "Creating a Report" section in Chapter 4.

Entering data for a game

The Batting Statistics database is designed to make it easy to enter the batting statistics for each game. If you enter the information as soon as possible after the game, your statistics will always be current and you won't have a pile of data to enter at the end of the season.

Entering the statistics for a complete game shouldn't take more than ten minutes or so. Here's the procedure:

1. Fire up Works and open the Batting Statistics database.

In the Works Task Launcher dialog box, click the Existing Documents tab, and then double-click the Batting Statistics database.

2. If the database is not already in list View, choose the View⇨List command to switch to list View.

3. Assign a number to the game whose statistics you want to record.

The easiest way to assign game numbers is to do them sequentially — your first game is game 1; the next game is game 2; and so on.

4. Working from the game scorebook, enter the batting statistics for the first batter listed in your lineup.

Type the batter's uniform number in the Number column, then press the Tab key and type the number of times that batter had at bat, then press the Tab key and type the number of hits the batter got.

Remember that if the batter received a walk, that time at bat does not count in the statistics. So only count those at-bats in which the batter either got a hit or was put out.

Also remember that a fielder's choice doesn't count as a hit. In other words, if a runner was on first and the batter hit to the shortstop who threw to make the out at second, the batter does not get credit for a hit even though he or she successfully made it to base. This does count as an at-bat, however, so it negatively affects the batter's batting average.

   5. Enter the statistics for the remaining batters in the same manner.

   6. After you enter all batters, choose the View⇨Reports command, select the Batting Average report, and click Preview. Then, if the report appears as you expected it to, click Print to print the current Batting Average report.

If you want to, you can use the Certificate Task Wizard to create certificates to honor your outstanding player's achievements.

PART V:

YOU

VOLUNTEERED

FOR

WHAT?

CHAPTER THIRTEEN

MASTER OF THE MAILING LIST

In This Chapter

- Keeping track of the membership
- Mailing form letters
- Creating a school directory

If you've accepted the thankless job of keeping track of your club or organization's membership, you'll appreciate the three projects in this chapter. These projects will show you how to create a powerful membership database using one of the built-in Works TaskWizards, how to use the membership database to send a personalized letter to everyone on the list, and — this is my favorite, because I usually get stuck doing it every year — how to create a school directory listing student names, addresses, and phone numbers sorted by classroom.

Project 20: Keeping the Membership Rolls

Every organization worth its salt has to appoint someone to keep track of the membership rolls. Churches, clubs, soccer leagues, PTA, even the local chapter of Save the Aardvarks needs an accurate and up-to-date membership list. This list is vital to the operation of any volunteer organization.

Fortunately, Works includes a TaskWizard that can create a pretty good membership list for you. All you have to do is enter all the data and keep the list current.

1. **Create the Membership database using the supplied Student & Membership Information TaskWizard.**
2. **Enter all the data. Yuch.**
3. **If you want, create a custom report that lists officers.**

Creating a Membership Roster database

To create a Membership Roster database, fire up Microsoft Works. When the Wo‌rks Task Launcher dialog box appears, click on Volunteer/Civic to reveal the list of te‌mplates for volunteer activities. Then select Student & Membership Information a‌nd click OK. You'll be asked whether to run the TaskWizard or display a list of existi‌ng documents. Click the "Yes, run the TaskWizard" button to start the Student & Me‌mbership Information TaskWizard, shown in Figure 13-1.

**Figure 13-1
The Student & Membership Information TaskWizard.**

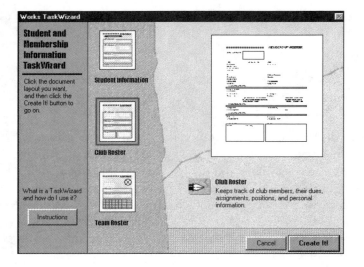

Like several other Works TaskWizards, this one lets you choose one of several var‌iations of a basic database design. In this case, you have three choices: a Student Inform‌ation database, a Club Roster database, and a Team Roster database. The Student Inf‌ormation database might be useful if you're running a private school, but it has far t‌oo much information for most volunteer record-keeping, even school-related. Likew‌ise for the Team Roster database: It might be useful if you're put in charge of the fr‌ont office of the New York Jets, but for keeping track of the membership of a recreational soccer league, it's a bit much. The Club Roster, however, is just right for many types of volunteer organizations. That's the one you want to choose. Click Club Roster, and then click the Create It! button.

Your computer's hard drive plays what sounds like a marching band cadence for a few moments, and then your screen displays a form for the first record of the Club Roster database, as shown in Figure 13-2.

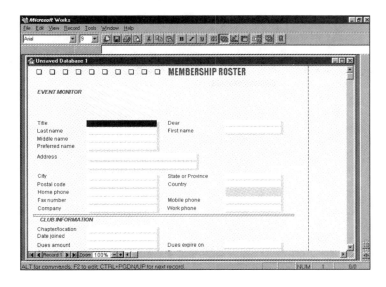

Figure 13-2
The Membership Roster database.

Before you start modifying the database or entering data into it, choose the File⇨Save command to save the database. Pick a meaningful name such as *Save the Aardvarks Membership* for the database.

Customizing the Membership Roster database

The Membership Roster database lets you record five categories of information about your club members:

- *Name and address information*, including phone numbers.
- *Club information*, including the club chapter or location, the date joined, the membership dues paid by the member and when the dues expire, and whether the member is an officer or serves on a committee.
- *Assignments*, which lets you record any special projects that the member may be assigned, along with a target and actual completion date.
- *Personal information*, including the member's birth date, spouse's name and birth date, names of children and their birthdays, and anniversary date.
- *Notes*, where you can enter any other information about the member.

You may find that the Membership Roster has too much detailed information for your needs, or it's missing key information you'd like to record. In that case, you can select the View↪Form Design command and add, remove, or rearrange the database fields in any way you want. Here are some suggestions for modifying the Membership Roster database:

- The name information stored in the Membership Roster is pretty formal. If you don't think you need to keep track of each member's middle name, title ("Mr.," "Mrs.," "Ms."), or preferred name, you can remove some or all of these fields.
- The Dear field is designed to use in the salutation of a form letter. If you want to use just the first name for your form letters, or a combination of Title and Last Name, you can delete the Dear field.

- The Club information section of the form assumes that your club has several locations or chapters. If that's not the case, you can delete the Chapter/Location field.

- If your club does not have dues, you can delete the Dues Amount and Dues Expire On fields.

- If you don't want to track the personal information (such as spouse's and children's names), delete that information as well.

- If your organization requires that new members be sponsored by an existing member, add a "Sponsor" field to the form.

Creating a committee list

One of the nice things about the Membership Roster database is that it lets you record who serves on what committee within your organization. Although the Membership Roster doesn't automatically create a report that lists committee memberships, you can easily create such a report by following the procedure described later in this section, "Creating a committee membership report."

For that report to be worthwhile, however, you must choose a standard way of designating the various committees of your organization *before* you start entering membership data. For example, if you have a "Ways and Means" committee, you should decide that you will always spell it "Ways and Means," not "Ways & Means." If you spell the committee name two different ways, Works will think you are referring to two different committees.

Thus, before you enter any data, come up with a simple list of committee names, and refer to this list whenever you enter data for a member of a committee. You may want to create a simple Word Processing document to hold your list, and print out a copy to keep by your computer when you enter membership information.

ENTERING THE MEMBERSHIP ROSTER DATA Typing in the Membership Roster is a monumental task if the organization has many members. Unfortunately, there's no easy way around it. All the information must be typed in, and it needs to be typed accurately.

When you type in the Membership Roster information (or any database information), remember these handy keyboard shortcuts:

KEYBOARD SHORTCUT	WHAT IT DOES
Tab	Moves to the next field on the form
Shift+Tab	Moves back one field on the form
Ctrl+PageDown	Moves to the next record
Ctrl+PageUp	Moves to the previous record

You don't have to worry about entering names in alphabetical order when you type the names for the Membership Roster database. You can always sort the database by choosing the Record➪Sort Records command. The Sort Records dialog box will appear. Select Last Name for the Sort By field and First Name for the Then By field, as shown in Figure 13-3. Then click OK to sort the database. The very first time you call up the Sort Records command, a first-timers dialog box appears. You can opt to take a brief tour of sorting, or you can click "To sort a database" to skip the tour.

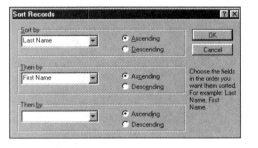

**Figure 13-3
Sorting the Membership Roster database.**

MEMBERSHIP ROSTER REPORTS The Membership Roster database includes several reports that you can print. To access these reports, choose the View➪Report command. A dialog box listing four reports will appear:

■ **Phone directory:** This report lists the entire membership list alphabetically. Each member's home and work phone numbers are listed, plus any office held by the member is listed. Figure 13-4 shows a sample of the Phone Directory report's output.

Figure 13-4
The Phone directory report.

MEMBERSHIP ROSTER

TELEPHONE DIRECTORY

NAME

Anderson, Betty Home phone: 555-2468
Office held: Committee assignment: Day phone: 555-7890
Cornwallis, Jeannie Home phone: 555-1234
Office held: Secretary Committee assignment: Administration Day phone: 555-5678
Edmonds, Janet Home phone: 555-3456
Office held: Membership Committee assignment: Administration Day phone: 555-7890
Henry, Jennifer Home phone: 555-2345
Office held: Vice President Committee assignment: Administration Day phone: 555-6789
Johansen, Mary Home phone: 555-6789
Office held: Committee assignment: Day phone: 555-5678
Johnson, Beth Home phone: 555-7890
Office held: Committee assignment: Day phone: 555-6789
Johnson, James Home phone: 555-1234
Office held: President Committee assignment: Administration Day phone: 555-2345
Jones, Renee Home phone: 555-4567
Office held: Historian Committee assignment: Administration Day phone: 555-8901
Klien, Amanda Home phone: 555-5678
Office held: Committee assignment: Day phone: 555-9012
Lowe, Bethany Home phone: 555-0123
Office held: Committee assignment: Day phone: 555-6789
Lowe, Sarah Home phone: 555-1357
Office held: Committee assignment: Day phone: 555-8901
Smith, Alice Home phone: 555-8901
Office held: Committee assignment: Day phone: 555-5678
Summers, Susie Home phone: 555-4680
Office held: Committee assignment: Day phone: 555-9012
Webb, Mary Home phone: 555-9876
Office held: Treasurer Committee assignment: Administration Day phone: 555-9382

■ **Events List:** This report lists any member who has a birthday, anniversary, unpaid dues, or an assignment coming up in the current month. It is illustrated in Figure 13-5.

Figure 13-5
The Event List report.

MEMBERSHIP ROSTER

EVENT LIST

The members listed in this report have a birthday or anniversary this month, have a past-due assignment, or are late paying their membership dues.

Henry, Jennifer

738 West, , Fresno, CA 93612
Home phone: 555-2345 Day phone: 555-6789

BIRTHDAYS	ANNIVERSARY	DUES EXPIRATION	ASSIGNMENTS
1 Birthday this month!			

Johnson, James

#6 Cherry Tree Lane, , Fresno, CA 93711
Home phone: 555-1234 Day phone: 555-2345

BIRTHDAYS	ANNIVERSARY	DUES EXPIRATION	ASSIGNMENTS
	Anniversary this month!		

■ **Birthday List:** This report is similar to the Events list except that it shows only those members who are celebrating a birthday in the family sometime in the current month. This report uses a combination of a fairly complex database function and a filter to determine whether the member, the member's spouse, or any of the member's children have a birthday in the current month.

■ **Addresses:** This report lists each member in alphabetical order, showing the member's address and phone number. It is shown in Figure 13-6.

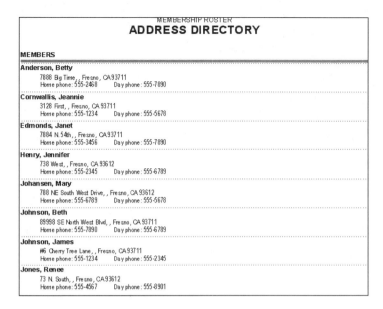

Figure 13-6
The Address Directory
report.

Creating a list of officers

One report that the Membership Roster database doesn't include is an Officers List report. But you can easily create an Officers List report by copying the Address List report and making a few simple modifications. Here's the procedure:

1. Choose the Tools⇨Duplicate Report command.
The Duplicate Report dialog box appears, as shown in Figure 13-7.

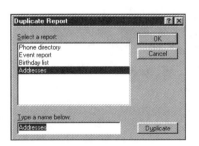

Figure 13-7
The Duplicate Report
dialog box.

2. Click "Addresses" in the Select a Report list box. Then type "Officers" in the Type a Name Below text box and click OK.
A duplicate copy of the Addresses report is created under the name *Officers*.

3. Choose the View⇨Report command. The View Report dialog box appears. Click "Officers" in the Select a Report list box, and then click Modify.
The newly created Officers report appears. As Figure 13-8 shows, it looks identical to the Addresses report from which it was copied.

Figure 13-8
The duplicated Officers report.

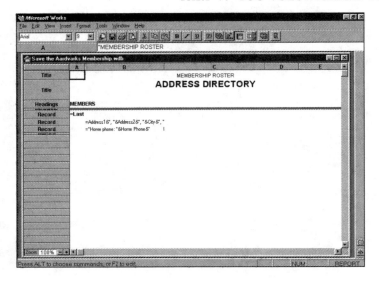

4. Select the A column in the second Title row. Then type "OFFICER DIRECTORY" and press Enter.

The title "MEMBERSHIP DIRECTORY" is replaced by "OFFICER DIRECTORY."

5. Select the A column in the Headings row. Then type "OFFICERS" and press Enter.

The heading "MEMBERS" is replaced by "OFFICERS."

6. Select the second Record row.

To select the entire row, click the Record heading to the left of the row.

7. Choose the Insert⇨Insert Row command.

The Insert Row dialog box appears, as shown in Figure 13-9.

Figure 13-9
The Insert Row dialog box.

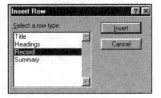

8. Select Record in the Select a Row Type list box, and then click Insert. A new Record row is inserted.

9. Select the A column in the first Record row and choose the Edit⇨Cut command.

Or, press Ctrl+X. Either way, the contents of the first Record row is obliterated.

10. Select the B column of the second Record row (the row you inserted in Step 7) and choose the Edit⇨Paste command.

Or press Ctrl+V. The data you cut in Step 9 is pasted.

11. Use the Font control in the toolbar to change the font to Arial Narrow, and click the Bold button to remove the bold formatting.

The text in the second Record row is formatted the same as the text in the third and fourth Record rows.

12. Select the A column in the first Record row, type "=Office", and then press Enter.

13. Click the Bold button to apply bold formatting.

14. Choose the Tools⇨Report Sorting command.

The Report Settings dialog box appears with the Sorting tab selected, as shown in Figure 13-10. As you can see in the figure, the Sorting options are set so that the report is sorted by Last Name, First Name, and Middle Name.

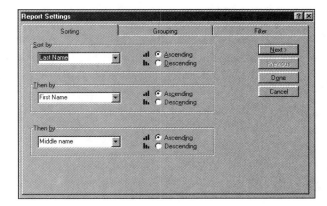

Figure 13-10
The Sorting options on the Report Settings dialog box.

15. Change the Sort by field to Office and the other fields (Then by and Then by) to (none).

Because the Membership Roster database contains so many fields, you'll have to scroll through a long list of field names to find the Sort and (none) options listed.

16. Click the Filter tab.

The Filter options are shown.

17. Click the Create New Filter button.

The Filter Name dialog box appears, asking for a name for your new filter.

18. Type "Officers" for the Filter Name, and then click OK.

The Filter dialog box appears, as shown in Figure 13-11.

Figure 13-11
The Filter dialog box.

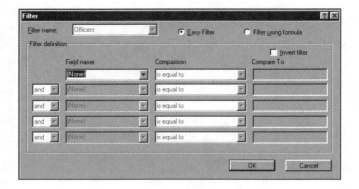

Figure 13-11
The Filter dialog box.

19. Select "Office" from the Field Name list box, and then select "is not blank" from the Comparison list box. Then click the OK button.

You are returned to the Report Settings dialog box.

20. Click Done.

The Report Settings dialog box is dismissed.

21. Choose the File⇨Save command.

The database file is saved with your new Officers report.

22. Click the Print Preview command to preview the Officer Directory report.

Figure 13-12 shows how the Officer Directory report should appear.

Figure 13-12
The Officer Directory report.

```
                            MEMBERSHIP ROSTER
                      OFFICER DIRECTORY

OFFICERS

Historian
       Jones, Renee
       73 N. South, , Fresno, CA 93612
       Home phone: 555-4567      Day phone: 555-8901

Membership
       Edmonds, Janet
       7884 N. 54th, , Fresno, CA 93711
       Home phone: 555-3456      Day phone: 555-7890

President
       Johnson, James
       #6 Cherry Tree Lane, , Fresno, CA 93711
       Home phone: 555-1234      Day phone: 555-2345

Secretary
       Cornwallis, Jeannie
       3128 First, , Fresno, CA 93711
       Home phone: 555-1234      Day phone: 555-5678

Treasurer
       Webb, Mary
       837 Lincoln, , Clovis, CA 93612
       Home phone: 555-9876      Day phone: 555-9382

Vice President
       Henry, Jennifer
       738 West, , Fresno, CA 93612
       Home phone: 555-2345      Day phone: 555-6789
```

Project 21: Mailing Form Letters

Junk mail is as much fun to send as it is to receive, especially if you have already created a database that contains the names and addresses of those poor hapless souls whom you want to bombard with your latest plea for funds, request for volunteers, or other personalized communication from your club or organization.

This project builds on the last project by showing you how to mail a personalized letter to everyone in your membership database. However, it can easily be adapted to work with any address-book-type database. It uses the Form Letter TaskWizard, which is one of Works' most powerful features.

FAST TRACK

1. **Use the Form Letter TaskWizard to create form letters to send to your mailing list.**
2. **That's all there is to it!**

FORM LETTERS

To create form letters to send to the addresses in your membership database, follow these steps:

1. From the Works Task Launcher, fire up the Form Letter TaskWizard. You'll find it in the TaskWizards tab, hidden under Correspondence. Click Correspondence to reveal the long list of Correspondence wizards. Click Form Letter, and then click OK.

2. When Works asks if you want to run the TaskWizard, click Yes. The Form Letter TaskWizard comes to life, as shown in Figure 13-13.

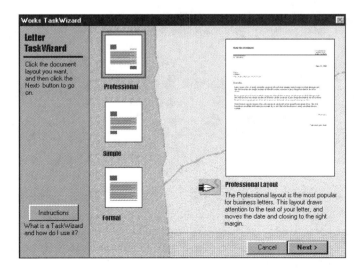

Figure 13-13
The Form Letter TaskWizard comes to life.

3. Select the letter format you want to use, and then click Next.

Works can create letters in three basic layouts: Professional, Simple, and Formal. As you click each style, the TaskWizard clarifies the specifics of the style in the lower-right corner of the Wizard dialog box.

When you click Next, the next screen of the TaskWizard appears, as shown in Figure 13-14.

Figure 13-14
The Form Letter Task Wizard lets you customize various aspects of your form letters.

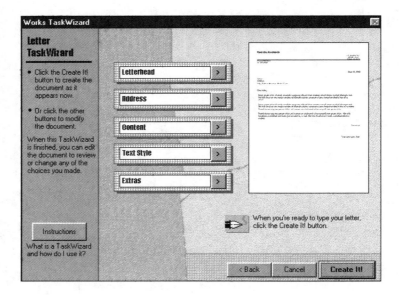

4. Click the Letterhead button in the Form Letter Wizard.

The Letterhead dialog box appears, as shown in Figure 13-15.

Figure 13-15
Picking a letterhead.

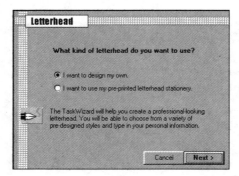

5. Select "I want to design my own" if it is not already selected, and then click Next. (If you want to use preprinted stationery, check "I want to use my pre-printed letterhead stationery" and skip ahead to step 11.)

The dialog box shown in Figure 13-16 presents several options for creating your letterhead.

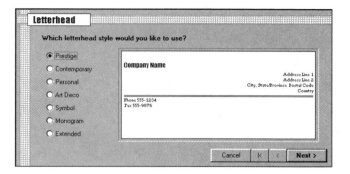

Figure 13-16
The Form Letter TaskWizard offers several alternative letterhead styles.

6. Pick the letterhead style you want, and then click Next.
You'll be asked to type your company name, as shown in Figure 13-17.

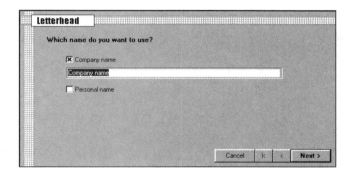

Figure 13-17
The Form Letter TaskWizard asks for your company name.

7. Type the name of your company, club, or organization, and then click Next.

You can also choose the Personal Name option button. If you do, a new text box appears into which you can type your name. If you want only the Personal Name to appear, be sure to uncheck the Company Name checkbox.

When you click Next, the TaskWizard asks for the address information, as shown in Figure 13-18.

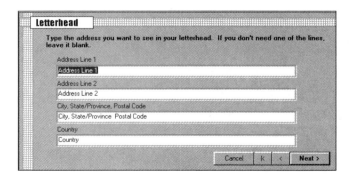

Figure 13-18
The TaskWizard asks for your address.

8. Type the address information, and then click Next.

Now the TaskWizard wants to know your phone number, as Figure 13-19 shows.

Figure 13-19
Now it wants your
phone number.

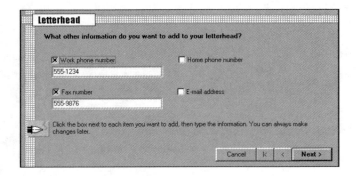

9. Type your phone numbers and e-mail address if you have one, and then click Next.

If you want your home phone number or e-mail address to appear on the letterhead, select those options and type the information into the text boxes that appear. Be sure to uncheck any boxes you don't need.

When you click Next, the TaskWizard presents a preview of your letterhead, as shown in Figure 13-20.

Figure 13-20
The TaskWizard gives
you a preview of your
letterhead.

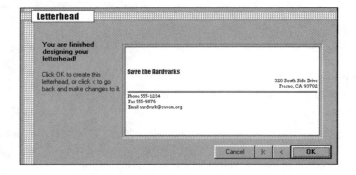

10. Click OK.

You are returned to the Form Letter TaskWizard (refer to Figure 13-14).

11. Click the Address button.

The Address dialog box appears, as shown in Figure 13-21.

Figure 13-21
The Address dialog box.

12. Click the "I want to use addresses from a Works database" option (after all, the Membership Roster is a database), and then click Next.

The dialog box shown in Figure 13-22 appears.

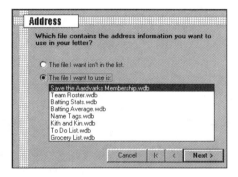

Figure 13-22
The TaskWizard asks which database to use for the letters.

13. Select the database from the list of databases that appears, and then click Next.

Although the TaskWizard allows you to proceed without selecting a database, it's best if you select the database now.

When you click Next, the TaskWizard retrieves information from the database, and then it displays the dialog box shown in Figure 13-23.

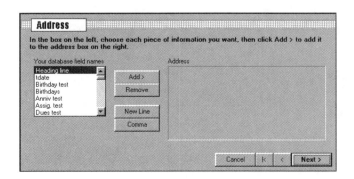

Figure 13-23
The TaskWizard is ready for you to compose the address area.

14. Compose the address area using the name and address fields from the database.

To add a database field to the address area, select the field from the list of database fields on the left and click the Add button. To start a new line in the address area, click the New Line button. You can also add a comma to the address area by clicking the comma button. If you make a mistake, click the Remove button to remove the last field you added.

To compose an address area using fields from the Membership Roster database that was created in Project 20, follow this sequence:

Click First Name, and then click Add.
Click Last Name, and then click Add.
Click New Line.
Click Address 1, and then click Add.
Click New Line.
Click Address 2, and then click Add.
Click New Line.
Click City, and then click Add.
Click State or prov, and then click Add.
Click Postal code, and then click Add.

When you finish, the address area should appear as shown in Figure 13-24.

Figure 13-24
A properly composed form letter address.

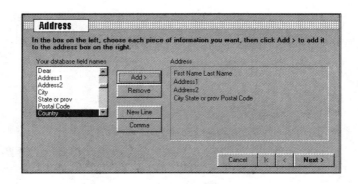

15. Click Next.
The dialog box shown in Figure 13-25 appears.

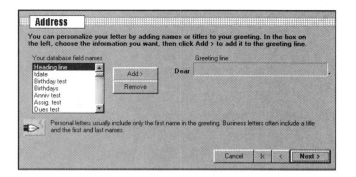

Figure 13-25
Now it's time to compose the salutation.

16. Select the field you want to use in the salutation, and then click Add.

The field is added to the salutation area. For the Membership Roster database, use the First Name field. This will create salutations such as "Dear John." If you want to be more formal, use the Title and Last Name fields to create salutations such as "Mr. Smith."

17. Click Next.

The dialog box shown in Figure 13-26 appears:

Figure 13-26
The address is finished.

18. Click OK.

You are once again returned to the TaskWizard.

19. Click the Content button.

The dialog box shown in Figure 13-27 appears.

Figure 13-27
Pick a letter, any letter.

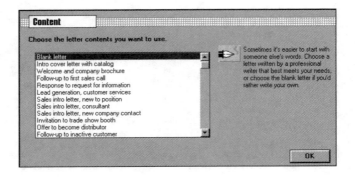

20. If one of the 100+ prewritten letters looks as if it might be appropriate for your form letter, select it and click OK. Otherwise, select "Blank Letter" at the top of the list and click OK.

You are yet again whisked back to the Task Wizard.

21. Have a snack.

This procedure is getting a bit long. Now would be a good time for a Twinkie or a cup of Mocha.

22. Click the Text Style button.

The Text Style dialog box appears, as shown in Figure 13-28. This dialog box lets you select the typeface that will be used for your letter.

Figure 13-28
One of these text styles is sure to please.

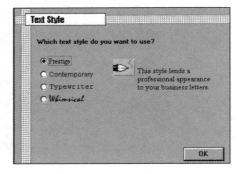

23. Select the text style you want to use for your letter, and then click OK.

For this example, I chose the Typewriter style. Once you select your favorite style, click OK to return again to the TaskWizard dialog box.

24. Click the Extras button.

The Extras dialog box appears, as shown in Figure 13-29.

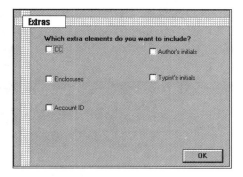

Figure 13-29
The TaskWizard lets
you add extras to the
bottom of your letter.

25. If you want the form letter to include one of the extras listed in the dialog box (CC, Enclosures, Account ID, Author's Initials, or Typist's Initials), check the appropriate checkbox and type the information requested into the text box that appears. Then click OK.

For example, if you want a CC (Courtesy Copy) line to appear in the letter, click the CC check box and type the name you want to appear on the CC line in the text box that appears beneath the CC checkbox. When you click OK, the Form Letter TaskWizard dialog box appears again.

26. Click the Create It! button.

The TaskWizard displays the dialog box shown in Figure 13-30, summarizing the choices you have made so far. If you discover a mistake in the Form Letter settings, you can click the Return to Wizard button to return to the TaskWizard, where you can change the settings you have selected.

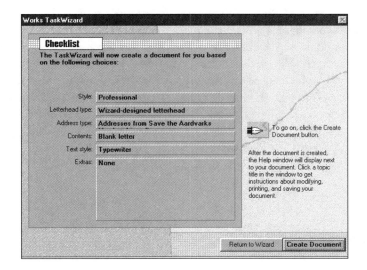

Figure 13-30
The TaskWizard lets
you add extras.

27. Click the Create Document button.

Your computer grinds and whirls for a moment, then it displays a skeleton mail merge letter similar to the one shown in Figure 13-31.

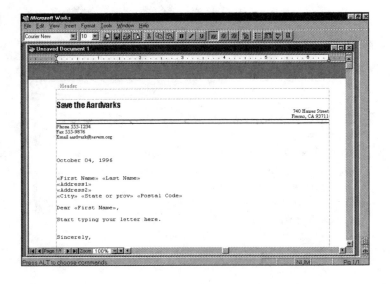

28. Save the file.

Choose the File➪Save command. When the Save As dialog box appears, type a reasonable file name for the file, and then click Save.

29. Type the body of your letter, replacing the "Start typing your letter here" placeholder that the TaskWizard inserted into the letter. Then scroll down a bit and replace the placeholder text "Your name goes here" with your actual name (or the name of the person you want to appear at the bottom of the letter).

If you chose one of the prewritten letters back in Step 20, this step will be easy: All you'll have to do is review the letter and make any necessary changes. If you started with a blank letter, you'll have to type the body of your letter from scratch.

Figure 13-32 shows what a letter might look like when finished.

Figure 13-32
A finished letter ready to be merged with names and addresses from the database.

30. Choose the File⇨Print command.

The Print dialog box appears, as shown in Figure 13-33.

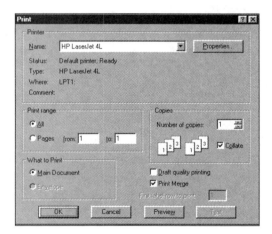

Figure 13-33
The Print dialog box.

31. Make sure the Print Merge option is checked, and then click the Preview button. When Works asks if you want to preview all records, click OK.

The merged letters appears in Print Preview mode, as shown in Figure 13-34.

Carefully review the appearance of the letter in the Print Preview screen. If the letter doesn't look right — for example, if there is too much white space above or below the letter, if the letter spills onto a second page to accommodate just one extra line of text, or if the names didn't merge correctly — click Cancel, then adjust the page margins (via the File⇨Page Setup command). Delete a sentence or two to get the letter to fit on one page, or add the correct merge fields to the letter (via the Insert⇨Database Field command).

Figure 13-34
Previewing the letters
before printing them.

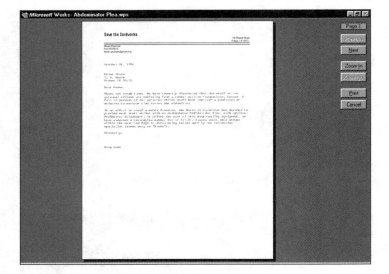

32. Double-check the letters to make sure they merged correctly. Then click Print to print the letters.

The form letters begin printing!

You can also use the Membership Roster database to print envelopes and labels. From the Task Wizards tab of the Works Task Launcher, choose the Envelopes or Labels Task Wizard, found under the Envelopes and Labels category.

Project 22: A School Directory

Some projects seem (at first) as if they are best suited for one of Works' tools but, after some thought, you find that a different tool altogether is more appropriate. A perfect example of this type of project is a school classroom directory that lists the names, addresses, and phone numbers of students by class, with each class appearing on a separate page.

For several years running now, my wife and I have been responsible for putting together this type of directory for our daughters' elementary school.

The school has roughly 20 classrooms, each with roughly 30 students, for a total of about 600 names, addresses, and phone numbers. This seems like a perfect candidate for a database. But the more you try to create a Works database to handle a class directory of this sort, the more you discover that the Works database can't handle it. Storing the names, addresses, and phone numbers is no problem. But creating a database report that lists the students by classroom is difficult if not impossible to do.

The problem is that each child may have one or two sets of parent or guardian addresses. If a child lives at home with both parents or at just one home with a single parent or guardian, only one line is needed for the child's listing in the directory. But if the child lives in a split family, two lines of address information need to be provided. In Works, there is no way to create a database report — at least that I know of — that prints one line for some database records but two lines for others. You can create a report that prints one line for each record, and you can create a report that prints two lines per record. But you can't mix and match.

So why not just print two lines for each student, whether two lines are needed? With thirty students per class, two lines apiece would require sixty lines, more than will fit on a single page unless you use itty bitty type.

A classroom directory such as this is best handled by the Spreadsheet program. You could create the directory using the Word Processor, but the Spreadsheet has the advantage of a Tools⇨Sort command. With this command, you can enter the students for a particular class in any order you want, and then quickly sort them into alphabetical order. If you opt for the Word Processor to create your directory, you'll have to manually sort the names into alphabetical order before typing them into the document.

This project is a bit different from most of the projects in this book; the procedure focuses more on the large-scale things you need to do to create a directory rather than on the details of how to use Works to actually create the document. For this type of project, the more difficult aspect of the project is figuring out how to gather the name and address information in a way that will make it easy for you to enter the information into the spreadsheet so the directory can be printed out.

1. **Create a directory information request form that can be sent home with students to obtain the basic address and phone number information and to secure the parents' or guardians' permission to include the information in the directory.**
2. **As the forms come back from the students, group them together by classroom.**
3. **When all (or most) of the forms are in, create a spreadsheet that has one page per classroom. As each class is entered, use the Tools⇨Sort command to sort the names into alphabetical order.**
4. **Print the directory spreadsheet to use as a master to make photocopied directories.**

FAST TRACK

SCHOOL DIRECTORY

Creating the permissions document

Your friendly, local public school won't simply give you the address and phone numbers of all the students at the school. That information is considered confidential and can be published in a directory only if the child's parents or guardians give you permission to do so. The best way to do that is to arrange to have an information form sent home to parents, with instructions to fill out the form and return it to school by a certain date. (It's best to allow only a few days to fill out and return the form; if you give 'em three weeks, they'll surely procrastinate and never get the form back to school!)

Figure 13-35 shows the form that I have used to gather this information at my daughters' school. As you can see, the form has a space for the student's name, grade, and room number, plus space for one or two parent or guardian names and addresses. In addition, the form has a space where the parent or guardian can sign to release permission for the address information to be included in the directory.

Figure 13-35
The Permission letter.

Dear Parents,

We are compiling a Figarden Elementary School phone directory. This directory is used solely for the purposes of communication between students, parents, and teachers at Figarden. It is very important that we have your number listed. There are many activities that your child will be involved in and we would like to make sure that everyone has been included in these special activities. Listing your phone number will help ensure that you are notified of the special happenings or needs of Figarden school. The directory is not available for use by any other groups or organizations.

Please return one form for each child by September 30, 1996.

Information Release

Name of Student _____ Grade ____ Room __

I hereby give permission to print my child's address and phone number information as listed below in the Figarden school directory.

Signature _____ Date _____

Parent or Guardian

Name _____
Address _____
City _____
Zip Code _____
Phone _____

Additional Parent or Guardian to be Listed

Name _____
Address _____
City _____
Zip Code _____
Phone _____

Because this letter is a fairly straightforward Word Processor document, I won't go into every detail of how I created it. I do, however, want to point out a few items:

- The blank spaces for the student's name, grade, and room number were created simply by typing the underscore character (the one you get when you hold down the Shift key and press the hyphen, next to the 0 key) repeatedly to fill out the space. Likewise for the Signature and Date lines.

■ The lines for the parent/guardian information were made by the creative use of tab stops. These paragraphs actually have three tab stops, and they are set up as follows:

1.125", right-aligned, no leader character.
1.25", left-aligned, no leader character.
5.5", right-aligned, leader style 3 (underlined).

Each paragraph in this section begins with a tab, then the heading text ("Name," "Address," and so on), followed by two more tabs. The first of these tabs creates ⅛" of space between the heading text and the start of the line; the second tab extends the leader underline across the page to the 5.5" tab stop.

■ To allow room for the parents to write between the lines, I added 0.25 lines of space after each paragraph in this section. You can add this space using the Format⇨Paragraph command, clicking the Spacing tab, and setting the After setting to 0.25l.

Not every student will return the information form, of course. In fact, you'll be lucky to get half of them back. As a result, you'll need to obtain a set of complete class rosters from the school office. This roster will include only the student's names — not their addresses and phone numbers; although the school office undoubtedly has that information, they'll be reluctant to give it to you for privacy reasons.

SETTING UP THE DIRECTORY You can start creating the directory even before you get the information forms back, since you must first enter all the names from the class rosters you obtained from the school. When you have the class rosters in hand, you can get started.

The first group of steps listed here (steps 1 through 18) show how to create the first page of the directory using names provided from the class roster:

1. Fire up Works and create a new Spreadsheet document.
From the Works Task Launcher, click the Works Tools tab, and then click the Spreadsheet button.

2. Select the entire spreadsheet by clicking the button at the upper-left corner of the spreadsheet window.

3. Choose the Format⇨Row Height command and set the row height to 15. Click OK to dismiss the Row Height dialog box.

4. Select the first row of the spreadsheet. Then set the font size to 14 and click the Bold button.
The first row of the spreadsheet is set up to accommodate the page heading.

5. Select the A, B, and C columns by clicking the "A" header above the first column and then holding down the mouse button and dragging it across the B and C columns as well.

6. Choose the Format⇨Column Width command and set the column width to 25. Click OK to dismiss the Column Width dialog box.

7. Select the D column. Then choose the Format⇨Column Width command and set the column width to 8.

8. Select the E column. Then choose the Format⇨Alignment command and set the horizontal alignment to Right. Click OK.

9. Click the A1 cell and type the room number for the first classroom you want to create. Press Enter.

For example, Room 4.

10. Click the B1 cell and type the name of the teacher for this classroom.

For example, Miss Barkley.

11. Select the B1 and C1 cells by holding down the Shift key and clicking both cells. Then choose the Format⇨Alignment command and select the Center Across Selection option and click OK.

The teacher's name is centered over the B and C columns.

12. Click the E1 cell and type the grade level for this class.

For example, Grade 1.

13. Select all of Row 3 by clicking on the "3" header to the left of the row. Then click the Bold button to format the entire row in boldface.

14. Enter the column headings in Row 3.

The following table shows the headings to enter for each cell:

CELL	HEADING TO ENTER
A3	Student
B3	Parent/Guardian
C3	Address
D3	Zip
E3	Phone

Figure 13-36 shows how the spreadsheet should appear at this point.

15. Choose the File⇨Save command to save the file.

Type a reasonable name for the file, such as Directory, and then click the Save button to save the file.

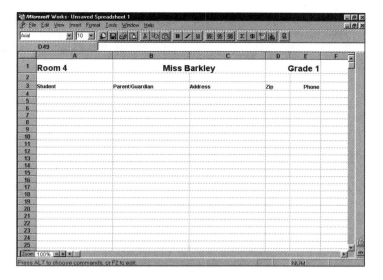

Figure 13-36
The class directory
after the first page of
headings has been
entered.

16. Working from the class roster provided by the school, type the name of each student (last name first) in the A column, starting in Row 4.

When you finish, the directory will resemble the one shown in Figure 13-37.

Figure 13-37
The class directory
after the student
names have been
entered.

17. If necessary, sort the student names by selecting all the names and choosing the Tools➪Sort command.

18. Save the file.

Choose the File⇨Save command, or click the Save button or press Ctrl+S.

The next group of steps (steps 19 through 29) show how to create subsequent pages by inserting page breaks, copying the heading rows, and typing names from the class roster.

19. Select the row immediately below the last row that contains a student name.

For example, if the last row of students is Row 35, select Row 36. Select the entire row by clicking the row heading to the left of the row.

20. Choose the Insert⇨Insert page break command.

A page break is entered above the selected row. It will appear in the spreadsheet as a dashed line.

21. Select rows 1 through 3 of the spreadsheet.

To select these rows, hold down the Shift key and click the row heading for Rows 1 through 3.

22. Choose the Edit⇨Copy command.

23. Select the row in which you inserted the page break.

This is the same row you selected in Step 18.

24. Choose the Edit⇨Paste command.

The headings from Rows 1 through 3 are pasted.

25. Edit the headings for the new class you want to enter.

For example, change the room number, teacher, and grade.

26. Enter the student names for the new class from the class roster provided by the school in the A column. Sort the names if necessary.

27. Save the file.

Use the File⇨Save command, click the Save button, or press Ctrl+S.

28. Repeat steps 19 through 27 for all remaining classes. Be sure to save your work often — at least when you finish each classroom, preferably after entering every 5 or 6 names.

When you have entered the names for all classrooms, print out a copy of the entire spreadsheet and carefully proof the names you entered against the class roster provided by the school. If you find any errors or omissions, now is the time to correct them.

Adding the addresses and phone numbers

As the information forms begin to come back, sort them into order by classroom. You can also sort each class alphabetically, which will make it easier to enter the addresses and phone numbers for each student.

When all the forms are in, start entering the parent/guardian names, addresses, and phone numbers. Leave these areas blank for students who did not return a form or whose forms are missing information or the parent/guardian signature.

It's very easy to get a row off during this step. Double-check each student as you enter his or her information to make sure you are entering the information on the correct row!

In those cases in which a student has two parent/guardian addresses listed, select the row beneath the student in question and choose the Insert⇨Insert Row command. Then use the new blank row to enter the second parent/guardian name, address, and phone number. Leave the name column blank for this row.

After you have created a second row for any student in the class, you cannot use the Tools⇨Sort command to sort the students for that class; the new row you created doesn't have a name in the A column. So make sure the students are listed in alphabetical order first.

Make sure you save your work after completing each class. This is tedious and time-consuming work, and you don't want to lose the whole thing if the dog happens to trip over the computer's power cord or if your four teenage daughters decide to run all their hair dryers at once.

Figure 13-38 shows how a directory should appear after addresses have been entered. Now it's simply a matter of printing the directory, taking it to a copy shop, and having 600 copies made. Then you can relax until next year.

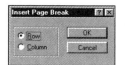

**Figure 13-38
A finished directory.**

CHAPTER FOURTEEN

MINDING MEETINGS

In This Chapter

- Creating an agenda
- Preparing the minutes

Call me a fool if you want (you won't be the first), but I kind of *like* meetings. I'm one of those parliamentary nuts who has actually read *Roberts Rules of Order* from cover to cover, twice.

If you're the chairperson or secretary of any organization that follows *Robert's Rules*, you'll appreciate the two projects in this chapter. The first project shows you how to create a proper *order of business* (commonly called an *agenda*) so you can keep your meetings on track. And the second project shows you how to prepare minutes.

Project 23: Creating an Agenda

An agenda — properly called the *Order of Business* according to Robert — outlines the business that is to be conducted at a meeting. Although *Robert's Rules* spells out the usual order of business that applies to most meetings, each organization has its own unique customs that affect how meetings proceed.

This project shows you how to create an Order of Business that is stored in a Works template that you can use to create agenda documents for upcoming meetings. The template provides a basic outline for the order of business, to which you can add additional items as necessary. We'll be talking about templates in this chapter and you'll get to put them to work.

FAST TRACK

AGENDA

1. **Create an agenda template to use as the basis for new agenda documents.**
2. **Create an agenda for an upcoming meeting by creating a new document based on the template.**

Creating an Agenda template

A *template* is a Works document that you use as the basis for new documents. Although Works comes with dozens of templates, it does not come with a template for creating agendas. So you'll have to create one yourself. Figure 14-1 shows an example of just such a template.

Figure 14-1
An agenda template.

> **Save the Aardvarks**
> Board of Directors Meeting
> (date)
> 7:00 pm
> Agenda
>
> **Call to Order**
>
> 1. **Reading and Approval of Minutes**
>
> 2. **Committee Reports**
>   a)   Treasurer
>   b)   Ways and Means
>   c)   Membership
>   d)   Nominating
>
> 3. **Reports of Special Committees**
>   a)
>   b)
>
> 4. **Unfinished Business**
>   a)
>   b)
>
> 5. **New Business**
>
> **Adjourn**

The following procedure shows how you can create your own agenda template:

1. Create a new word processing document.

From the Works Task Launcher, click the Works Tools tab, and then click the Word Processor button.

2. Create a heading that will appear on all your agendas.

For example, the heading in Figure 14-1 shows how the heading for the board of directors of an organization called *Save the Aardvarks* might appear. The heading is formatted in 12-point Arial, centered, and the first line is bold.

3. Type a sample outline for your meeting agenda.

The sample outline used in Figure 14-1 includes the elements of a standard order of business that are commonly used in informal organizations. It's not sufficient for Congress or the United Nations, but it will do for a PTA meeting.

Notice that I listed the standing committees that give reports at each meeting. Naturally, you should list the committees that apply to your organization here.

Also, notice that I included two empty paragraphs under both the "Reports of Special Committees" heading and the "Unfinished Business" heading.

Be sure to use tabs rather than spaces to line up the various elements of this document.

4. Choose the File⇨Save command.

The Save As dialog box appears, as shown in Figure 14-2.

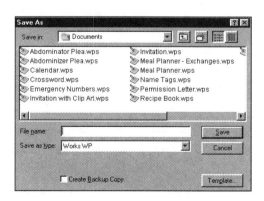

Figure 14-2
The Save As dialog box.

5. Click the Template button.

The Save As Template dialog box appears, as shown in Figure 14-3.

Figure 14-3
The Save As Template
dialog box.

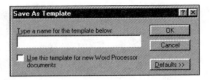

6. Type a name for the template.

I suggest Agenda.

7. Click OK.

The template is created, but the document remains open.

8. Choose the File⇨Close command.

That's all there is to it. You can now create new documents based on your Agenda template.

Using the Agenda template

To create a new document based on the Agenda template, follow these steps:

1. From the TaskWizards tab of the Works Task Launcher dialog box, click User Templates at the very end of the list.

The Agenda template appears in the list, along with any other templates you may have created, as shown in Figure 14-4.

Figure 14-4
The Agenda template
appears in the
TaskWizards list.

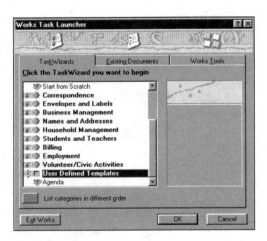

2. Click the Agenda template to select it, and then click OK.

Works creates a new document based on the template, as shown in Figure 14-5.

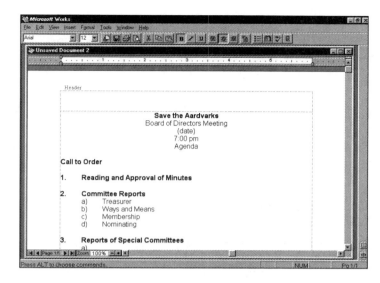

Figure 14-5
A document created from the Agenda template.

3. Type the meeting date in the heading area.

For example, replace "(date)" with December 10, 1996.

4. Add any specific items that need to be covered under "Reports of Special Committees" or "Unfinished Business."

If there are no items to go under these headings, delete the headings and renumber the agenda accordingly.

5. Use the File⇨Save command to save the file.

Type a file name that includes the meeting date. For example, Dec 96 Board Meeting Agenda.

6. Choose the File⇨Print command to print the agenda.

To print more than one copy of the agenda, set the Number of Copies field in the Print dialog box to the desired number, and then click OK.

7. Use the File⇨Close command to close the document.

Now that you've created an agenda, the only challenge that remains is to stick to it. Good luck.

Project 24: Preparing the Minutes

If you're the secretary or clerk of an organization that conducts formal meetings, your main mission in life is to keep accurate records of what goes on during the meetings so you can prepare the minutes.

The key to taking good notes for minutes is to remember that the minutes are intended to show actions that were taken during the meeting. You don't have to record who said what, who argued in favor of a motion and who argued against, or who had to leave early to get to their kid's soccer

game. In fact, you should *not* include such items in the minutes. The minutes are an official record of what actions were taken at a meeting; nothing more, nothing less.

1. Create a minutes template that you can use as the basis for new minutes documents.
2. Create the minutes for a meeting by creating a new document based on the minutes template.

Creating the minutes template

Minutes have a fairly simple format. About all you can do to create a template is type a heading and the opening paragraph, which should always contain the same information though the details vary from meeting to meeting.

The following procedure shows how to create a minutes template:

1. From the Works Task Launcher, click the Works Tools tab, and then click the Word Processor button.

The Word Processor comes to life, showing a blank document.

2. Type a title for the minutes, such as "Minutes of the Save the Aardvarks Board of Directors Meeting, <date>."

3. Choose the Format⇨Easy Formats command.

The Easy Formats dialog box appears, as shown in Figure 14-6.

**Figure 14-6
The Easy Formats
dialog box.**

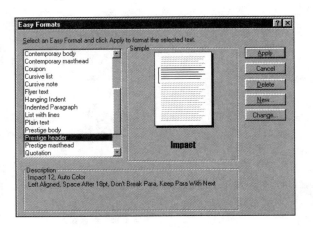

4. In the list of Easy Formats, select Prestige Header, and then click Apply.

The heading you just typed is formatted using 12-point Impact, and a line appears above the heading.

5. Press the Enter key to start a new paragraph. Then choose the Format⇨Easy Formats command again and apply the Plain Text format.

6. Change the font size to 10-point type.

Use the Font Size control in the toolbar to set the type size.

7. Type the text for your minutes, leaving placeholders for information that changes from meeting to meeting such as the date, time, location, and so on.

Here's an example:

```
The regular monthly meeting of the Board of
Directors of Save the Aardvarks was held on <day>,
<date>, at <time> at <location>. The President and
Secretary were present. The minutes were read and
approved as read.

<Type any actions taken here>

The meeting adjourned at <time>.

                                          Douglas
A. Lowe, Secretary
```

Notice that the last line appears near the right margin. You can create this effect simply by pressing the tab key several times (in this example, 8) or by right-aligning the paragraph by clicking the Right Align button.

Figure 14-7 shows how the template should appear after you type in this information.

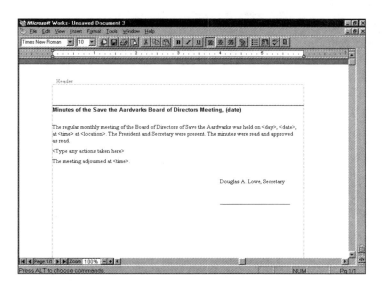

Figure 14-7
The Minutes template.

8. Choose the File⇨Save command, and then click the Template button. The Save As Template dialog box appears.

9. Type a name for the template.

I suggest Minutes.

10. Click OK, and then choose File⇨Close to close the document.

You are now ready to create new documents based on the Minutes template.

Using the Minutes template

To create a new document based on the Minutes template, follow these steps:

1. From the TaskWizards tab of the Works Task Launcher dialog box, click "User Defined Templates" at the very end of the list.

2. Click the Minutes template to select it, and then click OK.

Works creates a new document based on the template.

3. Replace the placeholder information in the heading and the opening paragraph with the meeting details.

For example, replace "(date)" with December 10, 1996.

4. Add a paragraph for each action that was taken at the meeting, replacing the <Type any actions taken here> placeholder.

See the following section, "Tips for minute takers" for advice on what to put in these paragraphs. Figure 14-8 shows an example.

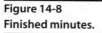

**Figure 14-8
Finished minutes.**

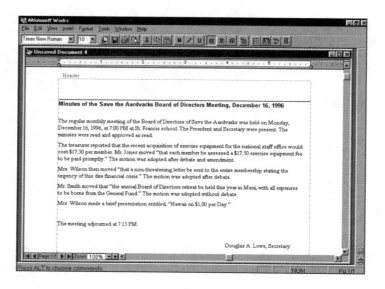

5. Use the File⇨Save command to save the file.

Type a file name that includes the meeting date. For example, Dec 96 Board Meeting Minutes.

6. Choose the File⇨Print command to print the agenda.

To print more than one copy of the minutes, set the Number of Copies field in the Print dialog box to the desired number, and then click OK.

7. Use the File⇨Close command to close the document.

Tips for minute takers

Although this book is not about parliamentary procedure, I do want to include a few pointers about what you should and shouldn't include in minutes. Keep in mind that the overriding principle is that the minutes should record the actions that were taken at the meeting — actions such as motions that were made, debated, and voted on. The minutes for most of the organizations that I've been a part of contain too much information.

Here's what should be included for each action taken at a meeting:

- The name of the person who made the motion.
- The complete, exact wording of the motion as it was voted on. (Note that this may be different from the original motion if amendments were made.)
- The disposition of the motion. If the motion was voted on, the results of the vote should be specified (for example, "the motion was carried" or "the motion was defeated.") If the motion is still pending for resolution at the next meeting, the status of the motion should be spelled out, including the status of any pending amendments.

Other information that should be recorded in the minutes includes:

- Any points of order that were raised, whether sustained or lost, along with the reason cited by the chair for the ruling.
- The results of votes taken by ballot, listing the total number of votes cast in favor and against the motion.
- The name and topic of any guest speaker. However, you shouldn't try to summarize the main points the speaker made. Just state the topic.

Information that should *not* be included in the minutes:

- The name of the person who seconded a motion.
- Motions to amend a primary motion. Instead, the minutes will record only the final wording of the motion after all amendments have been acted on.
- The names of those who spoke for or against a motion, or a summary of what was said.
- Committee reports, unless those reports include a motion or unless the board votes to have a report read into the minutes.
- Any opinion of the secretary, favorable or not, about what was said or done at the meeting.

PART VI:

DOING

HOMEWORK

WITH

WORKS

CHAPTER FIFTEEN

SCHOOL PROJECTS

In This Chapter

- Writing a term paper or report
- Creating signs for your science fair board

The projects in this chapter will help you complete homework assignments with class. Your teacher will think you're a computer genius, and you're bound to get high marks for neatness. And, as we all know, neatness counts.

Project 25: A School Report

One of the unavoidable facts of school life is writing reports. Starting in about the third grade, and continuing through graduate school, school reports are a constant chore. Fortunately, Works includes a TaskWizard specifically designed for school reports. And it can be used by third graders and graduate students alike.

1. **Use the School Reports/Thesis TaskWizard to create a skeleton report.**
2. **Fill in the blanks to complete your report.**
3. **If you want front matter such as a title page or a foreword with separate page numbering or no page numbers, create two documents: one for the front matter, the other for the body of the report.**
4. **Use Works' footnote feature to add footnotes to your report.**
5. **Don't forget to spell check before you print your final copy.**

Creating a report

To create a report, you must use the School Reports/Thesis TaskWizard, which you can find under the Students and Teachers heading in the Works Task Launcher dialog box.

When you start the School Reports/Thesis TaskWizard, the dialog box shown in Figure 15-1 appears.

**Figure 15-1
The School
Reports/Thesis
TaskWizard.**

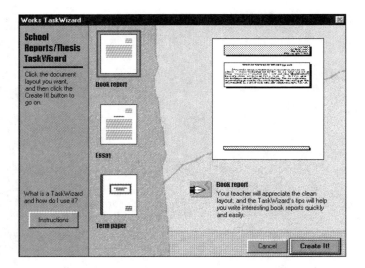

As you can see, the School Reports/Thesis TaskWizard can create three types of reports. To create a report, select the type of report you want to create, and then click the Create It! button.

The following sections describe the three types of reports you can create.

BOOK REPORT The Book Report option creates a simple, one-page report with an area at the top for your name, your teacher's name, and the date at the top of the page. Figure 15-2 shows a book report created by the TaskWizard.

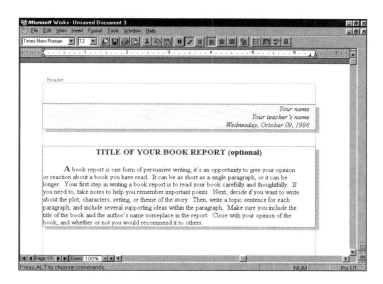

Figure 15-2
A book report created by the School Reports/Thesis TaskWizard.

As you can see, the book report includes a sample paragraph that gives you some pointers for how you ought to construct a book report. To finish the report, just type your name and your teacher's name in the heading area, and then type your book report in the main body of the document, replacing the sample text provided by the Wizard.

Of course, you also have to read the book. If Microsoft had really wanted to help you, they would have provided a Wizard that included a list of prewritten book reviews on such classics as *The Great Gatsby* or *Les Misérables.* Maybe in the next version.

ESSAY The Essay option of the School Reports/Thesis TaskWizard creates the document shown in Figure 15-3. It bears a striking resemblance to the Book Report document. In fact, the differences are only minor: The Essay document includes a place to type the name of the course in the heading area, and the main body of the document is not bordered as it is in the Book Report document.

Figure 15-3
An essay created by the
School Reports/Thesis
TaskWizard.

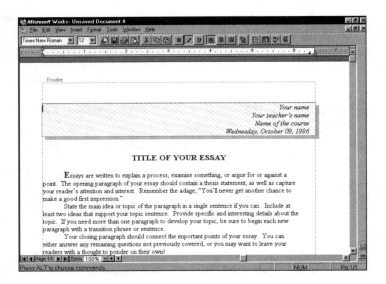

Figure 15-3
An essay created by the
School Reports/Thesis
TaskWizard.

To complete the essay, just replace the heading information with the correct information (your name, teacher's name, and course title). Next, replace "TITLE OF YOUR ESSAY" with the actual title of your essay. Then do the hard part: Type your essay.

TERM PAPER   The term paper is the most complicated of the three report options. While the Book Report and Essay options create single-page documents, the Term Paper option creates an eight-page document.

The first page is a title page, as shown in Figure 15-4. It includes placeholders where you can type the name of your school, the title of your paper, the name of the course, and your name.

The second page is intended to be left blank. However, it has the text "Leave this page blank" typed in the middle of it. Be sure to delete this text before printing your report.

The third page is a table of contents, as shown in Figure 15-5. Unlike more powerful word processing programs such as Microsoft Word, Works has no way to automatically generate a table of contents. So you'll have to type your chapter titles and page numbers. Of course, you won't know what page numbers to type until you finish the report, so hold off on the table of contents.

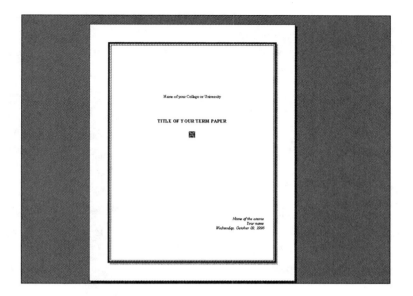

Figure 15-4
Title page for a
term paper.

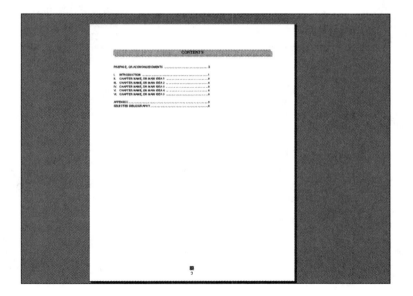

Figure 15-5
Table of contents for a
term paper.

The fourth and fifth pages of the term paper are a list of illustrations and a list of tables. If your report includes illustrations or tables, you'll need to type the correct information onto these pages. If not, you'll need to delete these pages.

Page 6 is the first page of the term paper itself, as shown in Figure 15-6. This is where you begin typing your paper. The sample text includes several examples of footnotes that you can use to create properly formatted bibliographic references.

Figure 15-6
The first page of text
for a term paper.

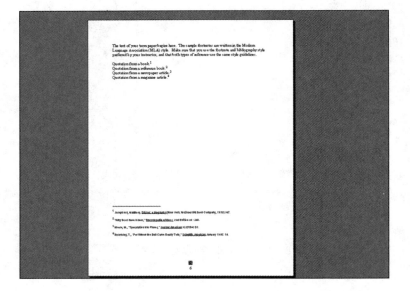

The last two pages are for an appendix and a bibliography. If your paper requires these elements, you'll need to type them here. If not, you'll need to delete these pages.

Dealing with page numbers

The term paper created by the TaskWizard is great, but it has a minor problem with its page numbering. If you'll look closely at the table of contents in Figure 15-5, you'll notice that the preface or acknowledgments is listed as starting on page ii — roman numerals for page 2. Then the first page of the term paper itself begins on page 1, which is actually page 6 in the document.

Unfortunately, Works cannot use roman numerals for its page numbering, nor can it restart the page numbers with 1 at the beginning of the text, several pages into the document.

To get the page numbering to work as described in the table of contents, you have to fake it. There are several ways to do that, but the easiest is to create the term paper as two separate documents. The first document will contain the *front matter*, including the title page, the blank page inside the title page, the table of contents, the list of illustrations, the list of tables, and the preface or acknowledgments, if any. Follow these steps to create this Front Matter document:

1. Fire up the School Report/Thesis TaskWizard and create a Term Paper document.

2. Delete pages 6, 7, and 8.

To do that, move to the bottom of page 5 and place the cursor on the page break mark that appears beneath the list of tables. Hold down the Ctrl and Shift keys, and then press the End key. The text from the bottom of page 5 to the end of the document is selected. Finally, press the Delete key.

3. Go to page 2 and delete the page numbers from the footer area.

To do that, scroll down to the bottom of the page until the footer area comes into view. Then highlight the page number field, which appears as *page* in the footer area and press Delete.

4. Go back to page 1 and type the report title and other information needed for the front matter.

5. To add a preface or acknowledgments, insert a page immediately after the blank page 2 by placing the cursor on the page break mark on page 2 and pressing Ctrl+Enter.

A new page 3 appears, where you can type your preface or acknowledgments.

6. Choose the File⇨Save command and save your report.

Make sure you include "front matter" or something similar in the file name so you'll be able to distinguish this file from the main text document for the report.

The front matter won't have page numbers, but most readers can figure out that the second page after the title page is page ii.

When you've created the Front Matter document, you can create another document to hold the main text of your report. Again, use the TaskWizard, but this time instead of deleting pages 6, 7, and 8, delete pages 1 through 5. Your text will begin on the first page of the document and will be properly numbered as page 1.

Creating footnotes

Most reports require footnotes. Fortunately, Works includes a handy footnote feature that makes creating footnotes easy. Here are the steps you can follow to create a footnote:

1. In the report, move the cursor to the point where you want the footnote mark to appear.

2. Choose the Insert⇨Footnote command.

The Insert Footnote dialog box appears, as shown in Figure 15-7.

Figure 15-7
The Insert Footnote
dialog box.

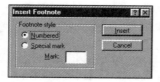

3. Click OK.

The footnote is inserted. If you are working in Page Layout view, you will be taken to the bottom of the page where you can type the text for the footnote, as shown in Figure 15-8. In normal view, a separate window opens in which you can type the footnote.

Figure 15-8
Inserting a footnote in
Page Layout view.

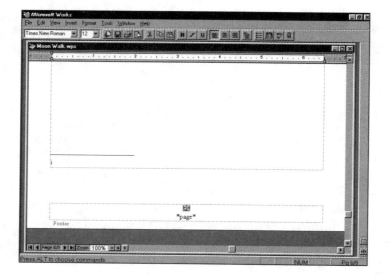

4. Type your footnote.

5. If you are working in Normal view, you can choose the View⇨Footnotes command to remove the footnote window.

Spell checking your report

If you use Works to type a report or term paper, be sure to run the spell checker to correct any spelling errors that might be in the document. Nothing will draw a teacher's ire more than a computer-printed report with spelling mistakes.

To spell check your report, choose the Tools⇨Spelling command, press F7, or click the Spelling button. Works checks your spelling word by word, looking up each word in its dictionary. If Works finds a misspelling, the dialog box shown in Figure 15-9 will appear.

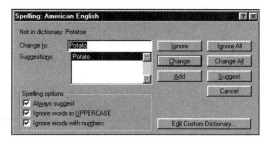

Figure 15-9
The Spelling
dialog box.

Choose the correct spelling from the list of suggested spellings that appears in the dialog box, and then click the Change button. If the correct spelling doesn't appear in the list, type the correct spelling in the Change To box and click the Change button. If Works is mistaken and the word is not misspelled (it happens), click Ignore. Or, click Ignore All to ignore not only this but also any other occurrences of the word.

Here are a few other tricks you can use to add spit and polish to your reports:

- If your teacher told you your book report has to be at least 500 words, use the Tools⇨Word Count command. It will display the number of words in the document.
- If you're not happy with a particular word, highlight the word and choose the Tools⇨Thesaurus command. This will bring up a list of alternate - er, surrogate, — I mean, substitute - words that have similar meaning.
- If you have the CD version of Works, you can also access the reference tools on Microsoft Bookshelf. In particular, you can use the dictionary to look up the definition of a word. Just highlight the word and choose the Tools⇨Lookup Reference command.

Project 26: Science Fair Projects

Science Fair projects are great fun. You get to fill the house with the aroma of seven different types of decomposing fertilizer, or you get to pop 37 varieties of popcorn to see which pops best (of course, you have to eat all the popcorn too!), or you get to play with model rockets.

Although Science Fair projects vary, all have one thing in common: the board. When you finish your experiment and have duly noted the results, you must create a project board to show off your work. Works can help you in several ways.

1. Use the Word Processor to create titles and signs.
2. Use the Spreadsheet to tabulate results and create graphs.
3. Use the School Reports/Thesis TaskWIzard to create your research paper.

Creating a title

A good Science Fair board must have a title, usually near the top of the board. The title should be large with large letters that your audience can easily read from a distance. In most cases, the title spans more than 11" — the size of standard computer paper. Unless you have a printer that can accept special continuous form paper, you'll have to print out the title on several pages, and then cut and paste the title together to create one long, continuous title.

Here's the procedure:

1. Create a new Word Processing document by selecting Word Processor from the Works Tools tab of the Works Task Launcher dialog box.

2. Choose the File⇨Page Setup command.

The Page Setup dialog box appears, as shown in Figure 15-10.

**Figure 15-10
The Page Setup
dialog box.**

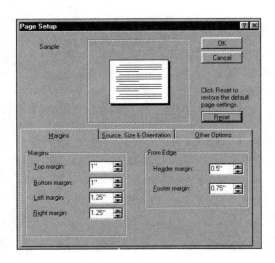

3. Change all margin settings to .5".

This allows for more room on the page in which to fit the title.

4. Click the Source, Size, and Orientation tab to display the dialog box shown in Figure 15-11.

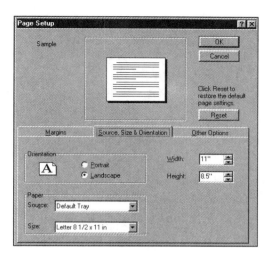

Figure 15-11
Setting the paper orientation.

5. Click Landscape.

6. If your printer will accept legal size paper (8.5"x14"), change the Size setting to Legal.

7. Click OK.

8. Click the zoom number in the zoom control at the bottom of the Works window, then choose Whole Page from the menu that appears.

This will reduce the zoom setting so that the entire page is visible on the screen.

9. Change the font size to 127.

10. Type as much of the title as will fit on the page. See Figure 15-12.

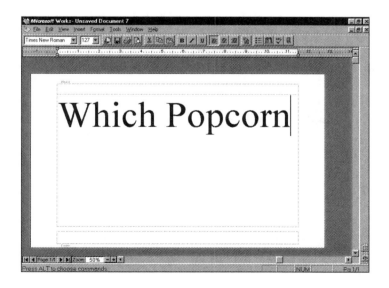

Figure 15-12
Print the title in pieces.

11. Press Ctrl+Enter to start a new page, then continue typing the title.

12. Repeat Step 11 as often as necessary until the entire title has been typed.

13. Choose File⇨Print to print the second part of the title.

14. Save the file if you want.

Because these files are so easy to recreate, I usually discard them.

15. Carefully cut the titles you printed, and then paste or tape them together to form one continuous, long title.

Project elements

All Science Fair projects have certain elements in common. Most teachers require that the projects include some or all of the following components:

- **Question** — the question to be explored by the project. For example, "Does one brand of popcorn outpop all others?"
- **Hypothesis** — the anticipated outcome, an educated guess at the answer to the question. For example, "Yes, Super MegaPop brand popcorn will outpop all other brands, just like it says on the box."
- **Research** — a summary of the research you conducted, on which you based your hypothesis.
- **Procedure** — how the experiment will be conducted.
- **Results** — the results of your experiment.
- **Graph** — the results are usually plotted as a chart.
- **Conclusion** — what you learned, including an assessment of your hypothesis and research.
- **Bibliography** — cites any sources used for the project.

You can create these project elements using a simple Word Processing document. I recommend you create just one document, placing each element on its own page. The only exception is the Graph, which is best created using the Spreadsheet program, as described in the section titled "Creating a chart."

Start by setting up the page layout to reduce margins to .5" on all four sides of the paper and, if you want, change the paper orientation to Landscape.

If you want to print some of the pages in Landscape orientation and others in Portrait, you must create two separate documents. Works won't let you switch from Landscape to Portrait midway through a document.

The typesize should be large enough to read comfortably from a distance, but not too large. Often, 36 point is a good size for the title of each page, with 24 point used for the text on that page.

Although the title of each page should be centered, the rest of the page should be left-aligned.

Figure 15-13 shows how a typical page might appear after it has been typed and formatted.

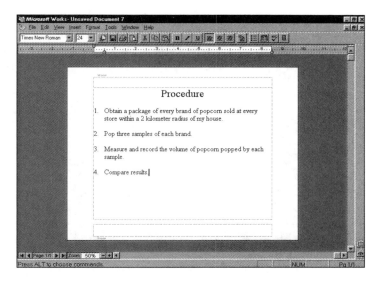

Figure 15-13
Typing pages to be displayed on the board.

Creating a chart

You can use Works' charting feature to create great looking charts to add to your science fair project. The details of creating charts are covered in Chapter 3, under the heading "Working with Charts." The main points are covered in the following procedure:

1. Type your results into a blank spreadsheet.

For example, Figure 15-14 shows sample results for a Science Fair project that compares different brands of popcorn.

2. Choose the File⇨Page Setup command and change the paper orientation to Landscape.

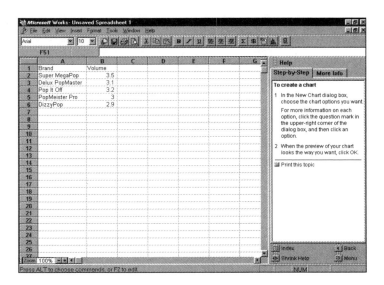

Figure 15-14
A spreadsheet with the Science Fair project results.

3. Select the cells that contain the data you want charted.

In the case of Figure 15-14, select cells A1 through B6.

4. Click the Chart button or use the Tools⇨Create New Chart command.

The New Chart dialog box appears, as shown in Figure 15-15.

Figure 15-15
The New Chart
dialog box.

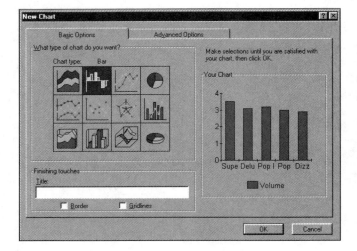

5. Select the chart style and chart options you want.

The various options you can select are described in Chapter 3.

6. Click OK.

The chart appears, as shown in Figure 15-16.

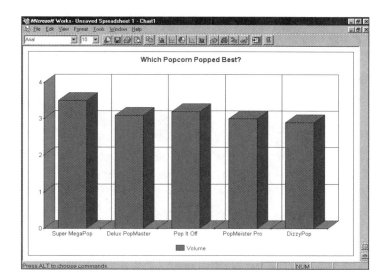

Figure 15-16
A finished chart.

7. Choose the File⇨Save command to save your work.
8. Use the File⇨Print command to print the chart.

CHAPTER SIXTEEN

STUDY HELPS

In This Chapter

- Creating a multiplication table
- Creating the Math Test Generator

S tudy is the key to success in school, and Works can be a great study companion. One way to use Works to help you in your studies is to use the Word Processor to create outlines of chapters as you read them. Another idea is to type notes (taken during a classroom lecture) into a Word Processing document; the mere act of retyping the notes will help reinforce them in your mind.

This chapter presents three simple Works projects that can help you in your studies. So put your nose to the grindstone and study, study, study!

Project 27: A Multiplication Table

Remember in the fourth grade when you had to memorize the multiplicatoin table up through 12x12? This project shows how you can create a simple times table that shows multiplication up through 12x12. However, you can easily adjust the size of the table to make it larger or smaller.

Figure 16-1 shows how the multiplication table will look when finished and printed.

**Figure 16-1
A multiplication table
created by the Works
Spreadsheet program.**

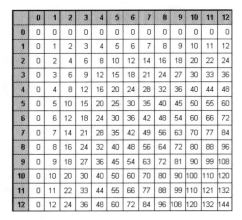

**TIMES
TABLE**
Use the Spreadsheet program to create a simple spreadsheet that shows multiplication answers up to 12x12.

Here's the procedure for creating a multiplication table:

1. Fire up the Spreadsheet program.

From the Works Task Launcher, click the Works <u>T</u>ools tab, and then click Spreadsheet. The spreadsheet program appears, with a blank spreadsheet in tow.

2. Select the range of cells from A1 to N14.

You can easily do this with the mouse by pointing at cell A1, pressing and holding the left mouse button, and dragging to cell N14. (Steps 3 through 9 of this procedure assume that this range of cells remains selected. If you accidentally deselect it while performing these steps, reselect them before proceeding.)

3. Choose the F<u>o</u>rmat⇨Column <u>W</u>idth command.

The Column Width dialog box appears, as shown in Figure 16-2.

**Figure 16-2
The Column Width
dialog box.**

4. Set the Column Width to 4, and then click OK.

The width of columns A through N is set to 4.

5. Choose the Format⇨Row Height command.

The Format Row Height dialog box appears, as shown in Figure 16-3.

Figure 16-3
The Format Row Height dialog box.

6. Set the Row Height to 20, and then click OK.

The height of rows 1 through 14 is set to 20. The cells in the range A1:N14 should now appear roughly square.

7. Click the Right Align button.

8. Choose the Format⇨Border command.

The Border settings of the Format Cells dialog box appear, as shown in Figure 16-4.

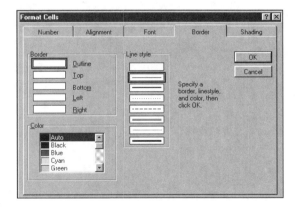

Figure 16-4
Setting the cell borders.

9. Click Outline, Top, Bottom, Left, and Right, and then click OK.

A grid pattern appears in the selected cells.

10. Type the numbers 0 through 12 in columns B through N of row 1.

11. Type the numbers 0 through 12 in rows 2 through 14 of column A.

12. Select the range A1:A14.

13. Choose the Format⇨Shading command.

The Shading settings of the Format Cells dialog box appear, as shown in Figure 16-5.

Figure 16-5
Setting the shading
options.

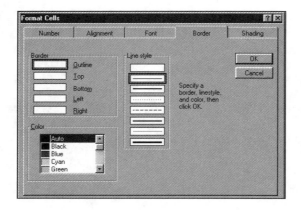

14. Choose the Solid (100%) shading in the Pattern list box, and then choose Light Gray for the Foreground Color list box and click OK.

15. Select the range A1:N1 and repeat Steps 13 and 14.

The spreadsheet should resemble Figure 16-6.

Figure 16-6
The spreadsheet so far.

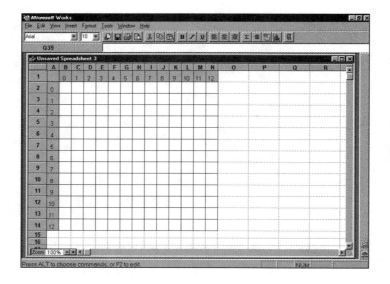

16. Click cell B2.

17. Type the formula =$A2*B$1 and press Enter.

The value 0 should appear in cell B2.

18. Copy the formula from cell B2 to the rest of the cells in column B.

To copy the formula, click cell B2. Then position the mouse pointer over the fill handle — the small rectangle that appears in the lower-right corner of the selection box. When the mouse is positioned over the fill handle, the mouse pointer changes to the word *fill.*" Press and hold the mouse button, and then drag the mouse all the way down to cell B14. When you release the mouse button, the formula in cell B2 will be copied into cells B3 through B14. Zeros should appear in these cells.

19. Copy the B2:B14 range over to the N column.

Leaving the B2:B14 range selected, position the mouse over the fill handle that appears at the bottom-right corner of cell B14. Press and hold the mouse button, and then drag the mouse all the way over to column N. When you release the mouse, the formulas are copied, and the multiplication table appears as if by magic (see Figure 16-7).

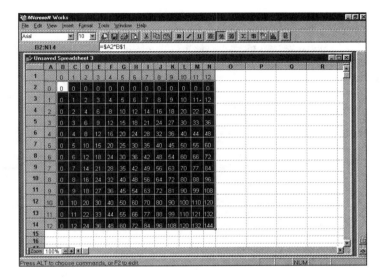

Figure 16-7
The multiplication table magically appears.

20. Save the file.

Choose the File⤷Save command. When the Save As dialog box appears, type a file name (such as Multiplication Table). Then click Save.

21. Print the file.

Although there are several ways to print a file, the easiest way is to click the Print button in the standard toolbar.

You're done! Show it to your kids. They're sure to love you for it.

Project 28: A Math Test Generator

This project is a little different from the others in this book. It is a relatively simple spreadsheet that creates a test of 20 arithmetic problems selected at random and prints an answer key on a separate page. You can tell the test generator what you would like to use as the largest number in the problem and whether you want to create addition, subtraction, multiplication, or division problems.

What's cool about this spreadsheet is that each test is different: If you run it 50 times, you get 50 different tests. So it's perfect for the kind of practice sessions that kids need to learn their math skills.

This project utilizes several of Works' more advanced spreadsheet features, such as the CHOOSE, INT, and RAND functions, cell protection, and circular formulas. Don't be discouraged if you don't understand every detail that goes into making this spreadsheet. If you follow the instructions exactly as they're listed here, the spreadsheet will work. When you get the spreadsheet working, you can study it if you want to figure out the details of how it works.

**MATH
TEST
GENERATOR**

1. Use the Spreadsheet program to create a spreadsheet that contains the formulas necessary to create the math tests.
2. To create a test, type the number you want to use as the largest number for the test, and indicate whether you want to create an addition, subtraction, multiplication, or division test. Then print pages 2 and 3 of the spreadsheet.

The procedure for creating the Math Test Generator is so long that I've broken it up into three parts.

Starting the Math Test Generator spreadsheet

To create the Math Test Generator, follow these steps:

1. Launch the Spreadsheet program.

From the Works Task Launcher, click the Works Tools tab, and then click Spreadsheet. The Spreadsheet program appears, ready to edit a blank spreadsheet.

2. Set the column widths for columns A through G.

To set the width of each column, select the column (or any cell in the column — you don't have to select the entire column) and choose the For-mat⇨Column Width command. In the Column Width dialog box, type the new size for the column, and then click OK.

Set the column widths for columns A through G according to the following table:

COLUMN	WIDTH
A	4
B	5
C	2
D	3
E	2
F	10
G	5

3. Select cell A1, and then type "Math Test Generator." Press Enter. Then click the Bold button in the toolbar to make the title bold.

4. In cell A3, type "Largest number to multiply:"

5. In cell A4, type "Type of test to generate:"

6. In cell A5, type "Press F9 to create a new test."

7. In cell H4, type "(1=Addition, 2=Subtraction, 3=Multiplication, 4=Division)."

8. Select cells G3 and G4.

To select both cells, click cell G3, hold down the Shift key, and then click cell G4.

9. Choose the Format⇨Border command.

The Border controls of the Format Cells dialog box are activated (refer to Figure 16-4).

10. Click Top, Bottom, Left, and Right, and then click OK.

Boxes are drawn around cells G3 and G4.

11. While cells G3 and G4 are still selected, choose the Format⇨Shading command.

The Shading portion of the Format Cells dialog box appears (refer to Figure 16-5).

12. Choose the Solid (100%) shading in the Pattern list box, and then choose Light Gray for the Foreground Color list box. Click OK.

Cells G3 and G4 appear with light gray shading.

13. While cells G3 and G4 are still selected, choose the Format⇨Protection command.

The Format Protection dialog box appears, as shown in Figure 16-8.

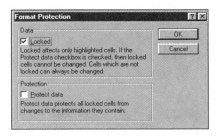

Figure 16-8
The Format Protection dialog box.

14. Click the Locked check box to uncheck it, and then click OK.

The two cells (G3 and G4) are now unprotected, which means that when you later protect the entire spreadsheet (see steps 15 and 16 of the procedure "Creating the answer portion of the spreadsheet"), these two cells will be the only two cells into which you will be able to type data. This feature prevents you from accidentally modifying the remaining cells in the spreadsheet.

15. Type any number you want in cell G3, and then type a number between 1 and 4 in cell G4.

16. Save your work.

Choose the File⇨Save command to display the Save As dialog box. Type a reasonable file name (such as Math Test Generator), and then click Save.

That's it for the first part of the Math Test Generator. The next part creates the cells that will actually generate a math test using random numbers.

Creating the Math Test

To create the math test portion of the Math Test Generator, follow these steps:

1. Select row 7.

Select the entire row by clicking the 7 left of the row.

2. Choose the Insert⇨Insert Page Break command.

A page break is inserted between rows 6 and 7 so that the body of the test — which you'll be working on in the next few steps — will print on a separate page from the information-gathering portion of the spreadsheet in rows 1 through 6.

3. Select cell A7, then type "Test" and click the Bold button to make the cell bold.

4. Select cell B7.

5. Type the formula =B7+1 in cell B7.

When you press the Enter key, Works complains about the formula being circular, displaying the dialog box shown in Figure 16-9. Works is quite right about the formula being circular — a circular formula is one that refers to the cell that contains the formula. However, in this case you *want* to create a circular formula, so just click OK to dismiss the dialog box.

The purpose of the circular formula in cell B7 is to provide a unique test number for each test that is created by the Math Test Generator. Each time the test is regenerated, one is added to the test number. This number will also appear on the answer key page, so you'll be able to match up tests with answer keys.

Figure 16-9
Works complains that your formula is circular. Laugh in its face and press on.

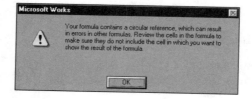

6. Type "Name" in cell I7. Click the Bold button to make the text bold, and then click the Right Align button to align the text to the right edge of the cell.

7. Type "Date" in cell I8, and then click the Bold and Right buttons.

8. Select cells J7 through O8. Choose the F<u>o</u>rmat⇨<u>B</u>order command, click Botto<u>m</u>, and then click OK.

Underlines appear in these cells so the person taking the test will have a place to write his or her name.

9. Select rows 7 through 50. Choose the F<u>o</u>rmat⇨Row <u>H</u>eight command, set the row height to 20, and then click OK.

10. Select cells A7 through B50, and then click the Right button to right align these cells.

11. Select cells C7 through C50, and then click the Center button.

12. Select cells D7 through D50, and then click the Left button.

13. Select cells E7 through E50, and then click the Center button.

14. Type "1)" in cell A9, "2)" in cell A10, "3)" in cell A11, and so on until you have typed "20)" in cell A28.

15. Type the following formula in cell B9:

```
=INT(RAND()*$G$3)+1
```

When you press the Enter key, a random number from 0 through whatever number you typed in cell Gs back in Step 15 of "Starting the Math Test Generator spreadsheet" appears.

16. Click cell B9 and choose <u>E</u>dit⇨<u>C</u>opy to copy the formula in cell B7 to the clipboard. Then click cell D9 and choose <u>E</u>dit⇨<u>P</u>aste to paste the same formula in cell D9.

Do not be alarmed if the number in cell B9 changes when you copy the formula to cell D9. Every time the spreadsheet recalculates itself — for example, whenever you add data to an empty cell or change the value of a cell — all the cells that have this formula (by the time you are finished, the formula will be copied to 40 cells) will change.

17. Click cell C9, and then type the following formula:

```
=CHOOSE($G$4,"","+","-","X","÷")
```

This formula is rather tricky because there is no division sign on the keyboard. When you get to this character in the formula, hold down the Alt key, and then type 246 on the numeric keypad — not the keys at the top of the keyboard, but the ones on the ten-key pad at the right of the keyboard - while continuing to hold down the Alt key. When you release the Alt key, the division mark appears. You can then continue typing the rest of the formula.

When you press the Enter key, the symbol that corresponds to the number you typed in cell G4 should appear.

18. Type an equal sign in cell E9.

19. Select cell F9. Choose the F<u>o</u>rmat⇨<u>B</u>orders command, click the Botto<u>m</u> check box, and then click OK.

The spreadsheet should resemble the one in Figure 16-10.

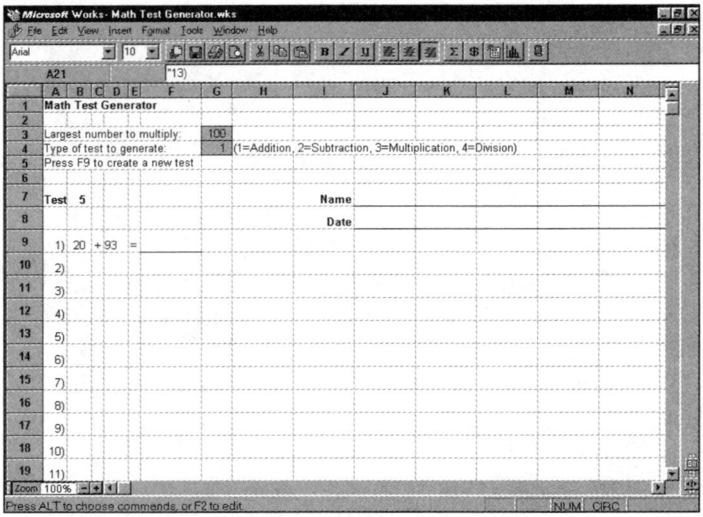

Figure 16-10
The Math Test Generator being constructed.

20. Select cells B9 through F9, and then drag the fill handle down to row 28.

When you release the mouse button, the formulas in cells B9 through F9 are copied to rows 10 through 28. The spreadsheet will resemble the one in Figure 16-11.

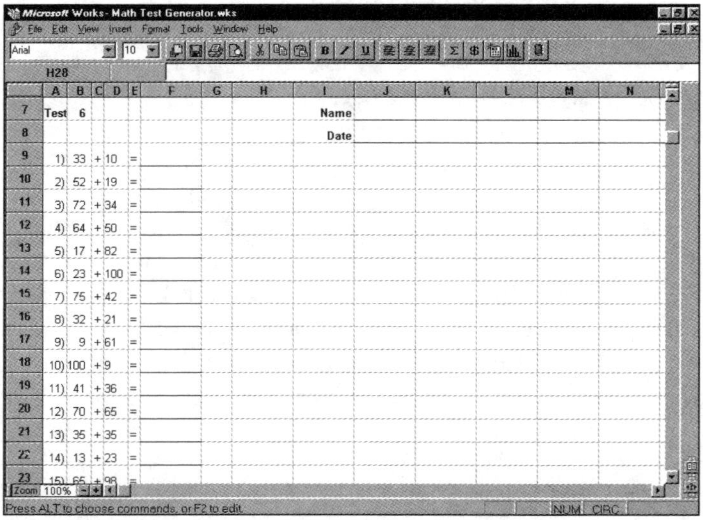

Figure 16-11
The Math Test Generator after the formulas have been copied.

21. Save the file again.

Just click the Save button or press Ctrl+S.

22. Type different values in cells G3 and G4 to make sure the formulas work.

The number you enter in cell G3 sets the limit for the largest numbers that will appear in the math problem. And cell G4 determines whether the test shows addition, subtraction, multiplication, or division. Try typing 1, 2, 3, and 4 in cell G4 to make sure the correct symbol appears in cells C9 through C28. If not, double-check the formula in cell B9 to make sure you typed it correctly.

Creating the Answer portion of the spreadsheet

The third and final part of the Math Test Generator is the answer key, which appears on a separate page. Here's the procedure to create it:

1. Select row 30A.
Select the entire row by clicking the 30 to the left of the row.
2. Choose the Insert↪Insert Page Break command.
3. Click cell A30. Type "Answers" in cell A30, and then click the Bold button.
4. Type "Test" in cell F30 and click the Bold button. Then click the Right Align button to right align this cell.
5. Type =B7 in cell G30 and click the Bold button.
6. Type =A9 in cell A31.
7. Type =B9 in cell B31.
8. Type =C9 in cell C31.
9. Type =D9 in cell D31.
10. Type =E9 in cell E31.
11. Type the following formula in cell F31:

```
=CHOOSE($G$4,"",B31+D31,B31-D31,B31*D31,B31/D31)
```

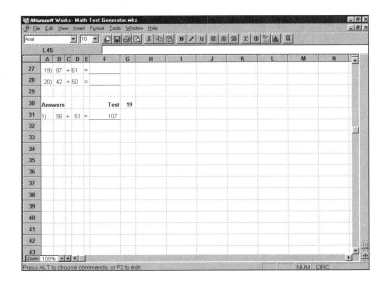

Figure 16-12
The first formula for the Answer portion of the spreadsheet has been entered.

12. Select cell F31, then choose the Format➪Border command to display the Format Cells dialog box. Click Bottom, and then click OK.

The Answers portion of the spreadsheet should resemble the one in Figure 16-12.

13. Select cells A31 through F31, and then use the fill handle to drag the selection down to row 50.

The formulas in columns A through F of row 31 are copied to rows 32 through 50. The spreadsheet should resemble the one in Figure 16-13.

Figure 16-13
The Math Test Generator is almost finished.

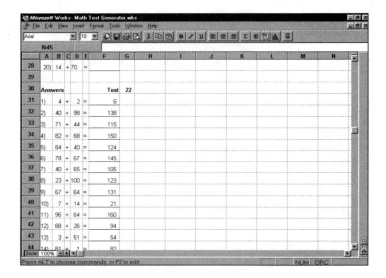

14. Check to make sure that the answers shown in column F match the problem spelled out in columns B, C, and D.

If the answers are wrong, double-check the formula in cell F31. You probably typed the formula incorrectly.

15. Choose the Format➪Protection command.

The Format Protection dialog box appears again (refer to Figure 16-8).

16. Click the Protect Data check box so that it is checked, and then click OK.

The spreadsheet is now protected so that the only two cells into which you can type data are cells G3 and G4.

17. Time to save the file again!

Use the File➪Save command or press Ctrl+S.

The Math Test Generator spreadsheet is done. The next section explains how to use it to print a math test.

Printing a math test

When you have created the Math Test Generator, you can use it to print a math test by following these steps:

1. Open the Math Test Generator spreadsheet.

From the Works Task Launcher dialog box, click the Existing Documents tab. Then select the Math Test Generator and click Open. The Math Test Generator appears along with that annoying message about the circular reference, as shown in Figure 16-14.

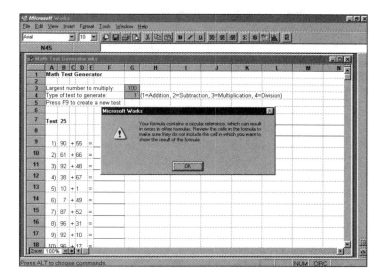

Figure 16-14
The Math Test Generator shows this annoying warning message whenever you open it.

2. Click OK.

3. Type the largest number you want to use in the math test in cell G3.

For example, if you want to practice multiplication problems through 12's, type 12 in cell G3.

4. Type 1, 2, 3, or 4 in cell G4 to indicate what type of problems you want to generate (addition, subtraction, multiplication, or division).

5. Choose the File⇨Print command.

The Print dialog box appears, as shown in Figure 16-15.

6. Click the Pages option button. Then type "2" in the From text box and "3" in the To text box. Click OK.

The test and answer key is printed on separate pages.

7. To print a different test, press F9, and then choose the File⇨Print command again.

When you press F9, Works recalculates the spreadsheet so that new random numbers are used for the test.

To print several copies of the test only, without the answer sheet, enter 2 for both the from and to page numbers and type the number of copies you want to print in the Number of copies field.

Enhancing the Math Test Generator

The Math Test Generator may be the most ambitious project in this book. However, there are ways you could modify this spreadsheet to make it even more ambitious if you want. The idea that comes to mind — which I offer as an extra credit project — is to present the test problems in columnar format, like this:

```
    6        10        7        9        6
  X 11      X 9      X 5      X 2      X 0
   66        90       35       18        0
```

It can be done, but copying cells requires a bit more work. Good luck!

PART VII:

THE

HOME

OFFICE

CHAPTER SEVENTEEN

HOW TO LOOK LIKE A BIG COMPANY ON A SHOESTRING BUDGET

In This Chapter

- Creating professional-looking letters and envelopes
- Making a brochure for your product or service

In business, image is everything. Just ask the folks who pay big-time basketball players millions of dollars to guzzle soft drinks on TV. Your company, be it large or small, is judged on its appearance. And every bit of communication you send out — letters, brochures, flyers, business cards, even faxes — convey an image.

The projects in this chapter show you how you can create a professional image for your letters and brochures.

Project 29: Creating Professional-Looking Letters

Works comes with an excellent Wizard for creating professional-looking letters. If you're still typing your letters from scratch, you need to check out this Wizard. In many cases, the Wizard can even write your letter for you, so all you have to do is change the names to protect the innocent.

FAST
TRACK

LETTER

1. **Use the Letter TaskWizard to create a letter.**
2. **Type your own content for the letter, or edit the letter written by the Wizard to suit your needs.**
3. **Print an envelope for your letter.**

Creating and printing the letter

The Letter TaskWizard leads you through the process of creating a profes-sional-looking letter, including setting up the letterhead and providing sam-ple text for common letters. To use the Letter TaskWizard, follow these steps:

1. Fire up the Letter TaskWizard from the Works Task Launcher.

You'll find the it in the TaskWizards tab, hidden under Correspondence. Click Correspondence to reveal the long list of Correspondence wizards. Click Letter and then click OK.

2. When Works asks if you want to run the TaskWizard, click <u>Y</u>es.

The Letter TaskWizard appears, as shown in Figure 17-1.

Figure 17-1
The Letter TaskWizard.

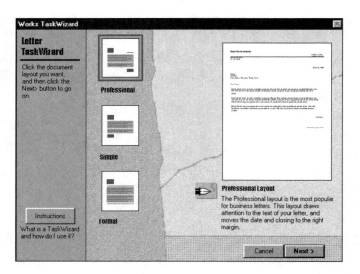

3. Select the letter style you want to use, and then click Next.

The Letter TaskWizard offers three basic letter styles: Professional, Sim-ple, and Formal. The text at the lower-right corner of the Works TaskWizard dialog box provides a description of each letter style, and the sample above it shows how the style looks.

When you click Next, the next screen of the TaskWizard appears, as shown in Figure 17-2.

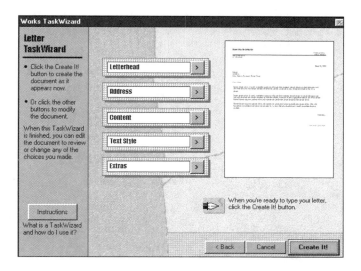

**Figure 17-2
You can customize several aspects of your letter.**

4. Click the Letterhead button.

The Letterhead dialog box appears, as shown in Figure 17-3.

**Figure 17-3
Picking the letterhead.**

5. Select "I want to design my own" if it is not already selected, and then click Next.

You are presented with several options for creating your letterhead, as shown in Figure 17-4.

If you use preprinted stationery, choose "I want to use my preprinted letterhead stationery" instead. The TaskWizard asks for the dimensions of your letterhead, after which you can skip ahead to Step 10.

Figure 17-4
Pick your letterhead
style.

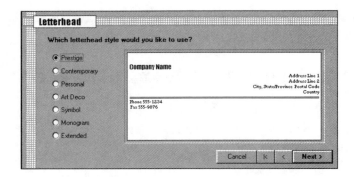

6. Choose the style you want to use for your letterhead, and then click Next.

The Letter TaskWizard asks for your company name, as shown in Figure 17-5.

Figure 17-5
Type your company
name.

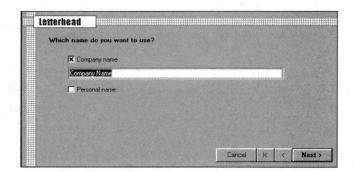

7. Type your name or the name of your company, and then click Next.

If you are creating a personal letter, choose the Personal Name option and uncheck the Company Name box. A new text box appears, in which you can type your name.

Figure 17-6
Now you have to type
your address.

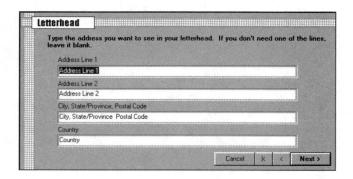

When you click Next, the TaskWizard displays the dialog box shown in Figure 17-6.

8. Type your address information, and then click Next.

You are asked for your phone number, as illustrated in Figure 17-7.

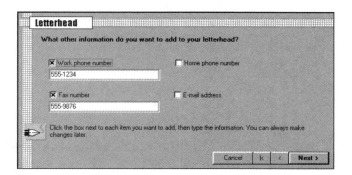

Figure 17-7
Your phone number is also required.

9. Type your phone numbers, and then click Next.

If you want to include your home phone number or e-mail address, choose those options and type the information into the text boxes that appear.

When you click Next, the Letter TaskWizard shows a preview of your letterhead, as shown in Figure 17-8.

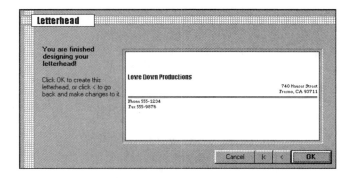

Figure 17-8
The Letter TaskWizard shows how your letterhead will appear.

10. Click OK.

You're returned to the Form Letter TaskWizard dialog box (refer to Figure 17-1).

11. Click the Address button.

The Address dialog box appears, as shown in Figure 17-9.

Figure 17-9
The Address dialog
box.

12. Choose "I want to type a single address" and click Next.
The dialog box shown in Figure 17-10 appears.

If you want to send the letter to a list of addresses stored in a database, choose the "I want to use addresses from a Works database" option. This will lead you into a mail merge, which you can learn more about in Project 21, "Mailing Form Letters" found in Chapter 13.

Figure 17-10
The TaskWizard asks for
an address.

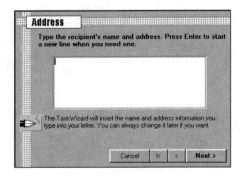

13. Type the name and address of the person to whome you want to send the letter, and then click Next.

The Letter TaskWizard asks for the greeting you want to use, as shown in Figure 17-11.

14. Type your greeting, and then click Next.

The Letter TaskWizard automatically stuffs the word *Dear* into the greeting. You can complete it by typing the recipient's name (for example, John), or you can delete *Dear* and type any greeting you want, such as Yo! or Hey You.

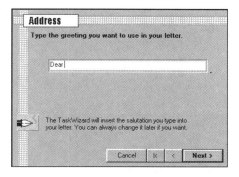

Figure 17-11
TheTaskWizard wants to know how you want to greet the recipient of your correspondence.

When you click Next, the TaskWizard announces you are finished with the address, in case you weren't sure. (See Figure 17-12.)

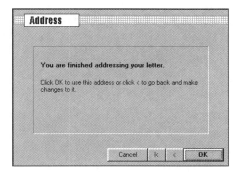

Figure 17-12
The address is finished.

15. Click OK.
The Letter TaskWizard dialog box appears again.
16. Click the Content button.
The dialog box shown in Figure 17-13 appears.

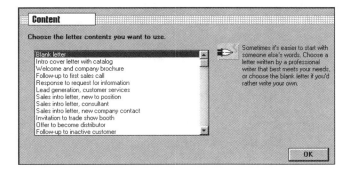

Figure 17-13
Works has a long list of prewritten letters.

17. If one of the prewritten letters is appropriate for the letter you are writing, select it and click OK. If not, select Blank Letter and click OK.

The Letter TaskWizard dialog box appears again.

18. Click the Text Style button.

The Text Style dialog box appears, as shown in Figure 17-14.

Figure 17-14
The Letter TaskWizard lets you pick a text style.

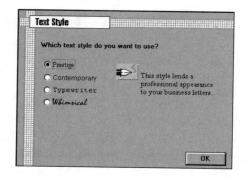

19. Choose a text style, and then click OK.

The Letter TaskWizard dialog box appears again.

20. Click the Extras button.

The Extras dialog box appears, as shown in Figure 17-15.

Figure 17-15
Extras you can add to your letters.

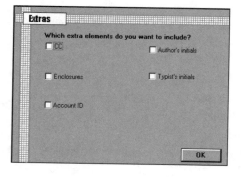

21. To include CC, Enclosures, Account ID, Author's Initials, or Typists Initials, check the appropriate check box and type the information requested into the text box that appears. Then click OK.

When you click OK, the Form Letter TaskWizard dialog box appears again.

22. Click the Create It! button.

The TaskWizard summarizes your choices, as shown in Figure 17-16.

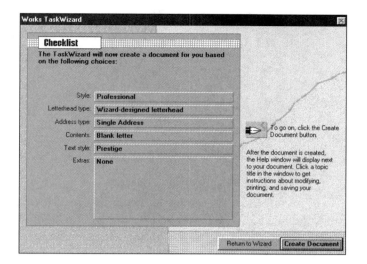

Figure 17-16
The TaskWizard is finally ready to create your letter.

23. Click the Create Document button.

The letter appears as a new word processing document, as shown in Figure 17-17.

Don't forget that you can change any part of this letter. Just because the Letter Wizard creates the letter a certain way, that doesn't mean you have to print the letter exactly as is.

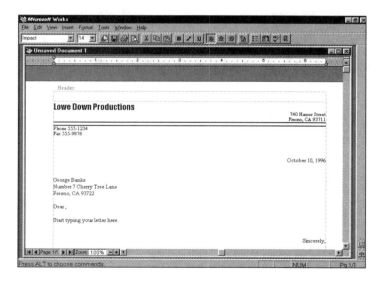

Figure 17-17
A letter created by the Letter TaskWizard.

24. Save the file.

Choose the File⇨Save command. When the Save As dialog box appears, type a reasonable file name for the file, and then click Save.

25. Type the body of your letter, replacing the "Start typing your letter here" placeholder that the TaskWizard inserted into the letter. Then scroll down a bit and replace the "Your name goes here" placeholder with your actual name (or the name of the person you want to appear at the bottom of the letter).

26. Save the file again.

27. Spell check the document.

Use the Tools⇨Spelling command.

For more information about spell checking, see the section "Spell Checking Your Document" in Chapter 2.

28. Choose the File⇨Print command to print your letter.

That's all there is to it!

Printing an envelope

After you have created your letter, you can print an envelope to mail the letter in by following this procedure:

1. In the letter you have composed, select the address of the recipient.

For example, the recipient's address is selected in Figure 17-18.

Figure 17-18
Highlight the address before you create the envelope.

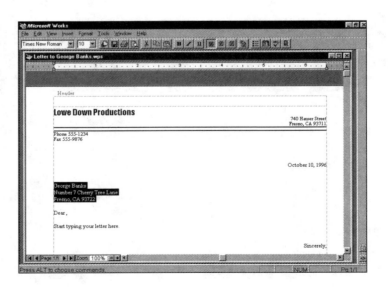

2. Choose the Tools⇨Envelopes command.

The Envelopes dialog box appears, listing the instructions for creating an envelope, as shown in Figure 17-19.

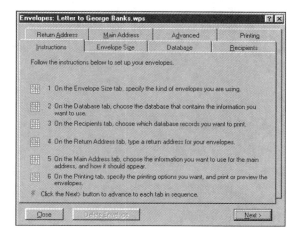

Figure 17-19
The Envelopes dialog box.

3. Click the Envelope Size tab.

The Envelope Size options appear, as shown in Figure 17-20.

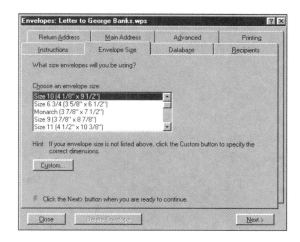

Figure 17-20
Setting the envelope size.

4. Pick an envelope size.

Size 10 is standard in the U.S.

5. Click the Return Address tab.

The Return Address options appear, as shown in Figure 17-21.

Figure 17-21
Setting the return
address.

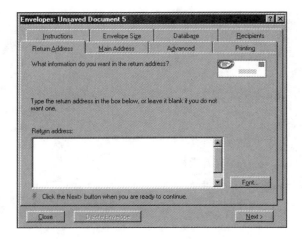

6. Type your return address in the box provided.
7. Click the Main Address tab.

The Main Address settings appear with the address already in place, as shown in Figure 17-22.

Figure 17-22
The main address is
already set for you.

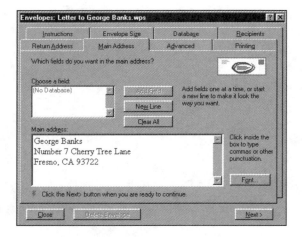

8. Edit the address if necessary, and then click the Printing tab.

The Printing options appear, as shown in Figure 17-23.

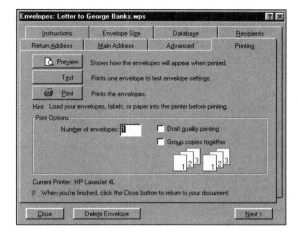

Figure 17-23
Ready to print the
envelope.

9. Insert an envelope into your printer.
10. Click the Print button.
The envelope is printed.

Project 30: Creating a Brochure

Works also comes with a Brochure TaskWizard that can create single- or double-folded brochures. Unfortunately, the TaskWizard won't actually write your brochure for you. But it can create a professional looking layout into which you can type your own sizzling advertising copy.

1. **Use the Brochure TaskWizard to create a skeleton brochure.**
2. **Type your own content for the brochure.**
3. **Print the brochure on separate pages, and then have the brochure photocopied onto both sides of a single page and folded.**

FAST TRACK LETTER

To create a brochure, run the Brochure TaskWizard. You'll find it on the TaskWizards tab of the Works Task Launcher dialog box, located under both Correspondence and Business Management. When you fire up the Brochure Task Wizard, the dialog box shown in Figure 17-24 appears.

**Figure 17-24
The Brochure
TaskWizard.**

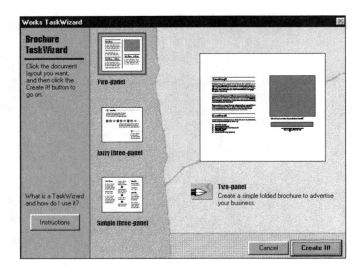

Select one of the three styles of brochures you want to create, and then click the Create It! button. Works creates a skeleton brochure for you based on the style you selected. For example, Figure 17-25 shows a simple, three-side brochure.

**Figure 17-25
A simple, three-sided
brochure.**

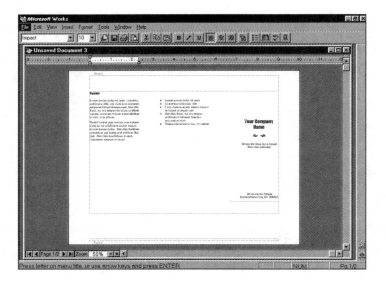

Whichever style you choose, Works creates the brochure as a two-page document. After the two pages of the brochure are copied back-to-back on a single page and the brochure is folded, the right third (or half, if you created a two-sided brochure) will appear as the front of the brochure.

The real work of creating a brochure, of course, is typing the content. The TaskWizard provides a sample layout and fills it full of Latin placeholder text. That's what all that "Lorem ipsum dolor" stuff is. Type your text directly over this placeholder text.

You'll find the brochure easier to work with if you increase the zoom factor to 75 or 100 percent. Be sure to save your work often.

When you finish typing the brochure, print it. Then take the pages to a copy shop and have the two pages of the brochure duplicated back-to-back on a single page. Use high-quality paper to create a more professional look.

CHAPTER EIGHTEEN

JOB HUNTING: TAKING
CARE OF BUSINESS

In This Chapter

- Polishing up that resume

My father-in-law got his first job throwing papers for the local newspaper in the 1940s. He liked the company so much he decided to stay until his retirement last year. (He did get a few promotions along the way.)

That used to be the way careers worked: You found a good company and stuck with it. But not anymore. These days, everyone needs a resume. Even if you're not actively looking for a job, a resume is still an important document. You never know when the right opportunity might come along, or when your current employer might suffer a setback.

This chapter has but one project: creating a professional-looking resume using the Works built-in Resume TaskWizard.

Project 31: Creating a Resume

Works comes with a helpful TaskWizard designed specifically for creating resumes. Whether you're in the job market or not, a complete and up-to-date resume is a good thing to have. Although the Resume TaskWizard

won't actually write your resume for you, it will create a skeleton resume based on your style and content preferences. All *you* have to do is fill in the blanks.

FAST
TRACK

RESUME

1. Use the Resume TaskWizard to create a skeleton resume.
2. Fill in the blanks, adding your own personal information, education, work experience, and other relevant items.

To use the Resume TaskWizard, follow these steps:

1. Start the Resume TaskWizard from the Works Task Launcher.

To find the Resume TaskWizard, click the TaskWizards tab in the Works Task Launcher. Click Employment, and then click Resume (CV). Click OK.

2. When Works asks if you want to run the TaskWizard, click Yes.

The Resume TaskWizard appears, as shown in Figure 18-1.

**Figure 18-1
The Resume
TaskWizard.**

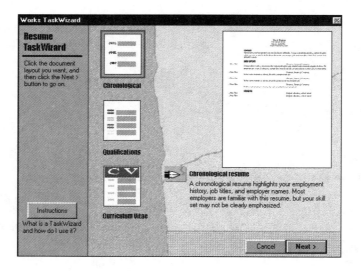

3. Select the style you want to use for your resume, and then click Next.

The Resume TaskWizard lets you choose from three basic resume styles: Chronological, Qualifications, and Curriculum Vitae. Chronological is the style most commonly used for resumes, but the other styles might be useful for specific situations.

When you click Next, the Resume TaskWizard displays the screen shown in Figure 18-2, which lets you customize several aspects of your resume.

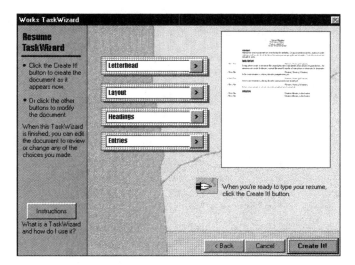

Figure 18-2
The Resume TaskWizard lets you customize your resume.

4. Click the Letterhead button.

The Letterhead dialog box appears, as shown in Figure 18-3.

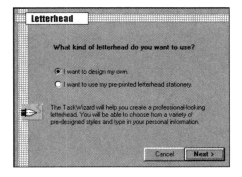

Figure 18-3
Choose your letterhead.

5. Select "I want to design my own" and click Next.

The Resume TaskWizard offers several choices for your letterhead style, as shown in Figure 18-4.

Choose "I want to use my preprinted letterhead stationery" if you want to use preprinted stationery instead of having Works print letterhead for you. The TaskWizard asks for the dimensions of your letterhead, after which you can skip ahead to Step 10.

Figure 18-4
Select the style you
want to use for your
letterhead.

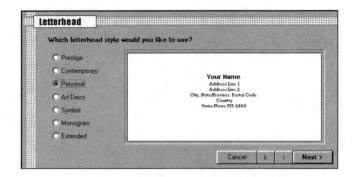

6. Choose the letterhead style you want to use, and then click Next.
The Resume TaskWizard asks for your name, as shown in Figure 18-5.

Figure 18-5
Type your name.

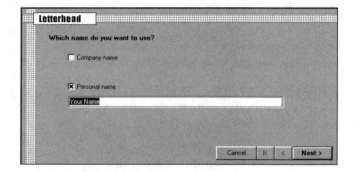

7. Type your name as you want it to appear on the resume, and then
click Next.
The Resume TaskWizard asks for your address, as illustrated in Figure
18-6.

Figure 18-6
Type your address.

8. Type your address, and then click Next.

The Resume TaskWizard asks for your phone number, as depicted in Figure 18-7.

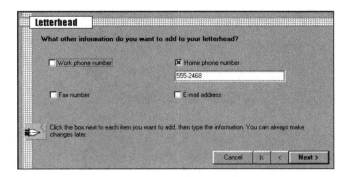

Figure 18-7
Type your phone
number.

9. Type your phone number, and then click Next.

If you want to include your business phone number, fax number, or e-mail address, choose those options and type the information into the text boxes that appear.

When you click Next, the Letter TaskWizard shows a preview of your letterhead, as shown in Figure 18-8.

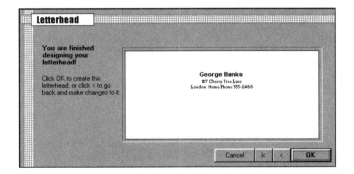

Figure 18-8
The Resume
TaskWizard provides
a preview of how your
resume's letterhead
will appear.

10. Click OK.

The Resume TaskWizard dialog box appears (refer to Figure 18-1).

11. Click the Layout button.

The Layout dialog box appears, as shown in Figure 18-9. This dialog box gives you four options for the format of your resume. Each option shows the formatting that will be used for both headings and body text.

Figure 18-9
The Layout dialog box.

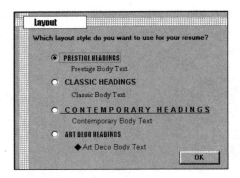

12. Choose the layout you want to use, and then click Next.

The Resume TaskWizard dialog box appears again.

13. Click the Headings button.

The dialog box shown in Figure 18-10 appears. This dialog box lists the headings that the TaskWizard will include in your resume. Note that the headings that are shown vary slightly depending on which resume style you selected back in Step 3.

Figure 18-10
The headings that you
can include in your
resume.

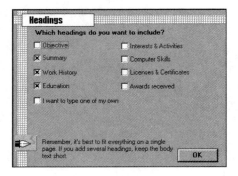

14. Select the headings you want to include.

Click a heading to select or deselect it.

15. To add a heading that is not on the list, click the "I want to type one of my own" option. Then type the heading you want to use in the text box that appears.

For example, Figure 18-11 shows how the dialog box appears after I selected the "I want to type one of my own" option and typed Professional Affiliations in the text box.

Although the Resume TaskWizard only allows you to insert one additional heading, you can always add more headings later using the Word Processor's Copy and Paste features.

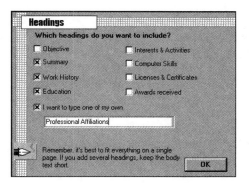

Figure 18-11
Adding a heading of your own.

16. Click OK.

The Resume TaskWizard dialog box appears again.

17. Click the Entries button.

The Entries dialog box appears, as shown in Figure 18-12.

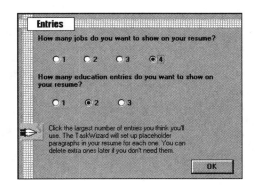

Figure 18-12
The Entries dialog box.

18. Indicate how many entries you want to include for jobs and work experience, and then click OK.

The Resume TaskWizard dialog box appears again.

19. Click the Create It! button.

The TaskWizard summarizes your choices, as shown in Figure 18-13.

Figure 18-13
The TaskWizard is
ready to create your
resume.

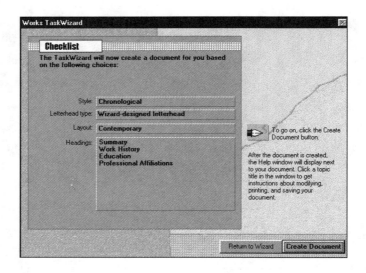

20. Click the Create Document button.

The resume appear as a new word processing document, as shown in Figure 18-14.

Figure 18-14
A resume created
by the Resume
TaskWizard.

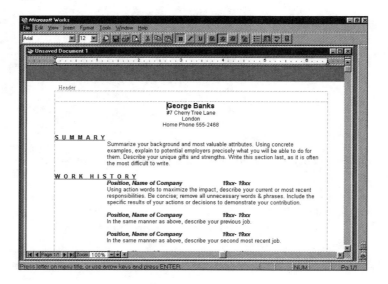

21. Save the file.

Choose the File⇨Save command. When the Save As dialog box appears, type a memorable file name for the file, such as My Resume, and then click Save.

22. Replace the resume's placeholder information with your actual job experience, educational credentials, and other noteworthy information.

This is of course the hard part. It's only Step 22 of a 26-step procedure, but it's the step on which you'll spend 90% of the time.

23. Save the file again.

24. Choose the File⇨Print command to print your resume.

25. Close the file.

Choose the File⇨Close command. The Works Task Launcher appears.

26. Create and print a cover letter.

Use the Letter TaskWizard, which you can also find under the Employment section of the TaskWizards tab in the Works Task Launcher dialog box. Project 29, which is found in Chapter 17, gives a step-by-step procedure for creating professional-looking letters, so I won't present that procedure again here.

The Letter TaskWizard includes two prewritten resume cover letters: "Resume cover letter" and "Resume cover letter with referral." Both letters provide an excellent starting point for your cover letter.

For more information about using the Word Processor, refer to Chapter 2.

INDEX

continued

continued

IDG BOOKS WORLDWIDE REGISTRATION CARD

RETURN THIS REGISTRATION CARD FOR FREE CATALOG

Title of this book: **At Home with Microsoft® Works**

My overall rating of this book: ❑ Very good [1] ❑ Good [2] ❑ Satisfactory [3] ❑ Fair [4] ❑ Poor [5]

How I first heard about this book:

❑ Found in bookstore; name: [6] _____

❑ Advertisement: [8] _____

❑ Word of mouth; heard about book from friend, co-worker, etc.: [10] _____

❑ Book review: [7] _____

❑ Catalog: [9] _____

❑ Other: [11] _____

What I liked most about this book:

_____

_____

_____

What I would change, add, delete, etc., in future editions of this book:

_____

_____

_____

Other comments:

_____

_____

Number of computer books I purchase in a year: ❑ 1 [12] ❑ 2-5 [13] ❑ 6-10 [14] ❑ More than 10 [15]

I would characterize my computer skills as: ❑ Beginner [16] ❑ Intermediate [17] ❑ Advanced [18] ❑ Professional [19]

I use ❑ DOS [20] ❑ Windows [21] ❑ OS/2 [22] ❑ Unix [23] ❑ Macintosh [24] ❑ Other: [25] _____

(please specify)

I would be interested in new books on the following subjects:

(please check all that apply, and use the spaces provided to identify specific software)

❑ Word processing: [26] _____

❑ Data bases: [28] _____

❑ File Utilities: [30] _____

❑ Networking: [32] _____

❑ Other: [34] _____

❑ Spreadsheets: [27] _____

❑ Desktop publishing: [29] _____

❑ Money management: [31] _____

❑ Programming languages: [33] _____

I use a PC at (please check all that apply): ❑ home [35] ❑ work [36] ❑ school [37] ❑ other: [38] _____

The disks I prefer to use are ❑ 5.25 [39] ❑ 3.5 [40] ❑ other: [41] _____

I have a CD ROM: ❑ yes [42] ❑ no [43]

I plan to buy or upgrade computer hardware this year: ❑ yes [44] ❑ no [45]

I plan to buy or upgrade computer software this year: ❑ yes [46] ❑ no [47]

Name: _____ Business title: [48] _____ Type of Business: [49] _____

Address (❑ home [50] ❑ work [51]/Company name: _____)

Street/Suite# _____

City [52]/State [53]/Zipcode [54]: _____ Country [55] _____

❑ **I liked this book!** You may quote me by name in future IDG Books Worldwide promotional materials.

My daytime phone number is _____

IDG BOOKS

THE WORLD OF COMPUTER KNOWLEDGE

 # YES!

Please keep me informed about IDG's World of Computer Knowledge.
Send me the latest IDG Books catalog.